IN FOR THE
LONG HAUL

A BUR OAK BOOK

IN FOR THE
LONG HAUL

THE LIFE OF JOHN RUAN

WILLIAM B. FRIEDRICKS

UNIVERSITY OF IOWA PRESS, IOWA CITY

University of Iowa Press, Iowa City 52242
www.uiowapress.org
Copyright © 2003 by Ruan, Incorporated
Originally published in 2003 by Iowa State Press,
a Blackwell Publishing Company
First University of Iowa Press paperback edition, 2010
Printed in the United States of America

The University of Iowa Press is a member of Green Press
Initiative and is committed to preserving natural resources.

Printed on acid-free paper

Library of Congress
Cataloging-in-Publication Data
Friedricks, William B., 1958–
In for the long haul: the life of John Ruan / by William B.
Friedricks.
p.   cm.—(A bur oak book)
Reprint. Originally published in 2003 by Iowa State Press.
Includes bibliographical references and index.
ISBN-13: 978-1-58729-917-9 (pbk.)
ISBN-10: 1-58729-917-8 (pbk.)
1. Ruan, John, 1914–   2. Businessmen—Iowa—Biography.
3. Philanthropists—Iowa—Biography.   I. Title.
HC102.5.R83F75   2010
388.3'24092—dc22
[B]   2010011470

For

Sarah and Emily

Contents

Acknowledgments

Many people deserve credit for making this book possible. Denise Dial informed me of the opportunity, and then my brother-in-law Jerry Crawford helped work out the details. Once begun, Jan Gillum, John Ruan's highly skilled and good-humored secretary/assistant for nearly 40 years, was essential in providing important background information, opening doors and introducing me to people, and keeping me from making mistakes in the manuscript.

A number of individuals at the Ruan companies and foundations made the project much easier. Especially cooperative were Tracey Ball, who put up with many questions and requests for documents, and Bill Giles, whose work on the Ruan Scrapbooks proved an invaluable introduction to John Ruan's life. Others who went out of their way to help included Virgil Anderson, Jan Douglas, Dan Golightly, Kent Havens, and Craig Winters.

John's friends and associates gave generously of their time. Most important were Ralph and Charlotte Schlenker, whom I'm now happy to call friends of mine as well. Howard Gregory, Ken Kendall, Herman and Jean Kilpper, and Scott Weiser also supplied important insights. B.J. Lester, Betty's longtime companion and attendant, was helpful as well.

All members of the Ruan family graciously endured my visits, phone calls, and many inquiries. Special thanks go to John and Betty Ruan, John III and Janis Ruan, Thomas Ruan, and Gary Fletcher, as well as John Lee Ruan, Ina Rae Ruan, Dorothy Nott, and Pattie Tidwell. I also appreciate the conversations I had with the Ruan grandchildren—John IV, Rachel, Jonathan, Stephen, Adam, and Philip.

Simpson College facilitated my work by granting me a sabbatical and then a leave of absence so I could finish the book. Bruce Haddox, our academic dean, was very supportive, as were the members of the history department—Owen Duncan, Nick Proctor, and Jennifer Hedda—who affably took up the slack while I was gone. Linda Sinclair, our building secretary, greatly simplified my task by transcribing all my interview tapes and sending out correspondence.

Numerous libraries provided much-needed assistance. Especially helpful were the librarians and archivists at Clear Lake Public Library, Des Moines Public Library, Drake University, Iowa State University, Kansas City Public Library, Oskaloosa Public Library, River Bluffs Regional Library, Simpson College, State Historical Society of Iowa, University of Iowa, Waterloo Public Library, and West Des Moines Public Library.

Tom Morain read the entire manuscript. He made incisive comments throughout, and I'm certain he made this a better book.

Once again, I had a great experience working with Iowa State Press. Gretchen Van Houten got the project going, Jill Anderson kept close track of everything, Lynne Bishop guided the manuscript to its final form, and editor Lori Meek Schuldt made the book more readable.

As always, my family was a source of constant support. My parents offered unflagging encouragement, reading and commenting on chapters as they were written. My father-in-law, who did business with the Ruan companies for years, made valuable suggestions along the way. My wife, Jackie, has lived with all of my book projects, and once again, her love and friendship allowed me to see this one through as well. Many times she set aside her own work to review mine, and her close reading and thoughtful questions undoubtedly improved the narrative. My daughters, Sarah and Emily, are likewise familiar with Dad working away on a book. S. and E., this one's for you. You've been wonderful. Thank you for giving me the time and space I needed. I hope someday you'll draw inspiration from the John Ruan story.

Introduction

On a hot and muggy July day in 1932, short and wiry Johnny Ruan drove his used Ford truck down a dusty, unpaved road in southern Iowa. The 18-year-old was headed back to the Des Moines River at Chillicothe for a last load of gravel. After delivering it to the road construction site, he returned to his campsite that evening and rested his weary body. The next day he was up early, shoveling yet another load of gravel into his truck bed.

Driving a truck was not Johnny's lifelong ambition. Several weeks earlier, he had been a freshman at Iowa State College, daydreaming about his future. Originally, he had thought of becoming a doctor, but by the time he enrolled, he planned on going into the forestry service, although several other possible careers soon interested him. But these ideas must have seemed miles away as Johnny and his payload of rock bounced and rattled along the state's country roads.

Like many other Iowans in the depths of the Great Depression, Johnny found himself facing difficult times. Foreclosures were forcing farmers from the land, and with businesses shutting down or cutting back, conditions in the cities and towns were no better. While thousands of Iowans looked for work, millions of unemployed people across the country were involved in a similar search. After completing his first year of college, there was no money left for further education; so that summer, John Ruan joined the throng of people needing a job. Following a tip that a road builder required gravel at his work site, John traded a family car for a truck and started the backbreaking labor of loading, hauling, and unloading the rock. Need pushed others to similarly tedious jobs; some remained destitute, some scraped by, and a smaller group found moderate success. John fell into none of these categories: he was among the select few who made it big.

Originally from a prominent family, John was not a rags-to-riches story, but he was a self-made man. Well before necessity drove him into trucking, John discovered a penchant for selling and a passion for making money. Making the money, more than the money itself, seemed to be what attracted him. Unwittingly encouraged by an overprotective

mother and overtly supported by his father, John developed his apti-
tude for sales and his interest in "making a buck" in childhood. These
qualities remained with him throughout his life, and they would serve
him well as he made his own way.

Once involved in trucking, John quickly captured the attention of
others with his pluck and dedication to hard work. Within a few
months, he bought two additional trucks, hired other drivers, and
switched to hauling coal. Several years later, when his small company
started to carry petroleum products, his operation began to take off.

From this modest and entirely unintended beginning, John Ruan
became one of the wealthiest and most powerful people in Des Moines
and Iowa, building a diversified business empire. His holdings
included interests in trucking, banking, financial services, real estate,
international trade, and a hotel. Most important of these were Ruan
Transportation Management Systems (RTMS), one of the nation's
largest trucking, leasing, and logistics firms, and Bankers Trust, the
largest independently owned bank in Iowa.

Good friend Joe Rosenfield frequently joked with John about the
latter's success. In his raspy voice, Joe often repeated, "You're not smart,
Johnny, you're just goddamn lucky."[1] John always chuckled when he
recounted Rosenfield's gibe, and he knew that good fortune was
important in his rise, but there were other critical factors as well. Interestingly, while John was building his business in the 1930s, Joseph
Schumpeter, a Harvard economist and sociologist, was studying char-
acteristics of entrepreneurs and their role in economic development.
He and John would never meet, but when Schumpeter identified
motivations of such businessmen, he could have been describing John.
"First of all," the scholar wrote, "there is the dream and the will to
found a private kingdom. . . . Then there is the will to conquer: the
impulse to fight, to prove oneself superior to others, to succeed for the
sake, not of the fruits of success, but of success itself. . . . Finally there
is the joy creating, of getting things done, or simply of exercising one's
energy and ingenuity."[2]

John often explained his success by stressing that he "never had any
specific dreams" or overall business plans but that he "just took one
thing after another and kept working."[3] Clearly, there was more to it

than that. From the outset, John exhibited a drive and a determination that set him apart from others. Harry Kemp, a former Oskaloosa trucker who knew John in his early hauling days, remembered, "He was aggressive, always moving. He pushed hard, and he never eased up."[4] John combined his resolve to succeed with a tremendous work ethic, which over the course of his career became legendary.

He began in the trucking industry by working 12- to 16-hour days, seven days a week, holidays included. These long days often started before dawn, and later in his career, he became famous for conducting early-morning breakfast meetings. James Cownie, then president of Heritage Communications, once recalled seeing John lobbying a local politician in a Des Moines restaurant at 4:30 A.M. John continued this pace well into his 70s, remaining convinced of the value of hard work: "I know people far smarter than me who could do far more than me, but they're content to sit back and not work very hard. What you don't have in intellect and other areas, you can make up for by putting in extra time. . . . There's no substitute for hard work."[5]

Not only did he have a great capacity for work, but he relished the labor. In a revealing moment, he once said, "Work is my hobby, work is my home. It's a habit. It's all I know."[6] Good friend Ralph Schlenker remembered just how committed John was to his work. The two men went quail hunting together early one Saturday morning. "After we'd been out a few hours," Schlenker recalled, "John said he'd had enough, went back to the car, and unzipped his coveralls. Underneath, he was ready for work. He was dressed in his standard bow tie and short-sleeve white shirt. After replacing his boots with black shoes, he drove down to his office." This was quintessential John, for no matter where he was or what he was doing, he was never completely divorced from his work.[7]

Much of his time was spent thinking about new business prospects. From the onset of his career, John exhibited a remarkable ability of seeing opportunities where others did not. Once he spotted something, he vigilantly jotted the idea on a note card. When out of the office, he carried a small leather address book, which included a pad of paper and a pencil, in his pants pocket so that even when hunting or playing golf, he could note possible opportunities so they would not "get away from him." John would later explain, "Most people see a lot of opportunities; I never let one go by."[8]

While he was a risk taker and seized what he saw as opportunities, he did not go into anything without considerable thought. Insurance executive Sam Kalainov believed John took "calculated risks," while Jan Gillum, his personal secretary and key assistant for nearly 40 years, observed, "He doesn't start something unless he's written a hundred notes. He doesn't just step into the batting cage and start swinging."[9]

After committing to an idea, John stayed the course and pursued it relentlessly. Former Des Moines city manager Richard Wilkey noted that once John took on a project, he would "stick to it" and "not waver in things." Similarly, Des Moines developer Bill Knapp explained, "With John, it's all the way or no way." Although he could be both abrasive and impatient with those who stood against him, his dogged determination and persistence more often than not wore down any opposition. In the words of Michael Gartner, a Pulitzer Prize–winning journalist, John was "a combative, bull-headed little fellow who will twist arms and bend ears and knock heads to get what he wants."[10]

It was this tough-as-nails businessman who guided his trucking company to new heights during World War II. With increased demand for truck and trailer combinations to haul petroleum products, Ruan Transport grew rapidly, becoming the nation's largest carrier of petroleum in the 1950s. This boom made John a millionaire and also led him into other businesses. His first foray was into local transportation—John bought the taxicab service in Des Moines and also established a rent-a-car operation that soon became the city's Avis Rent-A-Car franchise. Later in the decade, John and several fellow truckers founded a truck insurance business, and in the early 1960s, John went into banking, becoming the majority shareholder of Des Moines–based Bankers Trust.

The bank purchase was pivotal. It was John's first major investment completely unrelated to transportation, and it widened his horizons. As with the other businesses he held, John desired complete control, and over the years, he acquired the remaining shares of Bankers Trust stock. Because the bank was based in downtown Des Moines, John grew increasingly aware of the declining conditions of this business district. By the early 1970s, city planning director Robert Mickle characterized the downtown as wallowing in the "doldrums."[11]

Initially out of concern for his bank, John became much more active in the downtown community and eventually played a leading role in revitalizing the city center. Even as other companies were fleeing to the western suburbs, John saw potential in the city's core and gambled on the downtown, announcing his audacious plans for building the state's tallest building—the 36-story Ruan Center—in late 1972. With its trademark rusty exterior, the COR-TEN steel structure became the headquarters for his bank and trucking companies. Forever changing the skyline of Des Moines, the bold tower ushered in a new era in downtown redevelopment.

Following the construction of the Ruan Center, John's involvement in downtown development deepened, and leading the city's rejuvenation became one of his priorities. According to Walter Neumann of the Neumann Brothers contracting firm, John "was dedicated to downtown Des Moines." Neumann remembered John frequently saying, "Des Moines is a great city, and I owe a lot to Des Moines . . . you've got to put back what you take out."[12] With this belief, John gave the restoration of downtown Des Moines precedence. He played a key role in developing the nascent elevated skywalk system and as general partner won a long and contentious battle to build the 33-story downtown Marriott Hotel. In the early 1980s, he put up a second office building, the 14-story Carriers Building (later renamed Two Ruan Center) and shortly thereafter led the charge to establish the Des Moines Convention Center—now operated by the county and called the Polk County Convention Complex.

Speaking of John's downtown ventures, Andrew Mooney, onetime chief executive of the Greater Des Moines Chamber of Commerce, said of John, "He kept downtown Des Moines alive when it didn't look good." Robert Houser, former head of the Des Moines Development Corporation, considered John's work essential to the downtown's rejuvenation: "It could not have been done without the [Marriott] hotel and the [Ruan] center." Former Iowa Governor Robert Ray agreed:

"John Ruan is the father of the renaissance of Des Moines. Because of him, the city started to prosper and grow and come alive. We owe a lot to John."[13]

With his attention on the downtown, John's philanthropic work also expanded. As in the business world, his first major charitable undertaking was originally related to his personal interests. Since the late 1950s, John's wife Betty had been stricken with multiple sclerosis (MS), and fighting this neurological disease was the first major benevolent cause that attracted John. When the local chapter of the national MS society lost the corporate sponsor for its annual golf benefit, Mel Straub, its director, asked John for help. John readily agreed to back the affair, and the initial John Ruan MS Charity Golf Exhibition was held in summer 1975. That spring, several months before the event was held, John received tragic news: his daughter Jayne was also diagnosed with MS.

John now had that much more reason to take up the MS charity. Characteristically, he threw himself completely into the MS work. John gave the golf exhibition his full attention, and it soon became the largest one-day charity golf event in the United States. This success led to the charity's generous funding of research in experimental MS drugs at Rush-Presbyterian–St. Luke's Hospital in Chicago. Later, in order to bring first-class MS treatment to Des Moines, John provided $1 million for the establishment of the Ruan Neurological Center (now called the Ruan Rehabilitation Center) at Mercy Medical Center. Later he and his charity funded the Ruan Neurology Clinic as well.

If his MS endeavors started John thinking beyond his business concerns or the confines of Des Moines and Iowa, his support of the World Food Prize moved him to a global perspective. John had originally proposed a similar prize in the early 1980s as part of his effort to build an agriculturally oriented world trade center in Des Moines. The project as well as the prize did not get off the ground, but another Iowan, Nobel Prize winner Norman Borlaug, succeeded in getting the financial backing of General Foods, a subsidiary of Phillip Morris, and he established the World Food Prize in 1986. Three years later, when General Foods was merged with Kraft, the resulting firm announced it would no longer fund the prize. At that point, Borlaug and several others associated with the prize began looking for a new sponsor.

In early 1990, Borlaug and other World Food Prize representatives visited groups in several states that had expressed interested in sponsoring the prize. In March, they came to Des Moines and met with business and political leaders.[14] John attended the meeting and generally liked what he heard. After a couple of weeks, he decided to throw his financial support behind the prize. He later explained, "The World Food Prize was similar to what I had proposed earlier, and it was a great fit for Iowa." Then he added, "Of course, I also thought it might help me finally get the trade center."[15]

The trade center was never built, but the World Food Prize became John's obsession. Every year the award recognized an individual whose work greatly added to the "quality, quantity, or availability of food for the world." The international magnitude of improving food crops and their distribution and the significance of rewarding achievements in these areas were clear to the aging businessman. He explained it simply: "Food is the most important issue in the world. We can live without most of the things in our lives, but no one can live without food."[16] Always the salesman and the builder, John talked up the prize and its value whenever given the opportunity. Then in 1997, John assured the award's longevity and ties to Iowa with his wallet: he endowed the World Food Prize with a gift of $10 million.

Even into his 80s, John continued to work, refusing to enjoy a life of leisure. "Unless my health deserts me," he said, "I don't anticipate changing much what I'm doing right now." Although no longer putting in 16-hour days, he still went down to the office seven days a week. Likewise, his personality had mellowed over the years, but he still remained as driven as ever. What was different was his focus. As the 1990s progressed, he gradually moved away from concentrating on his companies to a preoccupation with the World Food Prize and an increasing dedication to the John Ruan MS Charity. With this shift in his attention, John handed over the running of his trucking company to his son John Ruan III in 1998. Yet he was unwilling to let go completely, and he stayed on as chairman of the two major corporate entities—Ruan Financial Corporation and Ruan, Incorporated—that controlled the family's holdings for a few more years.[17]

In 2002, *Worth* magazine dubbed John the "richest person in Des Moines" and estimated his "worth, conservatively [at] $500 million." Such success led many observers to conclude, "Whatever Ruan wanted, Ruan got." That, of course, was not the case, and while amassing the fortune, there were failures and personal tragedies, most notably the collapse of his insurance company and the death of his daughter. Through these and other troubles, though, John had a way of persevering and pushing himself forward into new schemes or projects. This was the figure the public saw: the hard-charging and aggressive entrepreneur who built a vast business empire.[18]

There was another side to John Ruan, but because he was very private, only a few close friends and associates saw it. To this inner circle, a very different man emerged. He loved, for instance, tramping about the timber during the spring in search of morels. A now-retired businessman remembered John's passion for the spongy wild mushrooms. "Not long after we had moved to Des Moines," former executive Bill Guy recalled, "John showed up at our door with a box full of freshly picked morels. When I told him I didn't know what the damn things were, he barged into the house, went into the kitchen, and prepared some mushrooms for us."[19] Guy was treated to John's longtime recipe for morels. After soaking the mushrooms in salt water for awhile, he dipped them in an egg-and-milk mixture, rolled them in crushed soda crackers, fried them until brown, and salted them.[20]

Along with his enthusiasm for morels, John enjoyed hunting and fishing. He also loved playing the piano, and later in life, he frequently serenaded friends with his fine voice. This interest in music was coupled with a penchant for off-color rhymes and a wry sense of humor. And when he was among those with whom he felt comfortable, John let down his gruff business face, revealing himself as sentimental, warm, and generous.

This complex man was honored time and again for his many commercial and civic achievements, yet one prize stood out above the rest: in 2001, John received the Iowa Award, the state's highest citizen award. So recognized, John was placed among an elite group of

Iowans, which included Norman Borlaug, George Gallup, Herbert
Hoover, and Henry A. Wallace, who had received the prize.

The award capped a 70-year career that saw John involved in
numerous enterprises. He had come a long way from hauling gravel
down rough rural roads and rose to cast a very long shadow. Propelled
by uncommon grit and hard work, John built his companies from a
one-truck beginning during the depression and made millions. Later
in life, he turned his attention to rebuilding his community, and
through his philanthropies, his impact was felt well beyond Iowa.

IN FOR THE

LONG HAUL

THE LIFE OF JOHN RUAN

1 Small-Town Beginnings: The Adventures of Johnny Ruan

From the second floor of the home where he was born in Beacon, Iowa, in 1914, young Johnny Ruan had a bird's-eye view of early-20th-century American life. Below him was the community's main street, and from the bedroom window, he watched small-town life unfold. Next door to the east was Nail's Confectionery Shop, where children often stopped for ice cream. Across the rutted dirt road shared by horse-drawn wagons, a streetcar line, and the occasional automobile stood one- and two-story wooden framed buildings. There, townspeople patronized such establishments as Perry's Grocery, Johnny T. Jones Grocery, and J. A. Jones Meat Market, where the enticing aroma of smoked sausage and ring bologna wafted from behind the counter to greet customers. Farther down the street stood a Knights of Pythias lodge, a blacksmith shop, and the post office. And because the streetcar track ended with a turnaround loop right in front of his house, Johnny got used to hearing the clanging bell of the passing trolley. A block north of the Ruan home was the livery stable, while the town's train depot was across the street to the west. A lively place, the station was served by three railroads at the time—the Chicago, Burlington, and Quincy; the Rock Island; and the Minneapolis and St. Louis—and offered news and goods from the larger world. Just off the main street, but not within Johnny's view, were the town's two austere, clapboard churches, one Baptist and one Methodist, where the faithful gathered on Sundays and for various social occasions.

It was here in Beacon, a small town in Mahaska County, Iowa, 70 miles southeast of Des Moines and two miles outside of Oskaloosa, that John Ruan spent the first years of his life. Situated amid rolling hills on the banks of Muchakinock Creek, Beacon had a population of approximately 500. Small towns like Beacon were commonplace across the United States in the late 19th to the early 20th century, and

American authors were especially intrigued by life in these communities. Mark Twain wrote of the benefits and drawbacks of village existence, but the joyful frolickings of Tom Sawyer and Huckleberry Finn were his most enduring images. Others, such as Sherwood Anderson and Sinclair Lewis, described these communities as crude places of limited opportunity, isolation, and cultural poverty, while Hamlin Garland remembered his small town fondly, as a place of supportive friends and family.[1]

Like other such communities, Beacon combined both the good and the bad aspects of small-town life. Economic opportunity, for instance, had been limited, largely tied to the local coal mining industry. But by the time Johnny Ruan was born, the town had seen better days. As construction of central Iowa railroads occurred from the 1860s through the 1880s, demand for coal rose and Beacon, located near rich veins of the commodity, soon prospered. By the mid-1890s, its population climbed to 971. Sixty percent of the town's workforce labored in the mines, while a good number of other jobs were supported by miners' dollars. Two decades later, Beacon had fallen on hard times, and its population had decreased by half. Demand for local coal fell off after World War I when a growing number of Iowans as well as the railroads began buying higher-quality, cleaner-burning coal from out of state, but by that time the town was already in decline. Initially, Beacon's demise was connected to its close proximity to Oskaloosa, a town of nearly 10,000, and eventually the rise of the automobile. With the larger neighboring city just two miles away, many essential businesses and services never developed in Beacon. Likewise, when the streetcar line that ran past the Ruan home connected the small town to Oskaloosa in 1906, further movement between the two centers occurred. Later, when automobiles became more common, people could commute to work from Oskaloosa, which had much to offer that Beacon did not.[2]

The town's misfortune did not adversely affect young John. In fact, he may have benefited from the community's demise. Historian Tom Morain noted that in small towns, a family's social identity was intimately tied to the male head of household's occupation. Not only was his father, John A. Ruan, a physician, he was the last remaining doctor in town. This occupation placed him and his family squarely among the elite in Beacon society.[3]

"Doc" Ruan's father had come to the United States in the 1850s, migrating with his father and two brothers from St. Croix, Danish West Indies, to New York City and then on to central Iowa. His mother's family, the Mendenhalls, had come to Iowa—where they had acquired land on which Beacon was established—from North Carolina and could trace their ancestors back to the Quakers who immigrated to Pennsylvania with William Penn.[4]

The son of a farmer and coal miner, John A. Ruan graduated from the Normal Institute of Mahaska County in 1888. He then taught at the Riverside School near Beacon for several years. The tenderhearted Ruan clearly cherished his teaching experience, and at least once, he wrote his students a poem before they parted for the summer. It ended with the lines: "Adieu kind scholars, we must part, and these are the thoughts of an aching heart. If in this school, some scholars dear, we ne'er should meet again, I still will kindly think of you, and now I bid you all a kind adieu."[5] But Ruan had greater ambitions, and in the late 1890s, he left teaching to study medicine at Central Medical College in St. Joseph, Missouri. He completed his doctor of medicine degree in 1900 and set up his practice in Beacon.[6] The young doctor soon established himself, and by the summer of 1904, observers noticed that Ruan "had been improving his place . . . No one could secure any satisfaction from him as to his intentions, and the air of mystery deepened as conflicting reports came into circulation and different domestic furnishings were seen to arrive at his place of business." The suspense ended on July 4 when several friends received wedding announcements. Two days later, on a stormy summer afternoon, the 34-year-old doctor married 28-year-old Rachel Llewellyn in a ceremony at the renovated Ruan home.[7]

Rachel Llewellyn was the daughter of Thomas Llewellyn and Elizabeth Jobe. The second of 15 children, she was born in Alton, Illinois, and settled with her family in Beacon, where her father worked as a coal miner. Rachel was known for her beauty and reserved disposition, and according to family lore, she once dated John L. Lewis, the eventual head of the United Mine Workers.[8]

The newlyweds soon settled into the rhythms of small-town life. Doc Ruan provided medical care out of his home—one of the largest in town—which had an office in the front half of the first floor and three rooms for patients on the second. As most doctors did at the time, he made frequent house calls, originally by buggy and later by automobile, one of the first owned by a Beacon resident. He was widely known as a compassionate and accommodating doctor. These traits were put to the test more than once. In an unusual case, a woman brought her injured pet pug to him for emergency care. Ruan gently explained that he knew nothing about treating animals and suggested she take the dog to a veterinarian. She countered that since he was her family's doctor and since the dog was part of the family, he needed to help the injured pet. He finally relented and treated the dog after the woman promised she would later seek veterinary care for her pet. And like many other physicians at the time, Doc Ruan often took items such as a ham or eggs in trade from people unable to pay for his services. Most commonly, patients offered chickens in lieu of money, and the coop behind the Ruan house was frequently filled with poultry given to the doctor. When not involved in his medical practice, Doc often entertained people by playing the piano and the violin. He also composed music, and at least one song, "She Always Had a Date," was published. In addition to his musical interests, he was a leader in the Methodist Church and a member of the Masons.[9]

Short, with a powerful, stocky build, the doctor sported a fashionable mustache, which originally had been grown to cover a scar above his lip that was the result of being kicked by a horse. His outgoing personality and jovial manner made him a popular figure, and as a member of the professional class, Ruan was active in civic affairs. Historian Lewis Atherton explained that in every small town, the elite's "personal interests were so tightly interwoven with those of the community at large that one cannot determine where self-interest ended and public spirit began."[10] Long concerned with the continuing decline of Beacon, Ruan once ran for mayor. He headed the Progressive ticket in 1916 and during the campaign drafted a handbill that began by asking a series of questions: "Do you believe your town could be made better? Would you like to see it better? . . . What have you done to make it better? . . . Have you laughed at town decay or have you given it any serious consideration?" The answer, according to the candidate, was the election of an "energetic Booster Council" and a "clean, honest mayor not afraid to do the right thing at the right time and place. Good clean, moral, active, citizens, who will hold up the town instead of knocking it down." In a closely contested election, which saw the heaviest voter turnout in a generation, Ruan lost the election by 10 votes.[11]

Ruan's wife, Rachel, could not help but comment on the election loss. Reminding her husband that his Democratic Party ties were not popular in the region, she joked, "You couldn't get elected dogcatcher in this area!"[12] People in the community, however, rarely witnessed her humor. Generally quiet, Rachel was strong and independent. Constrained by contemporary social standards, which dictated that proper women remain at home tending to the domestic chores, she was seldom seen in public. One of the few acceptable outlets for women was religion, and Rachel regularly participated in the activities of the local Methodist Church. Otherwise, from time to time she paid calls on a select group of neighbors. These few activities notwithstanding, villagers were struck by the differences between the gregarious Doc Ruan and his introverted wife, and local gossip often characterized her as standoffish and aloof.[13]

Although clearly opposites in personality, Rachel and her husband complemented each other, and in 1910, the couple was blessed with their first child, Jay Arthur. Characterized by those who knew him as a friendly, carefree youngster, Arthur reportedly lived for the moment and was a spendthrift who "couldn't hold a dime longer than it took to get to a place to spend it." He soon began running around town with a rowdy crowd of boys causing all sorts of mischief. Once, for instance, while playing up on the roof of his house with several friends, he knocked the chimney down. Such antics gave Arthur the reputation for being something of a prankster. Following Arthur by four years, John was born on February 11, 1914. The baby of the family, he was doted on by both parents, and Rachel soon became very protective of him. Whether to prevent John from emulating the wild behavior of Arthur or because he was a sickly child, Rachel kept him on a short rein.[14]

Ironically, during the Spanish influenza epidemic of 1918, it was not the flu virus that struck four-year-old John but pneumonia combined with whooping cough. In an era before antibiotics, the infection was often acute, and in this case, John's father performed emergency surgery on him at home. To ease his son's breathing, Doc Ruan removed a section of John's rib and inserted a tube to drain the mucus from his lungs. Following this serious illness, Rachel grew even more protective of John, and given the large number of relatives the family had living in town, keeping a close eye on young John was fairly easy.[15]

While trying to shield him from further debilitating illnesses, Rachel tightly restricted John's activities and allowed him to spend time with only a handful of the town's other prominent children. One youngster John frequently played with was Marie Ogden, the daughter of Beacon's postmaster. She remembered Mrs. Ruan as "very protective" of John. "He was allowed to come over to my house, but that was about the limit." Besides closely regulating his whereabouts, Rachel thought that the family's social position mandated a certain decorum. For John, this belief dictated that his wardrobe mirrored the fashion trends of the eastern establishment. "My mother used to dress me like Little Lord Fauntleroy. White blouse, knickers, and long stockings that came up and fastened to a garter belt under my shirt." Many of the town's young boys were put off by the ostentatious outfits, and they often picked on little Johnny Ruan. On several occasions, John recalled, he was "beaten up" because of his clothes.[16]

His outfits were not the only factor that set John apart from many boys his age. At his mother's insistence, John took years of piano lessons from a local woman named Jenny Frye. Such training merely isolated him further from most male playmates. Soon, John became somewhat of a loner, and he was drawn to another ostracized child, John Bedillon. Three years younger than John, Bedillon was from one of the few Catholic families in town. As post–World War I xenophobia swept the nation, Catholics generally fell under suspicion. The climate in Beacon was no exception, and, because of his religion, Bedillon was often harassed by town bullies. John clearly empathized with the younger boy's shabby treatment, and he defended him whenever he could. The two became good friends, with John playing the role of an older brother. He introduced Bedillon to various Halloween tricks, such as knocking down cornstalks. One of John's favorite pranks involved placing a knife which was connected to a tightly wound cord under a house's siding. After the twisted string had been pulled taut, John would let go. The knife would bang against the siding with "an awful racket" and startle the household's residents. When the two friends grew older, it was John who took Bedillon to his first shivaree.[17]

Not playing with many other children meant that much of John's time was spent with adults. He often traveled with his father on house calls, and he occasionally sat in the Mahaska County Hospital observation area while Doc Ruan performed surgeries. The youngster treasured these trips, and much to his father's delight, young John hoped to become a doctor as well. The two also enjoyed free time together, especially target shooting. Doc Ruan taught John to shoot skeet, and the son spent countless summer hours aiming at clay targets. When not in school or with his father, John sometimes sought out the company of Mike Monks, the local section foreman for the Rock Island Railroad, or Ned Owings, another railroad man. Often, when he was supposed to be in Sunday school, John sneaked down an alley to the railroad depot, met up with Monks and Owings, and the three of them took a handcar on safety inspection tours of the railway track. On other occasions, John was with a town character known as "Old Man Okey." In his 80s, Okey loved entertaining youngsters in front of his house, and John, who had inherited his father's love of music and singing, often joined the old man in song. Much to the delight of other children who gathered at Okey's house, John sang in a high falsetto while the old man sang the melody.[18]

Summers were usually passed at the family farm just south of town. Run by full-time manager Charlie Dixon, the 148-acre farm was a seasonal getaway for Rachel, Arthur, and John, while Doc Ruan, who remained in town to care for his patients, visited on weekends. Although John had numerous chores on the property—he mended fences, plowed corn, slopped hogs, and put hay up in the loft—the farm and the surrounding area provided a wonderful playground for the young boy. Here he pursued many of the outdoor activities fondly recalled in 1928 by another Iowan, then presidential candidate Herbert Hoover. Hoover's boyhood memories in West Branch, 10 miles east of Iowa City, included trapping rabbits, playing in the local swimming hole, and fishing in the river with willow poles. John had similar adventures. He hunted rabbits, squirrels, and quail and trapped muskrat, mink, and possum in the timber adjacent to the farm. He fished and swam in the creek, and it was here that he fell prey to one of his brother's pranks. John reminisced of a scene that could have been painted by Norman Rockwell: "Friends of our family from Ottumwa came to visit us [at the farm] each year, and the daughter who was my age was named Bernice Harper. She and I went swimming in the creek without any clothes . . . My brother came along and hid our clothes and we had to go to the house naked."[19]

But not all of John's activities were idle fun; many of his endeavors were pursued in an effort to make money. This passion may have been picked up from Doc Ruan, who was a risk taker when it came to investing. Some of the enterprises he had an interest in included several farms, a coal mine, South Dakota oil wells, and a wide variety of stocks. More likely, however, it grew out of John's frequent times alone. When other children were playing, he was often by himself because his mother tightly restricted his circle of friends. Left to his own devices, John soon found that he liked selling things and had a real knack for it. Early on, he engaged in various moneymaking schemes, doing, in his words, "whatever I could to make a nickel." And while John certainly appreciated seeing his earnings grow, he savored the process of making it much more.[20]

The hunting and trapping John enjoyed proved lucrative; pelts could bring the child up to 50 cents apiece. He picked blackberries and gooseberries and hunted wild morel mushrooms to sell to neighbors, and he gathered dandelion blooms for those who made wine. In town, he scavenged the back alleys for items of value, he popped corn, and he cleaned and prepared horseradish for sale. He also showed glimpses of entrepreneurial flair, though sometimes these tactics were less than honest. He collected rags, which were sold by the pound, in large gunnysacks. To make the bag weigh more, he sometimes wet down the rags at the bottom of the sack or hid a brick in it. In another incident,

John seemingly improved a product for sale. Egged on by local painter Peter Noter, he painted an old engine he had found with shiny aluminum-colored paint and sold it at a much higher price than the object was worth.[21]

As he grew up, he stopped following the clothing suggestions of his mother, and while searching for junk in town, he began donning overalls. His mother thought that wearing such clothing and rummaging around was beneath John's dignity, and when the overalls required patching, Rachel refused to do it, so John sewed them himself. Although his mother disapproved of John's moneymaking exploits, Doc Ruan, who was proud of his son's initiative and go-getting attitude, encouraged these efforts, and they continued.[22]

Unlike his brother, Arthur, who spent freely, John remembered being "tight" with his money and putting most of it in the Mahaska County State Bank. The savings mounted, and years later—apparently several weeks before the Iowa Bank Conservation Act became law in January 1933, allowing state banks to restrict withdrawals—John stopped by the Oskaloosa bank and closed his savings account, withdrawing nearly $300.[23] Of course, he did not bank all his money. Occasionally he bought ice cream or candy for friends such as Marie Ogden at Nail's Confectionery. More often he could be found thumbing through the latest Sears, Roebuck and Company catalog for products to buy. Over the years, John purchased numerous goods from the famous Chicago merchandiser. Once an item had been ordered, he ran to the train station every day with great anticipation until the much-expected package finally arrived. Rachel referred to the famous catalog as "John's bible" because he read it so frequently, and when John could not be found, she mused that her youngest son must be somewhere counting his money.[24]

One of his biggest purchases took place in the mid-1920s, when the young adolescent bought a 1921 Ford Model T Roadster pickup. It had been owned by an old bachelor in Beacon who had taken the engine apart but failed to put it back together. At the time, new Model T's started at about $300, while used ones generally sold for $50 to $75, but because this vehicle was disassembled and in poor condition, John bought it for a mere $10. With the aid of a manual he had ordered from a Kansas City trade school for mechanics, John restored the vehicle to running order in a couple of months. Although not yet a teenager, John wanted to use the truck to start a business, and with his father's blessing, he began a coal delivery service. He filled the bed of his pickup with 500 to 700 hundred pounds of nut coal—small lumps of screened coal often used in heating stoves—from a local mine and sold it door-to-door in and around Beacon for five cents a bushel.[25]

John continued his coal business for a couple of years, but he also started socializing more frequently with a wider range of young people. After going through the first eight grades in Beacon, he began attending high school in Oskaloosa, and because of his Model T, he was one of the few Beacon youngsters who drove himself and friends to and from school. As he became more involved in school, however, John eventually jettisoned his coal operation and ultimately sold his Model T at a profit. An honors student while at Oskaloosa, John excelled at his science courses and architectural drawing. He also indulged his interest in music and played the cornet in the high school band. Although he did not participate in any sport for the Oskaloosa Maroons, he played baseball at home in Beacon.[26]

As in many small towns throughout Iowa and the Midwest, baseball was an important activity in Beacon. Early on, John participated in pickup games with homemade baseballs consisting of string wound around corks and covered with black tape. Later, he joined the town's Twilight League team, which competed against teams from surrounding villages. Such baseball leagues built community spirit in small-town America, as was plainly the case in Beacon. John played outfield, and because of his small stature, which made it difficult for pitchers to throw him strikes, he usually was the leadoff batter. Crouching down while batting, John always made his strike zone even smaller, and he often got on base, whether through a walk, a wild pitch, or a hit.[27]

When not actually playing baseball or attending a game, Americans started listening to the sport on radio. Since the initial radios were expensive, only wealthier families acquired the early models—in 1921, for example, only 50,000 homes across the country had this new medium. Not surprisingly, the Ruans were among the first in Beacon to acquire one—a three-dial, "breadboard" Atwater Kent. By the mid-1920s, this radio was attracting many visitors to the Ruan household, especially friends of Doc Ruan who came over to listen to nationally broadcast baseball games. Now baseball fans across small-town Iowa could follow play-by-play accounts of their favorite teams. As the decade wore on and the price of radios fell, they became much more widespread. By 1929, more than 10 million American homes had radios. Residents in Beacon were part of this trend, and as more people in town acquired their own sets, the novelty of the Ruans' radio wore off. But enjoyment of the fellowship remained, and friends of the doctor continued gathering at his home to catch an occasional ball game.[28]

Such was the life of John Ruan through the summer of 1929. He had enjoyed a Tom Sawyeresque childhood and learned that hard work and ingenuity paid handsome monetary rewards. He was a good student and fully expected to follow his father in the practice of medicine. Circumstances, however, ultimately altered John's career plans and forever changed the family's trajectory. That fall, the stock market crash shook the nation, and it plummeted the Ruans into financial trouble. Wealthy by community standards, Doc Ruan was a gambler when it came to investing, and much of his cash was tied up in risky ventures. Like many others, he had also taken advantage of buying stock on margin. When the market collapsed and the loans were called in, it became clear that the town's last doctor was overextended. Already weakened with prostate trouble, Ruan took the news especially hard. Ashamed by his predicament, the doctor's long-standing prominence only made matters worse. Because of his social and economic position, Doc Ruan's life had been closely followed by the *Oskaloosa Herald*'s section on surrounding towns. Having earlier enjoyed the attention, he now shunned the spotlight.[29]

For a good part of the next year, Doc Ruan sold a number of assets and succeeded in paying off all his debts, but the monetary setback deeply embarrassed the doctor and destroyed his self-esteem. No longer able to face his friends and patients, Ruan decided a move was in order. After making several inquiries, the doctor decided to relocate to Des Moines, where he would join the practice of his friend Dr. Earl

D. McClean. Ruan sold the Beacon house, and with $3,300 and two automobiles, he moved the family to Des Moines in October 1930.[30]

Three thousand dollars of the family's money went into a new home, a large, white, two-story house at 1224 Ninth Street. On a streetcar line, the home was just a few blocks north of downtown Des Moines. Developed in the 1880s as the River Bend neighborhood, the area's prestige had begun to wear off as automobiles led people to build homes farther from the central part of the city. Although the residential district was past its prime, 16-year-old John thought his new environs were "pretty nice," and it was from here that Doc Ruan and his family made a fresh start.[31]

2 An Unexpected Turn in the Road: The Founding of Ruan Transport

Still distraught by the reversal of the family's fortunes, the Ruans tried to rebuild their lives in Des Moines. With $300 of savings left after purchasing their new home, Doc Ruan prepared to join Dr. McClean's medical practice, Rachel put the new house in order, Arthur looked for a job, and John started his senior year at North High School, about a mile north of their Ninth Street residence. Although difficulties were expected, everyone in the family anticipated an eventual return to monetary and social success—everyone, that is, except Doc Ruan.

The doctor's plans of practicing medicine with McClean did not materialize because Doc Ruan never recovered from the devastation of his financial debacle. Once vigorous and ebullient, he was now quiet and depressed. "Father was," John reminisced, "a broken man." His failure weighed heavily on him and worsened his already poor health. Several weeks after arriving in the capital city in October 1930, the doctor underwent surgery to remove his prostate. Soon thereafter, he suffered a stroke and remained incapacitated for the short remainder of his life. He died of pneumonia at Des Moines Lutheran Hospital in January 1931. Fittingly, funeral services for Doc Ruan were held in Oskaloosa, with the former Beacon Methodist minister presiding. Fellow members of Ruan's Tri-Luminar Masonic Lodge provided the order's ritualistic ceremony, and the small town's beloved doctor was laid to rest in Oskaloosa's Forest Cemetery.[1]

The man John had loved and admired, who had encouraged him in his moneymaking efforts and who hoped his son would follow him in the medical profession, was gone. Saddened by this loss, the high school senior buried himself in activity. New efforts at making money now became more urgent, and John started selling homemade potato chips for neighbor George Heiny, who had been laid off from his food brokerage job. Heiny produced the chips in his garage, where he had a potato slicer and deep fryer. Sales of the homemade chips were crisp, and John sometimes made as much as a dollar a day selling the snack food downtown to patrons at Northwestern Bell's lunchroom as well as to local grocers and restaurants.[2] As winter turned to spring, John began mowing lawns in his River Bend section of town. Caring for one yard, he remembered, took "half a day to mow and trim right, and I did it for a dime." Although that was not much in the way of payment, John well understood the value of money in depression-era America: "Well, you had a dime, or you didn't have a dime." As for his future, John had not given up on the possibility of a medical career, but it was becoming clear that this goal was really more his father's than his own. He now considered other professions, such as forestry, engineering, or writing, but the 17-year-old had not decided on his eventual vocation. Still, the young man applied himself at school and planned on attending Iowa State College the following year. The benefits from a life insurance policy that had been held by his father would make at least the first year of study there possible. [3]

John was also busy at home. Following the death of his father, the family had no income. Rachel, who had always been frugal with money, now instituted many household belt-tightening measures. At the same time, she thought about ways to make money and eventually came up with the notion of taking on boarders. Before that was possible, remodeling was necessary. Without any previous construction experience or carpentry training, John and Arthur reconfigured the second-floor bedrooms into three apartments. Their work was not perfect, but they succeeded in turning the upstairs of the house into passable boarding space. While Rachel was quite proud of her sons' efforts, John was surprised and noted, "It's funny what you can do when you have to."[4]

Not all his time was occupied with work, however. Instead of pursuing his musical interests with the school band, John decided he would participate in interscholastic sports, and he tried out for the North High baseball team, the Polar Bears. Coached by the very successful Johnny Johnson, the high-caliber team included some players who had already played semipro ball, while others were part of American Legion baseball. He made the squad, and according to teammate

Larry Hanes, John was well liked by his fellow players because of his competitiveness and congenial manner. Although not a starter, he saw action as a utility outfielder, usually occupying his familiar position of right field. Once, at an away game against a small school, John slipped and fell while chasing down a fly ball. He quickly got up, made the inning-ending catch, and trotted into the dugout. Angered by the right fielder's seemingly clumsy play, which apparently had made a routine catch difficult, Coach Johnson began yelling at John until he realized what had happened. Soon his shouting turned to raucous laughter. The opposing team's baseball diamond abutted a farm pasture, and no fence separated the two fields. While running to make the catch, John had slipped on a "cow pie," covering the front of his uniform with manure. Such comedy notwithstanding, the Polar Bears took their baseball seriously. Late that spring, the 1931 North High team won the first officially sanctioned high school state baseball championship by defeating a squad from Yale, Iowa, by the score of 4 to 2.[5]

John graduated from North High School in the spring of 1931. In the fall, he headed 30 miles north to Ames to start his education at Iowa State College. Like many students new at college and away from home for the first time, John spent nearly as much time involved in extracurricular activities as he did on his studies. Hoping to meet new friends, John pledged the Chi Phi fraternity. At a time when hazing was the norm, the new recruit was put through many humiliating activities before being initiated into the organization. One stunt landed John in the hospital. Required to sit on a block of ice for "a great long time," the pledge's bottom blistered so badly that he needed medical treatment. In another incident, John remembered, "They paddled my butt pretty darn hard" because he could not tie a bow tie. This demeaning punishment had lasting consequences and led to a permanent wardrobe alteration. He explained, "I decided then that if [wearing a bow tie] was that important, I figured I'd better start wearing them. I've been wearing bow ties since 1931."[6]

While he found the hazing "difficult and exasperating," John made new friends and took advantage of several opportunities afforded by his association with the fraternity. That fall, the Lawrence Welk Orchestra, which at the time was touring small towns in the Midwest, arrived in Ames to play at an Iowa State dance. For some reason, however, the group was without its piano player. Immediately, the search was on to find a local musician to substitute for the absent pianist. Aware of John's musical ability, an active fraternity member signed the pledge up for the job. The years of piano lessons paid off; John played so well that Lawrence Welk asked him to join the band. The freshman declined the offer, although John recalled, "I don't know if he meant it."[7]

Besides playing at the dance, John enjoyed the social scene his Chi Phi membership opened up for him, but he never stopped "looking for something to do to make a buck." In fact, the many parties and dances that were held gave him a lucrative idea. Sorority and fraternity members often attended several formal events a year. This meant they needed their dresses, suits, or tuxedos professionally cleaned. Because his brother worked at a dry cleaner in Des Moines, John knew that cleaning rates at that particular establishment were cheaper than in Ames. John thought he could take dirty clothes to the cleaners where Arthur was employed, get them cleaned, charge less than the going rate in Ames, and still make a tidy profit. He discussed the idea with friend and classmate John Varnell, who owned a Model A coupe. Varnell liked the plan, and the two went into business together. They modified the back of the coupe by adding a box to hang clothes and began running laundry to and from Des Moines. Just as John had expected, the money was good, and there was plenty of business. Soon, however, the city of Ames shut down their operation because Ruan and Varnell lacked a license required of those in the dry-cleaning business.[8]

As for academics, John registered as a forestry student and took the prescribed introductory courses for the major, which included yearlong sequences in botany, forestry, English, and military science, as well as courses in algebra, trigonometry, surveying, mechanical drawing, and economics. Given his fraternity activities and moneymaking schemes, he did not spend an inordinate amount of time on his studies. Nonetheless, his grades tended to be above average, and he excelled in classes he enjoyed, especially those involving writing or drawing. In fact, by his spring quarter, John began thinking about other career paths, possibly either journalism or architecture. Circumstances, however, forced him to shelve these plans.[9]

Near the end of his first year at Iowa State, John and fraternity brother Jack Melcher came to Des Moines for a visit. During the stay, Rachel Ruan told her son that there was not enough money left for him to continue at college unless he found a job to pay for it. John told Melcher the bad news, and his friend volunteered a suggestion. If John could persuade his mother to give him one of the two family cars—which the family could not afford to run anyway—he could trade it in on a truck and haul gravel for Melcher's father, who was a general contractor building roads in southern Iowa. John initially scoffed at the idea. "Hell," he said, "I don't know how to drive a truck." But Melcher quickly replied, "You can drive a car, can't you? Well, then you can drive a truck." So persuaded, John asked his mother for the Chevrolet and took it to a downtown car dealer. Working with salesman Paul Manning, John negotiated a deal for a 1930 Ford AA dump truck. Allowed $200 for the car, John was left owing $75, to be paid in 12 monthly installments.[10]

Early Monday afternoon, July 4, 1932, John loaded the truck with various provisions, including his tent, a gas stove, a rifle, and an ice chest his mother had packed with food. While others were enjoying the holiday, he drove 50 miles southeast to the promised opportunity in the small town of Chillicothe, situated along the Des Moines River. Even though it was the Fourth of July, John was eager to get started, and after hastily pitching his tent along the river, he headed down the road to Young and Harvey Gravel Company. Much to his good fortune, a skeleton crew was working, and it was late that afternoon that John picked up his first load of rock and hauled it to the road-building site. After making this maiden delivery, he returned to his camp that evening, ate his supper, and turned in early. The next morning, he was up before dawn and in his truck ready for a full day of hauling. After making several round-trips, he returned once again to his tent by the river. This process became a daily routine over the next few weeks. When not working, John took his rifle and hunted for food. Occasionally, he would "shoot a stray chicken, clean it, cook it up, and eat it about three times a day." And some weekends, he went home to Des Moines, checking in on his mother and brother.[11]

Entering the truck business in this fashion was actually quite common at the time. From the late 1920s to the early 1930s, approximately 150,000 independent truckers drove the highways for the first time. Commonly called "gypsies" or "wildcatters," these independent truckers in the 1920s were frequently farm boys fleeing rural life for the adventures of the city. Later and more similar to John's case, men impacted by worsening economic conditions joined the trucking industry to make money. Entry into the field was relatively easy. Truck dealers were eager to sell trucks, often accepting down payments as low as $125 and then offering buyers the opportunity to pay the balance over 18 months. A 1933 Ford dealer's advertisement in the *Des Moines Register*, for instance, read: "Remember, we carry our own paper, our terms are easy, and our trades liberal." Once a truck was owned, it could serve as one's livelihood, office, and home all rolled into one.[12]

Although similar to the rest of these independent truckers, John had a business savvy and work ethic that most others lacked. Only 18 years old, he had already run a couple of other successful businesses, and interestingly enough, his two biggest undertakings to date had been in hauling—his nut coal operation in Beacon and the short-lived laundry venture in college. In addition, he always liked working and making money. Thus, when many failed because they lacked basic business skills, had lazy work habits, or did not see opportunities, John succeeded.

After driving a little over a month, John took advantage of his first opportunity, and it immediately set him apart from most independent owner-operators. Albert Todd, a friend of the Ruan family and a salesman at the International Harvester dealer in Des Moines, offered John two used dump trucks that he could not sell. According to the arrangement, John had to find drivers for the trucks and pay the truck dealer all the money made with the two vehicles except the drivers' wages— the going rate at the time was $12.50 per week—and the cost of gasoline until the trucks were paid off. The novice trucker jumped at the deal and hired three drivers to alternate on the two additional trucks. Originally, brother Arthur, cousin Walter Carson Jr., and a young man named Ted Cartee joined the operation. Now, rather than working alone, John was managing a fledgling company. The Ruan truckers headed southeast to the Des Moines River and with the exuberance of youth, they were soon hauling more gravel than anyone else in the area. John recalled, "We were regular maniacs. We were reckless, drove people off in the ditch, but at least Wilson [the road boss] liked what we were doing."[13]

In fact, John had so impressed road superintendent Mike Wilson that as the end of the year approached, he suggested John get into the more lucrative coal business. Wilson was about to open a strip mine in Harvey, a small town about 10 miles west of Beacon, and he offered to sell John coal for $1 a ton. Beyond making coal available at a low price, Wilson also suggested a business plan: "If you put an ad in the paper in Des Moines, and cut the local price by fifty cents a ton, I think you can do business." Once again, John saw an opportunity and took it.[14]

His decision to go into coal distribution was far from unique. Throughout the East and Midwest, gypsy truckers "drove to the mines, loaded the trailers with ungraded coal, and delivered it direct to city customers, thus bypassing the retail coal dealer."[15] John had an edge in Iowa's capital city, however, because he was one of the first to sidestep coal retailers. As advised, the upstart Ruan firm advertised its coal at $3.50 a ton, undercutting the going rate in Des Moines by 50 cents.[16] John's mother began working—for the first time—for her son, and the Ruan home became the company's base of operations. Rachel took telephone orders for coal and kept track of the accounts, and the three young men began hauling coal. Throughout the winter, each of the Ruan truckers made three daily round-trips between the Harvey coal pit and Des Moines. John and his drivers worked long hours, sometimes from 4:00 A.M. to 11:00 P.M., hauling over 20 tons of coal a day. The work was grueling because it involved shoveling the coal twice, once on and once off the truck, but it proved profitable. John noted, "I made muscles and I made money at the same time."[17]

The price originally lured customers away from their regular coal vendors, and good service kept them with the Ruan company. One innovation John introduced facilitated the handling of consumers' wishes. Given the depression, many people wished to buy less than a ton of coal at a time, and John turned this situation into an opportunity. He put dividers in the truck beds, creating compartments of several sizes, so the drivers could supply different amounts of coal easily and efficiently. "We could deliver as little as half a ton, if that was all the customer could afford," John recalled.[18] When the weather turned warmer and demand for coal lessened, the Ruan company served as a general common carrier, hauling various other goods to various places. Frequent runs carrying scrap metal were made to Chicago, and if the trip required an overnight stay, John often saved money by sleeping in the cab. Besides driving in the Midwest, he also carried goods east. After renting a couple of refrigerated Fruehauf semi-trailers from Iowa Trailer Sales, John made several trips to the East Coast, transporting butter, eggs, meat, and poultry. Careful to avoid empty backhauls, he lined up finished goods for the return trip. More than once, for example, he brought tires from Lee Tire and Rubber in Pennsylvania back to Iowa. Those trips, he recalled, were, "a tough deal. We didn't have the kind of trucks they have today. . . . We had smaller trucks with loads beyond their engine capacity." Yet those trips produced much-needed revenue, introduced John to people who later proved helpful, and ultimately laid the groundwork for the firm's wide regulatory franchise.[19]

By the fall of 1933, Ruan's drivers returned to the coal enterprise, and initially the company's prosperity continued. "For its size, that was probably the most profitable business [I ever had]," John explained. Other independent truckers, however, soon noticed the potential of this market and went into retailing coal. Mounting competition drove down prices in Des Moines, while mine operators raised their whole-sale coal prices. By early 1934, profit margins in coal delivery were slim, and John pulled his infant company out of the business. Yet, even as John was considering other options, salesman and friend Albert Todd presented him with another possibility. Todd had been impressed with the young man's drive and initiative, so he offered a suggestion that could prove mutually beneficial.[20]

Since the 1920s, local cartage companies across the nation had been gradually replacing horses and wagons with trucks. Todd told John that he might have a chance to carry foodstuffs for Western Grocer. At that point, the food wholesaler was using Hawkeye Cartage, which still operated with horses and wagons. John visited with Western Grocer manager Cliff Demmon at the company warehouse in the Kurtz Build-ing on Court Avenue in Des Moines. After a short conversation, he signed a deal with Western Grocer promising 10 trucks for transporting its products. The contract specified that John would supply trucks and drivers for a fixed price per month. Once again, John saw a good prospect and took it. This time his hasty action was more daring, however. He had agreed to the contract without having the trucks (or funds to get the trucks) to fulfill his obligation. Undaunted, the young business owner went to a downtown bank for the necessary financing.[21]

John first stopped at Iowa–Des Moines National Bank and Trust and talked to a loan officer. The conversation was short, and it did not go well. The banker looked at the contract, sized up the 20-year-old customer, and decided that given the continuing depressed economy and the Ruan company's thin track record, the risk was too great. Turned down there, John went across the street to the office of George Jensen, president of the Euclid State Bank.[22] Known as "Major" Jensen because of the military rank he attained during World War I, the financier knew and trusted Demmon and had earlier worked with Western Grocer. More important, though, he liked John's boldness and self-assurance. He wrote the young man a check but gave a stern warning before handing it over. "Now Johnny," he cautioned, in a thick Danish accent, "you be careful with that goddamn money, that's mine." Thus began John's longtime policy of, whenever possible, using other people's money to build his business.[23]

With the loan secured in the spring of 1934, John traded in his current fleet of three dump trucks and purchased 10 new trucks from Todd at the International Harvester dealer. He then took the trucks to Brown Body Company at East Third and Locust to have special bodies designed and built for carrying groceries. The trucks were maintained and stored at Brown Body's lot, and John rented a small room from the body shop to serve as the new Ruan office. Since business was no longer conducted out of the Ninth Street home, Rachel ceased her involvement in company operations. John hired Ruth Johnson, his first secretary, to help run the office, while Maurice "Moze" Ferris was added to oversee the delivery trucks. These two employees kept an eye on the day-to-day operations of grocery distribution, and John spent time seeking out other business prospects.

One morning the following year, John was visiting with Bernie Evans, the owner of Iowa Trailer Sales, who had earlier leased John some trailers. During their conversation, they discussed Fruehauf Trailer

Company, which was in the midst of replacing independent dealers with its own branch outlets, so that Evans would no longer sell Fruehauf products. John mentioned that he had seen trucks bringing new Fruehauf trailers into town from Detroit, and he asked Evans who delivered them. When he was told that Fruehauf hauled its own trailers, John asked if he would have a chance at getting the contract. Evans thought so and put John in contact with Maury Pickering, the incoming Fruehauf branch manager. Pickering set up a meeting for John with the trailer company's regional vice president. The discussion went well. John soon convinced the Fruehauf representative that his firm would save money by letting Ruan Transport move the manufacturers' trailers, and John received a one-year contract. Once again, the young businessman's self-confidence and his capacity to persuade others of his ability paid off. These traits would serve John well for the rest of his life.[24]

While his Fruehauf operation was getting under way, the Motor Carrier Act (MCA) became law in the summer of 1935. This act placed the trucking industry under the jurisdiction of the Interstate Commerce Commission (ICC), and interstate common carriers were required "to obtain certificates of public convenience and necessity from the ICC. Established operators could get these as a matter of right under the act's 'grandfather clause,' a provision guaranteeing certification to common carriers that could show evidence of 'bona fide' operations as of June 1, 1935. New entries or carriers seeking additional rights, however, were sharply restrained."[25] As John recognized, he had gone "into the business at the right time." Now, because of his earlier and varied hauling experience, he applied for and received wide operating franchises through the MCA's grandfather clause.[26]

John used International tractors for hauling the Fruehauf trailers, which were financed by the truck manufacturer. He would employ such vendor financing many times through his career. With this equipment, the new operation began. It entailed picking up the trailers in Detroit and transporting them to contract manufacturers for finishing—tankers were added to trailer frames in Omaha; livestock racks were attached in Sioux City; and vans or reefers (refrigerated trailers) were affixed in Kansas City—or to branch outlets in the 14-state midwestern region. Although John had regular drivers for the transfer of

Fruehauf equipment, he sometimes transported trailers himself. On one trip to pick up a finished tanker in Omaha, John arrived at Independent Metal Products without gas money for the return trip to Des Moines. Jake Bernstein, the owner of company that built tankers on Fruehauf trailers, gave John a two-dollar bill for gas. From that point on, every time Bernstein saw John, he presented the trucker with a two-dollar bill. When Bernstein died, John gave his widow the pile of two-dollar bills he had received from her husband over the years. After that, John began what became a tradition—handing out two-dollar bills as his personal calling card.[27]

By the end of the contract period, John had 12 tractors moving Fruehauf trailers. These additional trucks made it necessary for Ruan Transport to seek larger facilities. Jesse Brown, the owner of Brown Body, had become annoyed at all the space the trucks were occupying and was pleased when John began scouting new locations. In 1937, the problem was solved with John's purchase of land at 11th and Market Streets. The property, located across the railroad tracks that ran along the southern edge of downtown Des Moines, soon housed the company office and terminal. Brother Arthur initially ran the new office before Van Marin took over as its manager.[28]

By the time the Fruehauf contract expired, John was netting more money hauling trailers than some Fruehauf managers made. When several of them complained, top officials at the company decided it was best not to extend the Ruan contract. Fruehauf bought John's 12 tractors and returned to hauling its own trailers. To ease the transition, John and his drivers worked for this Fruehauf "drive-away" operation delivering its equipment for six months before bowing out completely. Although Fruehauf leadership did not realize it at the time, taking back its internal transit operation would to be a financial mistake, and within a decade, John Ruan would be asked to return.[29]

Besides affording business opportunities, John's association with the trailer company also put him in contact with Roy Fruehauf, one of the younger sons of the family who had been sent to the firm's Des Moines branch outlet to learn the business. John and Roy became fast friends, and over the years, they shared a number of exciting escapades. One trip in the late 1930s stands out because John did very little socializing during the decade, preferring to work long hours and build his business. During a trip to Omaha to look over the Independent Metal Products facility, John and Roy decided to fly to San Francisco for a vacation. The plane had a stopover in Las Vegas, and Roy convinced John to head downtown for some gambling. After only 12 hours in town, John recalled, he had won $25,000 shooting craps. They then headed for California, spent several days at the St. Francis Hotel, and returned to Omaha. Before heading back to Des Moines, John stopped to see Lou Thomas, a Fruehauf engineer, and the two went to an illegal gambling establishment called Chez Paree on Carter Lake, just on the Iowa side of the Missouri River. John remembered his amazing luck continuing, and again shooting craps, he won an astonishing $58,000 before leaving for home.[30]

Gambling, in fact, was one of the few activities that diverted John from his nearly constant attention to trucking. Besides returning to Chez Paree from time to time, he frequented two of Des Moines's gaming establishments—Pete Rand's Mainliner on Fleur Drive and the Grant Club on High Street. One evening, following a long day of work, John went to the Grant Club with Lou Thomas. Soon after arriving, he became involved in an angry exchange with another bar patron. As the conflict heated up, Thomas stepped in and reminded John of the gun he still had in the shoulder holster under his coat. He then suggested they leave before the situation got out of hand. John had completely forgotten about the .38 caliber pistol he was carrying, and he and his friend left without incident. The gun had nothing to do with John's gambling; it was business related. Ever since his Western Grocer drivers began returning at night to the 11th Street terminal with cash payments, John usually had a lot of money at Ruan Transport. He kept the money in his office desk, and because he often worked alone late into the night, John sometimes worried about being robbed. To ward off such a crime and for sheer peace of mind, John purchased the pistol for protection. For several years, it was a standard part of his business attire.[31]

Roy Fruehauf remained one of John's steadfast gambling buddies, and their friendship continued unabated, but since he lost the Fruehauf Trailer contract in 1937, John aggressively searched for other business possibilities. Once again, the advice of associates opened doors to new ventures. That year, a friend named Joe Hall, an insurance agent, informed John that McCoy Trucking of Waterloo, Iowa, was on the verge of bankruptcy. The company owed the insurance man several thousand dollars, and Hall thought that if he and John took it over, he might recover his money. After investigating the company and visiting with owner Harvey McCoy, John bought the majority share of the common carrier, which served Iowa, Illinois, Minnesota, and Nebraska. Joe Hall purchased the remaining 30 percent of the business. Over the next six months, John lived in Waterloo rebuilding the troubled company's operations. Focusing on McCoy Trucking's restoration gave John a familiarity with the general freight business and led him to expand in this area. In 1941, John established Ruan Motor Freight with the purchase of Central Freightways, a common carrier in Iowa. The operation was soon enlarged with acquisition of Leonard Lines, serving both Iowa and Minnesota.[32]

Up to this point, all the suggestions John had followed proved helpful in building his trucking enterprise. Yet, the next tip had much greater significance: it put him in on the ground floor of petroleum transportation. In this highly specialized type of hauling, Ruan Transport would grow into the industry leader. In the fall of 1937, John was talking to E. E. "Chub" Amsberry about the trucking business. A Ruan family friend, Amsberry had run a DeSoto and Plymouth automobile dealership in Oskaloosa before moving to Des Moines in 1935 and taking a sales position at Fruehauf Trailer. He had also been associated with the Shell Oil Company, and it was this latter connection that gave him some valuable information, which he passed on to John. Shell Oil, he noted, was planning to transport petroleum by barge up the Mississippi from a refinery at Wood River, Illinois, to Burlington and Bettendorf, Iowa, and on to St. Paul, Minnesota. Given this new program, Amsberry suggested that Shell might need someone to haul the gasoline out of the new depots to bulk facilities around the state. John saw potential in this idea, and Amsberry arranged a meeting for his young friend with Shell Oil manager Howard Swanson at the company's Des Moines division office in the Valley Bank Building. John signed a contract with Shell to provide five tractors and tanker trailers with a capacity of 4,000 gallons each. The tankers, built by Independent Metal Products in Omaha, were put atop Fruehauf frames, and John took delivery in December.[33]

All seemed to be going well for Ruan Transport. John explained his success simply: "The more I put out, the more opportunities that were offered."[34] Hard work, tips, and luck along the way had indeed propelled the small company, but that was only part of the story. Gone unstated was John's willingness to act on ideas others thought too risky. His intrepid nature was put to the test in 1939, however. A year into carrying gasoline for Shell, the Iowa Legislature began to consider a wide-ranging bill designed to overhaul state trucking regulations. Part of the proposal suggested either limiting the amount of cargo that trucks could transport or assessing a penalty for those exceeding the limit. If the cutoff point was less than 4,000 gallons for fuel, John could not use his recently purchased tankers, and that would put him in real financial trouble. In response, John went into action trying to cajole the legislature into voting down the limitation on cargoes. John recalled, "I'd wined them [the legislators], I'd dined them, and I'd taken them out to my house and cooked steaks and so on and so on." As the legislative session wound down, John thought he had lost, and he went to talk to a representative from Audubon County. The state legislator told him, "I think you're smart about a lot of things, but you sure are dumb about this. They [legislators] just used you as a meal ticket; they killed that [weight limit section of the] bill this morning."[35]

This first attempt at influencing legislation led John to take politics more seriously. He now understood the importance of scrutinizing government action closely. The event also solidified his political leanings. Although his father had been a Democrat, John was heavily influenced by his mother, a dyed-in-the-wool Republican, and given his business sensibilities, he had joined the Republican Party. His views were still malleable, however, until his lobbying efforts brought him into contact with state representatives from both camps. These various conversations convinced John his political affiliation was correct. He would remain a lifelong Republican and in later years become a large donor and important fund-raiser for the party.[36]

With the battle over the weight limit legislation behind him, John returned his full attention to running his company, focusing largely on the tanker operation. In 1938, just as his trucks started moving gaso-line, John sent his brother to eastern Iowa to supervise the operation.[37] Initially, Ruan Transport was hauling Shell Oil products from Burlington to tank farms and wholesale facilities throughout Iowa and Illinois, but the business soon expanded. The following year, Socony-Vacuum Oil, Paraland, and Standard Oil of Indiana added terminals in Bettendorf, and Ruan Transport began hauling petroleum for them as well. After a couple of years, it was clear that company growth man-dated larger quarters, and in 1941, the transit firm built a new termi-nal in Bettendorf.[38]

Over these four years, Ruan Transport's petroleum-hauling division had grown from five to seven trucks, and gallons carried rose from 10 to 18 million. Its gross revenues moved from $75,000 to $100,000, but net profits dipped slightly, falling from $9,000 to $8,200. Although still running a small operation, John had his foot in the sec-tor's door and was making a name for himself in the region. Heavy demand for petroleum during World War II would provide a major boost for the young company.[39]

As his company increased in size, John started looking for a home in a more fashionable Des Moines neighborhood. In October 1938, he and his mother moved into a new four-bedroom house on Lincoln Place Drive in the elegant south-of-Grand section of town. Rachel, who had always been especially fond and protective of her youngest son, would live with John through 1940. Earlier that year, another woman had captured John's attention.

One morning, on his way to the office on Eleventh Street, the bachelor stopped for breakfast at a diner on the first floor of an apart-ment building on Grand Avenue. There he met Rose Alice Duffy, a tenant of the complex. Two years older than John, the dark-eyed, dark-haired beauty had worked for Western Mutual Fire Insurance for nearly a decade, first as a clerk, then as a business machine operator. Rose's striking looks must have attracted many suitors, but it was with John that a romance blossomed. Just as John behaved in business, he worked hard and fast at the courtship. After a few months of dating, the couple eloped to avoid the required Iowa waiting period. They traveled to Sioux Falls, South Dakota, where they were wed on Octo-ber 5, 1940. Friends Claude Rudy, the Des Moines Fruehauf manager, and his wife, Peggy, accompanied them and attended the ceremony. Afterward, the two couples headed west to Absarokee, Montana, about 75 miles east of Yellowstone National Park, for a short vacation and, for the Ruans, honeymoon. There, John and Claude enjoyed elk hunting, and the women went on sight-seeing trips.[40]

Upon returning to Des Moines, John and Rose settled into married life. Unfortunately, given the vagaries of the international situation, establishing a normal routine was difficult. By late 1941, it appeared as if the United States was moving toward war. This fact already had an impact on John and Rose: during their honeymoon in Montana, John had registered for the draft. Ultimately, he would not serve in the armed forces but remain in Des Moines and work for a wartime federal agency.[41]

As war loomed on the horizon, John could look back over the past 10 years with satisfaction. In the midst of the Great Depression, family tragedy, and financial difficulty, he had set out on his own with nothing but a job lead, a used truck, and sheer determination. As many in the nation struggled—some of whom would never recover—John etched out a small trucking operation, which over the 1930s rose from hauling gravel, coal, and groceries to transporting trailers, shipping freight, and finally carrying gasoline. With the U.S. entry into and subsequent participation in World War II, Ruan Transport would be shaped and refashioned to take advantage of new markets and opportunities in the upcoming postwar years.

3 The War and Its Aftermath

Several times over the course of the depression years, John had the fortune of being in the right place at the right time. Trusted friends had given him good advice, and he seized the opportunities presented. Such chutzpah turned the young independent trucker into an owner of a growing enterprise, and by 1942, he once again found himself in an advantageous situation. He also maintained his exceptional work ethic. "I'm no smarter than a lot of guys in town," he once said, "but I work harder."[1] These elements combined to take John and his firm to even greater heights through the 1940s.

World War II increased energy demands, and because John had gotten into the petroleum-carrying business before the war, this division of his company was well positioned to expand with the nation's growing fuel requirements. His expertise in handling petroleum products also kept him from being drafted. This specialized background led John to be declared "essential" to the war effort, and instead of serving in the military, he was appointed to a position with the Office of the Petroleum Coordinator for War—soon renamed the Petroleum Administration for War (PAW)—in 1942. The agency oversaw all aspects of the wartime petroleum industry including use, conservation, market allocation, and shipping. John was assigned to the 15-state Midwestern District, and not surprisingly, he worked in its supply and transportation division.[2]

John was among those charged with ensuring that petroleum shipments moved throughout his district. Most of his time was spent addressing problems in the Midwest, but once or twice a month he traveled to Washington, D.C., for meetings or committee appearances or to obtain necessary clearances. His job was complicated, because many railroad tank cars that were usually deployed in the Midwest had been sent east to replace tanker ships. Prior to the war, ships had delivered most of the Atlantic seaboard's fuel and heating oil, but once the United States became involved in the war, these ships were vulnerable to attacks by German submarines. In addition, the Office of Defense Transportation decreed that shipments by railroad tank cars "be lim-

ited to a minimum of 200 miles from the point of origin." This ruling was based on an estimate "that one large tank truck could ade-
quately replace 12 railroad tank cars for hauls up to 200 miles."[3] For
John, it meant that all of the short hauls (less than 200 miles) and
some of the longer hauls of petroleum made within his district were
moved by truck, and he often pulled strings to get the tank trucks to
their destinations. On New Year's Eve 1944, for instance, he called
Iowa governor Bourke Hickenlooper out of a party because one of his
trucks carrying fuel oil was stopped at the scales in northeast Des
Moines. The truck had been accidentally overfilled at the bulk plant,
and the weight master demanded that the product be drained off until
the truck met weight limitations. When John threatened to call a
newspaper and have photographs taken of valuable fuel being
dumped, Hickenlooper intervened, and the fully loaded truck was
sent on its way.[4]

While John's time at the PAW served the interests of the nation, it
also proved beneficial for his company. Since the job did not require
him to move from Des Moines, John could oversee his own company's
operations when not concentrating on government work. That was
important because of the tremendous growth the firm experienced
during the war years. In addition, John's work in the agency's transportation division introduced him to numerous people in the oil business. One prominent figure he met was Frank Phillips, the founder of
Phillips Petroleum, who briefly served as the chairman of the midwestern region for the Office of the Petroleum Coordinator.[5] Such
connections often proved valuable in obtaining future business contracts. Furthermore, discussions with various oil representatives made
the trucker aware of problems and concerns they had about the transit and delivery of their products. John's "key-stop system"—a major
innovation in the tank truck industry that allowed Ruan Transport drivers to pick up and deliver petroleum at any time of the day or night—
grew out concern for efficiency.

For years, railroad tank cars had delivered the majority of petroleum products from terminals to bulk stations, and a system had been
developed that allowed them to transfer their cargo to wholesale storage facilities regardless of whether they were open. As the war pro-

gressed and tank trucks were used for short hauls of petroleum goods, John thought that truck drivers should have the same freedom as the railroads had to make pickups and deliveries at unattended facilities. To do so, John developed the "key-load" and "key-stop" system. Through the new Ruan program, clients had the option of having their product loaded onto or delivered by Ruan trucks at unattended terminals, plants, or service stations. The idea was actually quite simple—John's drivers carried keys that unlocked certain valves at patrons' facilities. With this access, they could fulfill customers' needs around the clock. This practice had started in 1943 but initially was used only by Shell Oil and a few other small Ruan accounts.[6]

The same year that "key-stop" was getting under way, John hired two managers who would play critical roles in the years ahead. In March 1943, Ray Denkhoff joined Ruan Transport as general office manager. John had met Denkhoff years before, when Denkhoff had been the credit manager for the International Harvester branch in Des Moines. Known for his easygoing personality and coolness under pressure, Denkhoff was immediately well liked and respected within the company. After serving as general manager for seven years, he was promoted to operations manager, overseeing the transportation services at all the company's terminals. In this position, Denkhoff reported directly to Robert (Bob) Root, who also joined the trucking enterprise in 1943. Root and John became acquainted in 1939 when he moved to the city's south-of-Grand area, two houses down from John on Lincoln Place Drive. Root's background was amazingly similar to his new employer's. Like John, he was from a professional family in southeastern Iowa. Both were from small towns, and both started, but neither finished, college. By the time the two men met, however, their worlds had diverged: Root was a successful bond salesman and John was in the hauling business. As the neighbors became friends, John told Root of the bright future in trucking and tried to hire him. John's cajoling notwithstanding, Root was not yet ready to leave the investment world. He stayed in the bond business, joined the firm of William Blair and Company, and was sent to Chicago.[7]

The friendship between the two men continued during Root's time in Chicago. While there, he began helping John with "specialized" freight. Two of John's good friends, Sam McGinn, part owner of the Hotel Fort Des Moines, and Joe Rosenfield, an attorney, prevailed upon the trucker to buy liquor in Chicago and transport it to Des Moines. Root bought the liquor and had it hidden in the nose of a Ruan trailer. It was then sent to Des Moines. Although Iowa did not prohibit alcohol, the state was the sole wholesaler, and bringing such cargo in from Illinois was illegal. From 1941 to 1943, the years Root was in Chicago, several of these shipments were made. The liquor was stored on the eleventh floor of the Hotel Fort Des Moines. Once, when it was discovered that the establishment was about to be raided, John had driver Hap Tulk pick up the alcohol and load it on a trailer at a Ruan lot several blocks south of the hotel at 10th and Cherry Streets. It remained hidden there for over a year before being returned to McGinn's hostelry. Law enforcement officials never discovered any of the illegal liquor, and over the years, every time Sam McGinn passed the former Ruan lot, he would smile and say to himself, "God bless John Ruan."[8]

Following several of these liquor deals, John had worn down Root's resistance to joining the trucking business, and in August 1943, Root came to Ruan Transport as vice president. An elegant, intelligent, and respected gentleman with good connections to the financial world, Root served as the company's outside liaison, providing John with an entrée to lenders. He was the consummate salesman, and when not talking to bankers, he was recruiting new customers. So important was selling, thought Root, that he once wrote for the *Ruan Transreporter:* "The sales department is not the whole company, but the whole company should be the sales department." Selling the company's services and winning over new clients kept Root on the road much of the time, and before office space was readied for him, he worked at the end of John's desk. This also suggested the close relationship between the two men. With Denkhoff and now Root on board, John had two close, trusted friends and associates who would help him manage and extend the company.[9]

Because the Second World War brought about many changes in American society, running a company during the period was sometimes challenging. In Iowa, as with the nation, many positive transformations occurred. Agricultural production rose, farm income jumped, and tractors increasingly replaced animals as the motive power in the fields. Many existing industrial establishments expanded, and many new ones were created to fill wartime production needs. In 1939, Iowa had 2,541 manufacturing firms; by 1947, that number had risen to 2,965. This growth increased fuel requirements, and John's business expanded with it. Meanwhile, the presence of military bases in the state also affected Iowa. In fact, a proposed army base that would stretch across southern Iowa and northern Missouri had a direct impact on Ruan Transport.[10]

In the fall of 1940, Clifford Demmon of Western Grocer contacted John about establishing a grocery store in Corydon, a small Iowa town 75 miles southeast of Des Moines. According to reports, the military appeared likely to build a 40,000-acre training camp on a site spreading across Iowa's Wayne and Decatur counties and southward into Missouri. Estimates suggested that up to 25,000 troops would be stationed at the base. In addition, 500 houses were to be constructed—half in the town of Leon and half in Corydon—for noncommissioned officers. As plans progressed, many expected a boom in Corydon, and Western Grocer wanted in on the bonanza. A new Corydon grocery supplied by his wholesale firm, Demmon believed, could take advantage of the population increase. Initially, John was not interested because he "didn't know a thing about running a grocery," but when Demmon suggested he might drop Ruan Transport in favor of another cartage firm for hauling the company's wholesale products, John relented. In November 1940, he announced the opening of his Corydon Jack Sprat Food Store on the west side of the town square. The market was to be managed by two men from Des Moines.[11]

Ironically, the same day the Corydon newspaper reported the opening of John's new grocery, it also ran a story calling the proposed military camp "uncertain." A month later, on December 5, 1940, the paper explained that plans for the new Iowa base were being scrapped in favor of a fort in southern Missouri. Without the installation, the increased demand for food did not develop. Furthermore, the Ruan store faced stiff competition from established Corydon retailers such as an A&P, Piper Grocery, Sheets Cash Grocery, and the Supply Store (a forerunner of Hy-Vee Foods). With no improvement in sight, John closed the market after operating for only 11 months. On one level, the venture was clearly a failure: John went into a business that never made money and shut down in less than a year. On another level, however, even though the store never turned a profit, it was worthwhile because John succeeded in keeping Western Grocer as a client. This would not be the last time John was pressured into a bad business move by an important customer.[12]

Although Iowa lost this army post to southern Missouri, the state's economy still received a boost when its four active military sites—the naval training facility in Ottumwa, a B-17 training base in Sioux City, the Women's Army Corps (WAC) at Fort Des Moines, and the Women Accepted for Volunteer Emergency Services (WAVES) center at Cedar Falls—swelled with personnel during the war. One young naval officer who went on to an infamous political career spent a short time on an Iowa base and became friendly with John Ruan. The 29-year-old lieutenant was Richard Nixon. In the fall of 1942, Nixon's orders sent him to the Ottumwa Naval Air Station, which he later referred to as "a runway that stopped abruptly in the middle of a cornfield." Nixon served as an administrative aide at the air station, while his wife, Pat, took a job as a teller at Ottumwa's Union Bank and Trust. Because the Nixons saw the small farming town as a "deadening backwater," they looked to Des Moines for a cultural respite. Early on during the Nixons' six months at the air station, Max von Schrader, whose family owned Union Bank and Trust, took them to Des Moines for dinner and introduced them to John Ruan, a friend and bank customer. From late 1942 until the Nixons left Iowa the following spring, John met them for lunch or dinner "several times" and found them to be "very nice people." Years later, during his 1972 presidential reelection campaign, Nixon would recall this wartime acquaintance and successfully solicit John's assistance as a fund-raiser.[13]

The war, of course, also brought both challenges and opportunities for John and other business owners. Initially, trucking was hit hard. In 1942, the Office of Defense Transportation, the government agency overseeing American wartime transit, required that all trucking firms obtain a Certificate of Necessity. Because Ruan Transport was hauling a growing amount of petroleum, it quickly received this authority to operate. Meanwhile, tire rationing, regional gasoline rationing, and then the halting of civilian truck and trailer production created

headaches for the industry. Shortages in replacement parts made ser-
vicing tractor fleets tough, and the lack of tires resulted in a growing
number of drivers hitting the road without spares. Later that year, the
War Production Board recognized five classes of users who could buy
trucks. Of the 33,000 applications received, only 640 users (including
Ruan) qualified. Even with access to equipment, Ruan Transport also
faced wartime personnel shortages, especially of qualified drivers. Not
surprisingly, when a load had to go out and no driver was available,
John stepped into the tractor and made the delivery himself.[14]

John's biggest challenge during the war was keeping up with the
increasing business. In the early 1940s, the Great Lakes Pipe Line—a
common carrier of refined petroleum products such as diesel fuel, heating oil, and gasoline, which was owned and principally used by Continental Oil, Mid-Continent Petroleum, Skelly Oil, Texas Company,
Pure Oil, Phillips, Cities Service, and Sinclair Refining—began adding
depots in Iowa. The pipeline originated in Tulsa, Oklahoma, and ran
to Kansas City, where it divided into two branches. One branch
headed through central Iowa, sending a line east to Illinois and north
to Minneapolis, while the other ran along the western border of Iowa
and continued up to North Dakota. In 1942, Great Lakes Pipe Line
established a terminal in Des Moines, and later that year, it added
another terminal in Coralville, a small town just west of Iowa City. The
following year, pipeline terminals were completed in Sioux City and
Council Bluffs, and a station in Clear Lake (about 120 miles north of
Des Moines) was up and operating by early 1945. As the pipeline grew,
John added facilities near each of the pipeline's terminals. By the war's
end, he had trucks operating out of buildings in each of the afore-
mentioned five communities plus his marine terminal in Bettendorf.[15]
Meanwhile, several other companies operated their own pipelines
throughout the area. Standard Oil of Indiana had two such lines. One
originated at its refinery in Sugar Creek, Missouri, and ran north
through Kansas City into Iowa, reaching Council Bluffs, Sioux City,
and Des Moines. The other extended from its refinery at Whiting,
Indiana, northwest to Dubuque, Iowa, and Minneapolis, Minnesota.
Sinclair Refining's pipeline came north from its facility just south of
Kansas City to Fort Madison, Iowa, and then to Peoria, Illinois.
Socony-Vacuum's pipeline began outside of Wichita, Kansas, and

headed north to Omaha, Nebraska, and Sioux Falls, South Dakota, while Champlin Refining operated a line from McPherson, Kansas, northward to Rock Rapids, Iowa. By the end of the 1940s, all of these pipelines were served by Ruan out of one of its already established terminals or at new ones added in Dubuque, Iowa (1947), Mankato, Minnesota (1947), Spring Valley, Minnesota (1948), and Pekin, Illinois (1948).[16]

These new terminals and the additional truck and trailer combinations needed for the mounting business required substantial borrowing. International Harvester carried loans for the trucks, Fruehauf provided credit for the trailers, and much of the other money was borrowed from Central National Bank in Des Moines. In late 1942, Edwin Buckley, president of Central National, demanded that Ruan Transport's financial books be reviewed by an independent accountant before he loaned John more money. Up to this point, the trucker had focused on building the business and paid little attention to keeping company records. Buckley recommended that the local firm of Bemis, Ream, and Knobbe, which handled the accounting work for several other truck lines, do the audit. Partner Lester Ream, whose family had come from John's hometown of Beacon, examined the company's financial statements. Among other things, he recommended that the business be incorporated. Buckley concurred, and John followed the advice. In April 1943, Ruan Transport Corporation was born. Initial directors were John, his brother, Arthur, and John's wife, Rose.[17]

As John's business increased with the new pipeline terminals and rising demand, his family experienced growth as well. Rose gave birth to a baby boy at Iowa Methodist Hospital in Des Moines on May 10, 1943. The baby, named John Ruan III, was healthy, but Rose was not. Although the pregnancy had been uneventful, the birth was difficult. Rose had hemorrhaged, and doctors could not control the bleeding. When she was brought back to the hospital room, a doctor told John his wife's situation was grave, and she was not expected to live much longer. John was sitting in the drab room with his pale wife when she took his hand and whispered, "Johnny, I don't want to die." Following those last words, Rose closed her eyes. Within an hour, she was dead. Grief-stricken, John was left to raise his hours-old son on his own.[18]

The memorial service was held at Dunn's funeral home, and Rose was buried at Resthaven Cemetery in West Des Moines. Following the interment, an acquaintance began talking with John and suggested that religion could provide comfort in this time of sorrow. When it became clear that the young widower could not get out of the conversation, his aunt, Mayme Carson, stepped in and pulled her nephew aside. After thanking her for rescuing him, John suggested he would seek solace in work, not religion. "I'm just going to go out and make a million dollars," he told her.[19]

This statement was telling. Although John had been raised in the Methodist Church, religion had become less important to him once his family moved to Des Moines. After John entered trucking in 1932, organized religion no longer played a significant role in his life. Sunday became just another day to work and seek new opportunities.

Meanwhile, since childhood, John had often chosen work over play, and money was clearly a motivating factor. Over the years, he found that for himself, there was a correlation between hard work and financial reward. He also found that labor had intrinsic value. Looking back over his life, John explained, "I like working. If you didn't like it, why, well, why would you do it?"[20] And work for John helped him through times of despair. Concentrating on various odd jobs and school activities had carried him through the period following his father's death. With the loss of Rose, John again tried chasing away the gloom by throwing himself into work.

Work helped John through the heartbreak, but he now had an infant to think about as well. Johnny, or John III (pronounced "John Three"), as he would later be called, was cared for by a full-time nanny. Rachel Ruan, John's mother, understood the pain John was suffering, and she soon came to help as well. Never really happy about "losing" her son to marriage anyway, she gladly returned to John's home to share his life and once again run the household on Lincoln Place Drive.

Early in his young son's life, John sometimes combined work and pleasure trips. In April 1945, John, Rachel, Johnny, the nanny, and Bob Root all headed up to Clear Lake. John and his vice president were reviewing arrangements to put trucks in a new Clear Lake facility to serve the Great Lakes Pipe Line's terminal that had recently opened.

Meanwhile, the Ruans were vacationing. During the visit, John ran into Charlie Strickland, president of Mason City Gas and Electric. Strickland was irritated about Ruan Transport's entry in the area because it would compete with the utility's railroad—which ran from Clear Lake to Mason City—for the pipeline terminal's petroleum business.

To settle their differences, the two men sat down over drinks. After being "seasoned with booze," Strickland's anger subsided, and he suggested that if John's company was coming to town, he might as well buy a vacation home on the lake. Since he dabbled in real estate, Strickland knew of an available lakefront property. He took John to see the cottage, but in his inebriated state, he had forgotten the door key. Not to be stopped, Strickland kicked in the door. John liked what he saw and was also intrigued by its history—the home sat on land originally owned by Grenville Dodge, civil engineer, Civil War soldier, and later politician, who served as chief engineer for construction of the Union Pacific Railroad during its drive west to create the first transcontinental railroad. Sensing a sale, Strickland called John Corsaut, the homeowner, and put John on the line. Strickland asked Corsaut bluntly, "What do you want for it [the house]?" Corsaut replied, "$10,000," and John responded simply, "It's a deal." Over the years, the Clear Lake property served as both a summer destination for the Ruan family and a center for entertaining customers and company parties.[21]

Several months before the Clear Lake trip, Root had been actively recruiting more customers. He was especially interested in the local division of Standard Oil of Indiana. C. & W. Transport hauled all the company's petroleum products from its Des Moines pipeline terminal. Root met with Joe Honomichael, the oil company's division manager, several times and promised that Ruan Transport could provide Standard Oil better service than it was currently receiving. Finally, Honomichael called John in for a meeting. When he arrived, the Standard Oil manager was sitting with Sigfred Carlson, one of the owners of C. & W. Honomichael said that he was going to give Ruan Transport 15 loads a day for a month and compare its service head-to-head with C. & W. If John's company proved better, it would receive an even greater share of Standard Oil's business. When the trial period was over, Honomichael was indeed happier with the Ruan firm, and he upped its allocation to 25 loads a day. Soon, both Carlson and partner Lanceford Wood saw the difficulty in competing with Ruan, and they sold C. & W. Transport to John in February 1945.[22]

With this acquisition, Ruan Transport's dominance as the leading Des Moines-based for-hire carrier of petroleum products grew, and after just six years in the business, it was the largest such independent hauler in Iowa. Expansion of its petroleum business was nothing short of extraordinary. Revenues rose fivefold, increasing from $300,000 in 1942 to $1.67 million in 1945, while the number of trucks employed jumped from 18 to 78. Meanwhile, John also ran two freight firms: the smaller Ruan Motor Freight saw revenues rise from $38,200 in 1942 to $63,800 in 1944, while McCoy Truck Lines' revenues fell from $427,900 to $387,200 over the same period.[23]

In the midst of this wartime growth, Roy Fruehauf offered John a great opportunity. Fruehauf was one of the trucker's best friends, and John once said he and Roy "were closer than two brothers."[24] Often impulsive, Fruehauf told John, "If we ever get out of this war, by God, I want you to come back and haul these trailers." From 1937 to 1941, Fruehauf moved its own trailers, and to management's chagrin, it proved much more expensive than contracting for this service. When civilian trailer production was curtailed in 1942, such a move was obviously not necessary. Fruehauf was looking ahead to whenever normal conditions returned. He wanted his company to concentrate on what it did best and farm out other operations. John, on the other hand, remembered how profitable his relationship with Fruehauf had been, and he readily agreed that when the war was over, he would take back the trailer transit business.[25]

Even though the war in Europe was nearing its end by the spring of 1945, John did not spend much time thinking about his soon-to-be-renewed contract with Fruehauf. In addition to running his own companies, he remained busy with PAW duties. In early April, he received a telephone call from friend Sam Majors. John had met Majors several years earlier because both were in the trucking business. This call, however, was social. Majors was from a prominent Democratic family, and he was planning to have lunch and spend an afternoon with Vice President Harry Truman later that month. He invited John to join them. John turned down the offer because it conflicted with an appearance he had scheduled before the War Production Board. Early on the morning of April 13, Majors again called John. "Ruan," he said, "you'll go down in history as the only guy who was too busy to have lunch with the President of the United States." The previous afternoon, Franklin D. Roosevelt had died of a cerebral hemorrhage in Warm Springs, Georgia, and Truman was sworn in as president that evening.[26]

When the war finally ended, John happily surrendered his PAW position and returned full time to his business. As his firm had rapidly expanded, John had become more and more apprehensive about releasing company information. This concern grew out of the premium he had always placed on privacy. Although he often made speeches at events such as trucking conventions, John generally shunned the spotlight and rarely gave interviews. Following World War II, this interest in maintaining as much confidentiality as possible led to new corporate entities. After consultations with top management and accountants, John created two additional enterprises. The new firms and their relationship with Ruan Transport were part of a strategy designed to shield income from public scrutiny. In May 1946, Terminal and Supply Corporation was established, and the following March, John founded Eastside Service Corporation. Much of Ruan's property—real estate, terminal buildings, tractors, trucks, and trailers—was transferred to Terminal and Supply, which then leased it back to the trucking company at rates set by management. Eastside Service was founded to buy and stock truck parts and tires, which it then sold to Ruan Transport. John owned all the stock of these two enterprises as well as 100 percent of the transport firm, but the new companies had no corporate connections with the trucking enterprise. Unlike the operating entity of Ruan Transport, which was required to disclose its financial records because it fell under the jurisdiction of the ICC, these two recently created corporations were not so obligated.[27]

Not all of John's time was occupied with business, however. In the spring of 1946, John was introduced to an attractive young woman named Elizabeth "Betty" Jayne Adams. Betty's neighbors Earl and Edna Rush, who for months had been trying to get Betty to meet John, finally succeeded in bringing the two together. Long employed at Firestone Tires, Earl had recently started working at Ruan Transport, and he told John about the delightful young woman. A dinner party was eventually arranged at John's house, and the Rushes brought Betty Adams with them.[28]

Betty was the youngest of three daughters born to Tom and Matilda Adams of Valley Junction (a community renamed West Des Moines in 1938). A talented tap dancer, she was an attractive and popular student at Valley High School. After graduating in 1942, Betty and friend Norma Jeann Gordon formed a dance duo and took their act on the road. Calling themselves "the Gordon Sisters," they entertained throughout the Midwest at various small towns, military bases, and eventually Chicago. Although the two loved dancing, they were both homesick and returned to Iowa in 1945. Once back, both entered the Miss Iowa Pageant: Jeann won, and Betty was named runner-up.[29]

Once introduced to John, Betty was charmed by the businessman's sense of humor and dynamic personality.[30] He was also intrigued and recognized Betty as the Chicago dancer who had caught his eye a year earlier during one of her performances. For her, it was "love at first sight." John was interested, but he was a littler slower to come around. As he jokingly recalled, "She'd say to me two times a day, every day, let's get married. She beat me down."[31] Actually, John did not require much convincing. The two dated for only a few months before John contacted friend Sam Majors about making wedding arrangements for him in Kansas City, Kansas. Like his first wedding, once John decided to marry, he wanted to wed immediately, and Kansas (similar to South Dakota before) required no waiting period before marriage. On September 6, 1946, John and Betty were married at Washington Avenue Methodist Church with his good friends Ray and Marge Denkhoff in attendance. Following the ceremony, the Ruans and the Denkhoffs went to dinner, where they were joined by Bob and Dorothy Root. John and Betty then retired to the Bellerive Hotel, where they spent their wedding night. Unfortunately, the newlyweds did not enjoy a quiet, blissful night. John recalled, "We had an awful time getting to sleep or anything else we had in mind because people kept trying to get into our room. There were telephone calls and beating on the door until I was almost out of my mind. I finally went to the door and jerked it open, and the people trying to get in our room apologized when they discovered someone was already there."[32] The next day John and Betty left Kansas City and drove to the cottage at Clear Lake, where the couple enjoyed some solitude. After a weeklong honeymoon, they returned to Des Moines. Once back in town, they lived at John's house on Lincoln Place Drive for a month before moving into a larger home several blocks southwest on 34th Street.[33]

Marriage transformed much of John's life, but it did not alter his devotion to his work and company. The first major change involved Rachel. When it appeared that John and Betty's relationship was heading toward marriage, his mother moved out rather than share her "little boy" with another woman. She took an apartment at the Commodore Hotel on Grand Avenue. Although out of the house, Rachel was less than a mile away, and she remained intimately involved in her son's life. Roughly a year later, on August 11, 1947, Betty gave birth to Elizabeth Jayne Ruan. While John remained a workaholic and was often away on business, Jayne immediately transformed the hardnosed businessman into a doting father. The warm and close relationship that developed between father and daughter contrasted with the way John interacted with his son, Johnny. Whether he unconsciously blamed his son for the death of his wife Rose or because in his despondency he had trouble expressing love for the child, a formal and distant relationship between father and son evolved.[34]

As John's postwar family was growing, so too was his company. From 1946 through 1949, the firm's petroleum-hauling business continued its rapid growth. Following the war, John and his vice president, Bob Root, saw that the efficiency of "key-load" and "key-stop" service could be used to keep current customers and attract others. The procedures were selling points because they offered oil companies a flexibility of delivery generally available only to those who owned and operated their own tank trucks. At the same time, it provided Ruan Transport greater efficiencies. "Key-stops" were made between 8:00 P.M. and 6:00 A.M., while the routine deliveries took place during the day. Mechanics were stationed at terminals around the clock, and the firm's equipment was therefore kept running 24 hours a day. Fifty customers were taking advantage of "key-stop" by 1946, up from a handful when the idea was introduced in 1943. With more firms contracting for these services, full-time oversight was required, and Moze Ferris was tapped for the new position. "Key-load" and "key-stop" garnered much attention and succeeded in attracting additional customers. By early 1950, one-third of Ruan Transport's petroleum deliveries employed this system. In all, 850 bulk facilities and service stations of 15 major oil companies were using these programs.[35]

"Key-stop" service to gas stations was soon improved when Ruan became the first for-hire carrier in the Midwest to add meters to its tankers. The meters allowed for delivery to several service stations with one truckload. They accurately measured the amount of fuel dispensed at each station and then printed a ticket that confirmed the transaction. These automated receipts were left at customers' offices. Such meters allowed for any size delivery, and therefore Ruan saved money because the tank trailers did not need to be compartmentalized. Similarly, the printed receipts cut down on patrons' bookkeeping responsibilities.[36]

The convenience of "key-load" and "key-stop" were but only two of the company's offerings that appealed to customers. In the midst of completing a study of the company in 1950, industrial analysts Duff, Anderson, and Clark conducted a survey of major shippers using Ruan Transport. Results indicated that customers regarded Ruan's service as excellent. L. H. Cowles, general traffic manager for Standard Oil of Indiana, which accounted for 48 percent of Ruan Transport's freight revenue, noted that "the company [Ruan Transport] is one of the best, if not the best, of all motor carriers used by Standard Oil." He praised the firm's "favorable terminal locations which permit an effective trans-fer of equipment" and referred to Ruan management as "capable, young and energetic." L. W. White, traffic manager for Mid-Conti-nent Petroleum, had similar feelings: "As a group they [Ruan man-agers] . . . have a record and reputation of fair dealing with shippers equaled by few companies and certainly not excelled by any." The responses to the survey were overwhelmingly positive and could be summed up in the words of a Phillips Petroleum representative. He found Ruan Transport "to be extremely competent . . . with a keen grasp of transportation conditions." It was, he thought, "one of the better transporters in the nation."[37]

With increased attention on moving petroleum products and plans being readied for the renewal of business with Fruehauf, John decided to drop his freight operations. In July 1947, he sold his share of McCoy Truck Lines to partner Joe Hall. Several months later, in

December, he sold Ruan Motor Freight to Birney Baker, owner of Des Moines Transportation Company. Nevertheless, John maintained his grocery division, which still hauled canned goods, fruits, and vegetables for Western Grocer. Added to this comparatively small operation was a large truck that made deliveries to Younkers department stores throughout the state. In 1947, however, Western Grocer was purchased by the larger Consolidated Grocer, and by the end of 1949, it opted out of its contract with Ruan Transport. Almost a decade earlier, John had worked hard at keeping the Western Grocer account; now, with his petroleum business booming, he was happy to close down the division.[38]

These changes in Ruan's businesses were related to changing company quarters. By 1943, the company had outgrown its office and terminal space on Southwest 11th Street, but plans to build on property it owned at Second Street and University Avenue were thwarted because of flooding. While the Grocery and Younkers Division remained at the old 11th Street facility, the company divided its larger operations between two new locations. Ruan Transport moved to 30th and Scott, a couple of miles from the Great Lakes Pipe Line terminal, and the freight companies worked out of a building at 10th and Cherry streets. In 1945, a small terminal building was erected at Southeast 30th Street, and in 1947, construction of a two-story addition began. As the new building went up, Ruan Transport temporarily shared the 10th Street site with its freight division. When the structure was finished, Ruan Transport moved to its new headquarters at Southeast 30th and Scott streets.[39]

As the company set up shop in larger and more modern quarters, further acquisitions occurred. Ruan's share of the state and regional petroleum-carrying business grew when the firm took over Schaefer Transport Company—out of Coralville—and the Des Moines and Coralville operations of Sam Majors's St. Louis–based American Petroleum Transports. In Council Bluffs, John added equipment and business by buying Terminal Transport's tractors and contracts based at that pipeline location. Farther west, Ruan Transport bought M & S Transport Company, which had intrastate carrying rights in Nebraska.[40]

These additions and the aggressive selling of company programs such as "key-stop" occurred during the beginnings of the postwar economic boom. Millions of Americans who had long been deprived of consumer goods used wartime savings to buy new automobiles, build homes in suburbia, and fill these new dwellings with the latest appliances. With the baby boom further fueling consumer spending and the cold war keeping defense allocations high, the economy continued its upward trend. John looked back over the 1940s and explained the rapid rise of his trucking business: "We met a demand with a service that was needed and we've grown with the demand."[41]

Keeping up with this demand meant that Ruan Transport's tractors logged millions of miles a year. In 1948, for instance, the firm's 150 trucks traveled 13.4 million miles, delivering various types of petroleum products. Such heavy usage was hard on the fleet, and keeping older trucks operating was costly. John therefore opted for new trucks. In what was said at the time to be "one of the largest equipment deals in the history of Iowa motor transportation," Ruan Transport bought 65 International tandem tractors and 11 White tandem tractors. John called the purchase "a good investment, not only for safe and efficient operation, but also for the future security of the business and the employees."[42]

By the end of 1949, Ruan Transport was running its fleet out of 10 terminals strategically located in Iowa, Illinois, and Minnesota. It employed 330 people and operated more than 150 tractor-trailer combinations, up from 90 in 1946. Revenues climbed rapidly as well, moving from $1.84 million to $4.44 million. Net income, meanwhile, soared from $68,000 in 1946 to $452,000 in 1949.[43]

This was not the only growth, however. John's trucking enterprise was experiencing expansion on another front as well. Roy Fruehauf made good on his pledge to give John his firm's trailer-hauling business. In the summer of 1946, Ruan Equipment Company was formed to convey Fruehauf products between the manufacturer and contract builders, from factories to dealers, or directly to customers. With its primary facility near the Fruehauf plant in Fort Wayne, Indiana, Ruan Equipment established other terminals close to Fruehauf trailer factories in Detroit, Michigan, and Kansas City and Springfield, Missouri. From the beginning, this was a sizable operation. Ruan Equipment was running approximately 140 tractors; roughly 45 to 50 of them were based at both Fort Wayne and Detroit, with fewer operating out of

Kansas City and Springfield. In order to remain near major Fruehauf sites, several Ruan Equipment terminals were closed and new ones added as they followed the larger Fruehauf plants around the country. Before the end of the decade, the Ruan terminals in Detroit and Springfield were shut down and new ones were added in Avon Lake (Cleveland area), Ohio; Memphis, Tennessee; and Los Angeles, California. In addition to hauling trailers from these locations, Ruan Equipment picked up trailers in Omaha, Nebraska, and Seattle, Washington.[44]

These distant terminals, combined with the growth of Ruan Transport and John's penchant for hands-on management, meant that the expanding company's president was often away on business trips. To make travel more convenient, Terminal and Supply Corporation purchased a twin-engine Beechcraft in 1946. With room for seven passengers, this plane was the first of a number of company aircraft. It was flown approximately 100,000 miles per year through the remainder of the decade. Besides John, Root and other top executives used the plane to visit company terminals, see vendors or shippers, recruit new customers, or make appearances before the Interstate Commerce Commission.[45]

Besides his large operations, John entered smaller businesses as well. In 1947, C. Earl Fletcher, owner of a used-car lot and auto body shop, and several minority investors founded G. I. Taxicab Company in Des Moines. With 13 Packard taxis, the new firm was smaller than its two established competitors. McGrevey Cab Company had 25 taxis, while the much larger Yellow Cab owned 117. After several months of struggling against the two other companies, G. I. Cab remained in the red, and Fletcher decided he preferred concentrating on his other businesses. While a buyer was being sought, Claude Rudy, former Fruehauf branch manager and now a White Truck dealer who owned several shares of G. I., told his friend John that the cab company was a good opportunity. This conversation led to a meeting between John and Fletcher, and in early 1948, John bought the taxi firm for $18,500. The name was immediately changed to Ruan Cab Company, but turning a profit remained illusive. Although John would not make money with this operation for several years, Ruan

Cab did expand his company's name recognition. Through various gestures of community goodwill, such as working with the Polk County Society for Crippled and Disabled Children, the company helped build good public relations. Early on, in the summer of 1949, Ruan Cab provided free transportation to a camp for disabled children at Grandview Park in Des Moines.[46]

Community outreach and goodwill were attained in other ways as well. In 1947, a Ruan petroleum tank driver, L. H. "Lum" Edwards, began coaching a neighborhood group of boys playing baseball. The following year, he approached John about sponsoring this team in the Junior City League. Having long enjoyed baseball, he agreed, and the Ruan Cardinals were born. Practices were scheduled in between Coach Edwards's trucking runs. In 1948, the Cardinals won the city title in their division. The next season, the boys were moved up to the more competitive city league, and again, they won the championship. After their second consecutive title, the Cardinals were advanced once more, this time landing in American Legion baseball, "the toughest competition outside of organized baseball." Here, the Cardinals remained a top team and kept the Ruan name associated with the community good.[47]

Another public relations effort was more directly related to the trucking business and much more important. The company's safety program was designed, in John's words, to "first, protect the thousands of motorists who meet Ruan transports on the highway each day; and second, to protect the tanker drivers themselves and the company's equipment." Ruan Transport began an effort to enhance safety in the mid-1940s, but the program did not hit full stride until 1949. The campaign had a $40,000 annual budget, and manager George Hutchison was appointed its administrator. Before joining Ruan in 1945, Hutchison had been in charge of dock and driver personnel at McCoy Truck Lines.[48]

At decade's end, the Ruan safety program consisted of the following. First, four driver supervisors—each responsible for two or three terminals—were put in charge of all company drivers. These managers hired and trained new drivers, retrained old drivers, and continually evaluated the drivers on their knowledge of traffic laws and their driving skills. Second, Hutchison led quarterly safety meetings at each terminal. Third, drivers' families were involved in the program with weekly mailings home and the inclusion of the in-house publication, the *Ruan Transreporter*, with the monthly paycheck. Fourth, a preventive maintenance program for each tractor-trailer was established, calling for weekly inspections and overhauls at regular mileage intervals. Fifth, annual awards banquets were held at each terminal to recognize drivers for their safety record. Finally, cash bonuses, first given out in 1946, were given annually to drivers for accident-free driving, maintenance of their equipment, adherence to schedules, and personal appearance and attitude. In 1949, $6,000 in safety bonuses was distributed among 150 Ruan drivers.[49]

John was delighted when the *National Petroleum News* noted in 1949 that the Ruan driver safety program was "recognized by the trucking industry as one of the best." Certainly pleased about the resulting safer roads and good public relations, he was clearly happiest about the enhanced bottom line. The *Iowa Oil Spout* explained that the strategy actually increased profits: "By preventing damage to equipment, saving on man hours and insurance costs, it has increased the over-all efficiency of the transport service."[50]

The company's tractors themselves also augmented the safety program. Ruan Transport worked closely with its suppliers, most often International Harvester, to equip the trucks with the latest safety devices. The new trucks purchased in 1949 came with tandem axles, which provided greater traction and braking on slippery roads; a two-speed auxiliary transmission with more forward speeds for greater hill-climbing ability; a Ruan-designed device that helped prevent jackknifing; and tachometers and tachographs that recorded the drivers' speed and stops. Air brakes, air horns, and CO_2 fire extinguishers furnished further security.[51]

Highway safety and good public relations combined yet again. In the summer of 1949, Ruan Transport distributed more than 1,100 copies of Emily Post's *Motor Manners*—a book on driving and traffic etiquette—around the state to Iowa's schools and colleges. An additional 400 copies were handed out to all Ruan employees. Sent with the books was a letter to school superintendents and librarians from John Ruan. It said, in part:

Though there is not a commercial line in the book, we do have a selfish interest in presenting it to your school. We want your students to think of the trucking industry as what it is: an industry doing everything in its power to prevent accidents and encourage courtesy on the highways. But more important, we feel sure that "Motor Manners" will be read by your students with keen interest—and will do much to put across the fact that good manners behind the wheel are a means of saving lives. Perhaps I have a special weakness for trucks, but truck drivers are gentlemen of the highway. They have fewer accidents. They are professional drivers. They have learned from experience that good motor manners pay dividends in safer, more efficient transportation.[52]

Ruan's distribution of Post's new work was widely reported and extolled by Iowa newspapers. Most important was the *Des Moines Register*'s response. By 1949, the *Register*'s wide circulation made it the state's most influential newspaper. It praised both Ruan's gift and the manual itself in a lead editorial. Written as a poem, the piece was accompanied by a *Motor Manners* cartoon.[53]

The impact of the safety program was also reflected in the company's minimal number of driving accidents, and the industry soon acknowledged this accomplishment. In the fall of 1949, winners of the first annual National Tank Truck Safety Contest were announced. Within the group of largest operators—those logging more than 5 million miles annually—Ruan Transport, with .618 accidents per 100,000 miles, placed a close second to the smaller Dugan Oil Transport, whose accident ratio was .545 per 100,000 miles. Compared with the national average of 3.4 accidents per 100,000 miles for all commercial carriers, both Dugan and Ruan had maintained outstanding safety records. This was the first national safety award Ruan Transport received; a long line of additional such trophies would be added in the upcoming years.[54]

Also in the fall of 1949, John Ruan was recognized by fellow truckers as the first Iowan to hold one of the top general offices of the American Trucking Associations (ATA). He was elected fourth vice president of the ATA by a unanimous vote at the organization's annual convention in Boston. Previously, John had served on the association's executive committee and as the Iowa Motor Truck Association (IMTA) representative to the ATA. In fact, he had been a founding member of the state organization. John and 11 other Iowa trucking executives had met at the Kirkwood Hotel in December 1942. They decided that because lobbying was of growing importance, the state's truckers would be better served speaking with one unified voice. Therefore, they agreed to merge the state's three motor carrier groups—Independent Truckers of Iowa, the Iowa Motor Carriers Conference, and Northwestern Truckers, Inc.—into the IMTA. John was elected treasurer of the newly consolidated association, a behind-the-scenes job he held for the next 40 years.[55]

These positions in both the state and the national organizations, coupled with the safety award, seemed to signal John's arrival on the national trucking scene. Revenues from his petroleum-hauling operation merely confirmed John's growing significance. By 1948, Ruan Transport was the second largest petroleum carrier in the United States, and by the end of the decade, it was within $100,000 of overtaking the leader, Leaman Tank Lines of Pennsylvania.[56]

Much had changed for John over this eight-year period from 1942 through 1949, and yet, much had also stayed the same. Personally, John was deeply wounded by the tragic death of his wife Rose, while at the same time he became a father for the first time. Although he literally worked through his grief, the loss of his wife in childbirth strained the father-son relationship between John and Johnny. Three years later, John remarried and was soon a very proud and devoted parent to his second child, Jayne. Family life was new, but John remained dedicated to his company. Long hours at work continued as he built an organization that took advantage of the increased demand for petroleum. Company growth was phenomenal, and many people in his position would have sat back and enjoyed the fruits of their labor, but not John. He was not one to dwell on past accomplishments but was always pushing forward and seeking new challenges. Over the next few years, John tried several new ventures with varying degrees of success, but he would easily reach his self-proclaimed goal of making a million dollars.[57]

John's father, Dr. John A. Ruan, ca. 1906. Courtesy of John Ruan.

John's mother, Rachel Ruan, ca. 1905. Courtesy of John Ruan.

Trolley car sitting in front of the Ruan home (left) in Beacon, Iowa, ca. 1914. Courtesy of John R. Jacobs.

Across the street from the Ruan home in Beacon, ca. 1914.
Courtesy of John R. Jacobs.

John Ruan as a baby, 1914. Courtesy of John Ruan.

John Ruan as a
senior in high school,
1931. Courtesy of
North High School,
Des Moines, Iowa.

North High School State Championship Baseball Team, 1931. John Ruan
is standing in the upper left corner. Courtesy of North High School,
Des Moines, Iowa.

John Ruan (lower right) walks past his fleet of three
trucks parked alongside his Ninth Street home in
Des Moines, 1934. Courtesy of John Ruan.

John behind the wheel of one of his trucks devoted to hauling
for Western Grocer, ca. 1936. Courtesy of John Ruan.

Ruan tractors and drivers in front of the Des Moines Fruehauf office, 1936.
Courtesy of David Irving.

John's first wife, Rose (Duffy) Ruan
in the 1930s. Courtesy of
John Ruan III.

John holding his one-year-old son,
John III, 1944. Courtesy of John
Ruan.

Betty Adams (later Ruan; right), during her dancing days in the early
1940s with partner Jeann Gordon. Courtesy of John Ruan.

Betty and John Ruan
on their wedding day,
September 6, 1946.
Courtesy of John Ruan.

Ruan gasoline transport in a Des Moines parade, 1946.
Courtesy of John Ruan.

The Ruan Clear Lake cottage as it looked in 1947. Courtesy of John Ruan.

The Clear Lake cottage in 2002. Author's collection.

Betty Ruan and children, Johnny and Jayne, in the family's boat at Clear Lake, Iowa, ca. 1952. Courtesy of John Ruan.

Ruan Transportation's new general offices and home terminal at East 30th Street and Scott Avenue, Des Moines, Iowa, 1948. Courtesy of John Ruan.

Ruan Cab Company providing transportation for the Polk County Society for the Crippled at the Disabled Children's Summer Camp, 1949. Courtesy of John Ruan.

Ruan Transport's "key-stop" director, Moze Ferris (left), working with a Shell Oil employee in Des Moines as they ready facility for off-hours, "key-stop" deliveries of petroleum, 1949. Courtesy of John Ruan.

John playing the piano at the first annual Ruan Transport Five Year Club banquet, 1951. Courtesy of John Ruan.

John's Grumman Mallard airplane dropping off guests for fishing trip, 1951.
Courtesy of John Ruan.

Ruan petroleum tanker taking on a load at a pipeline terminal, 1951.
Courtesy of John Ruan.

John visiting with a Ruan
Transport driver, 1952.
Courtesy of John Ruan.

Good friend Roy
Fruehauf and John
shake hands at the
1954 National Tank
Truck Carriers, Inc.,
convention. Courtesy
of John Ruan.

4   Into the Big Time

Dick Herman, a former owner of Herman Brothers Tank Lines—a small company that competed head-to-head with Ruan Transport in parts of Iowa and Nebraska during the 1950s—believed John Ruan became successful because "he was a fierce competitor and tough businessman." Equally important was John's charm, which he frequently employed while recruiting potential customers. According to Herman, "John used entertainment better than anyone in the industry." Early in the decade, guests were taken to the Clear Lake cottage or flown on the company's airplane to a remote lake in Canada for fishing and camping. Later, after Ruan Transport acquired an island property on Brule Lake in northern Minnesota, it became the company's primary site for entertaining. Guests enjoyed a warm camaraderie in this pristine wilderness, and here John worked his magic. With his wry sense of humor and self-confidence, he cut business deals, assuaged disgruntled shippers, wooed new customers, and maintained good relations with suppliers.[1]

Yet this "hail fellow well met" personality he so readily turned on for business functions was somewhat a facade. Fairly shy and very private, John kept his distance from most people, and few ever knew him well. Instead, John preferred a small circle of close friends. Through the 1950s, his closest associates remained Bob Root and Ray Denkhoff at work, while those outside the company included Tom Bannister, Charlie Bendixen, Howard Gregory, Evert "Hud" Weeks, and lawyer and business executive Joe Rosenfield. John was at ease with these intimate friends, but often their recreational time together turned to business matters. Even his hobbies, such as hunting, golfing, or playing the piano, were usually enjoyed at business functions or company events. When these diversions took place on a Saturday or Sunday and were purely for pleasure, they invariably followed several hours of work. Margaret Ann Bastian remembered, "John and Tom [her late husband, Tom Bannister] loved quail hunting together, but John always went down to the office for awhile before meeting my husband to go hunting."[2] With single-mindedness, John worked. Rosenfield explained: "It isn't only money. It's energy and persistence. Hard work. Hard work. He works all the time . . . Ruan takes the prize for effort."[3]

This effort played a central role in the rise of Ruan Transport. According to a 1950 appraisal conducted by accountants Ream, Martin, Cloutier, and Sanderson, Ruan Transport and Terminal and Supply Corporation owned tractors, trucks, and cars appraised at $855,000; tank trailers worth $1,077,000; and operating rights valued between $900,000 and $1,200,000. These figures did not include any company-owned real estate or other operations such as Ruan Equipment or Ruan Cab Company. As the sole stockholder of all these businesses, John must have been pleased with these numbers: he had surpassed the $1 million plateau he set for himself at Rose's funeral.[4]

His drive and focus remained undiminished, and John continued to press forward through the 1950s. Petroleum hauling, which expanded through enlisting additional customers and acquiring competitors, remained the core of his business. This growth made Ruan the nation's largest hauler of petroleum products by 1957 and provided the foundation for diversification into long-distance freight, insurance, and the transit of other bulk goods such as chemicals and cement.[5] Meanwhile, possibly pushed to succeed where his father had failed, John used his increasing profits to try his hand at various speculative investments. And when not specifically focusing on his firm or portfolio, he spent countless hours looking out for the trucking industry through various trade associations.

In his own company, John remained a firm believer in hands-on management. Leading by example, he "put in the hours," and a company culture developed that dictated employees do the same. Many in the Des Moines office started their workday at 7:00 A.M., but not John. If he was in town, he had already been at his desk an hour or two before others began arriving at the 30th Street headquarters. For John, the workweek always included hours at the office on Saturday and Sunday as well. On Sunday, he expected to be alone at the office, but Saturday was another story. According to LeRoy Brown, a Ruan manager who at the time was in charge of keypunch operators and tabulating machines, "John wanted everybody on Saturday to be there, and you'd put in some time on Saturday . . . By God, we were all there, and we found things to clean up that didn't get done during the week."[6]

John's time at the office habitually included holidays, even Christmas Day. He remembered, "I'd go down and spend a few hours at the office either before or after we opened presents." His work ethic became legendary, and when he was not on the job, it was newsworthy. Sidelined with appendicitis, John had surgery, but his recovery was slow. When John's absence reached 10 days, the *Ruan Transreporter*, the company's in-house magazine, wrote tongue in cheek: "Believe it or not, readers, this is the longest period the 'Pres' has ever been away from his office and the business that bears his name."[7]

This Ruan employee publication had been upgraded from a small, typed pamphlet to a magazine format in 1949. Issues of the *Ruan Transreporter* included news from each terminal, introductions of new employees, and information on company events. The publication also featured photographs, short humor stories, cartoons, and brief monthly "letters" from John Ruan.

After recuperating from surgery, John was back at the office putting in his long hours. His work frequently extended into the night, and although he did not often mix with his employees, late-night strolls through the building sometimes led to impromptu encounters. One evening, for instance, LeRoy Brown and James Gabriel from accounting were running punch cards through a tabulating machine when janitor Sam Bradley tried to persuade them to take a break and shoot craps. At that point, John walked in and demanded, "What the hell are you doing, Sam? Are you bothering these guys back here trying to work?" Then his tone lightened, and he said, "Alright, Sam, do you want to roll those goddamn dice? Put your damn money down, we're gonna roll right here." With that, John and his janitor started playing craps. The game lasted about half an hour, and when it was over, John had all Sam's money. LeRoy Brown was astonished: "I couldn't believe that here's the president of the company down there rolling dice . . . he was just as much a regular person as anybody that night." Clearly, Brown was not surprised to see John at the office late at night, but watching the boss take a break and gamble with an employee caught him off guard. Such interactions occurred from time to time, but they were clearly the exception.[8]

If John's hours on the job were extraordinary, his knowledge of company operations was also exceptional. He demanded up-to-date information from his top lieutenants, and while the management team was small, these updates were generally accomplished through informal discussions. Vice president Root was clearly second in command, overseeing both sales and operations. Denkhoff, the operations manager, had charge of the terminals and reported directly to Root. George Hutchinson, the safety director, and Moze Ferris, manager of customer relations and the "key-load"/"key-stop" system, were also responsible to Root. Bill Gorgas, head of accounting, reported to John, but when it came to those in charge of company shops, engineering, and public relations, the lines of authority blurred. Theoretically these three department heads were within Denkhoff's jurisdiction, but they were also directly under John's supervision. Such a structure had worked as the company was growing, but it was clear that full responsibility for the firm's success or failure rested with John. An independent analysis of the company conducted by Duff, Anderson, and Clark in 1950 discussed this point and noted that this overreliance on a single individual could prove problematic. It suggested a revamping of the management structure with clearer lines of authority. The subtle message was that as the company expanded, John should continue to hire good people and work on further delegating responsibility.[9]

Not surprisingly, John took only part of the recommendation to heart—he did not delegate any decision-making power, but he added managers as Ruan Transport grew. Besides increasing business with current customers and winning new ones, the company expanded through an orderly acquisition program. Early in the decade, two purchases opened up new territory for the company. In August 1950, John signed an agreement to buy Union Service Company, a petroleum-hauling truck company based in Wood River, Illinois (a few miles north of St. Louis on the Mississippi River). Initially run as a wholly owned subsidiary, Union Service had operating rights in Illinois and parts of Missouri, and it vastly expanded John's business in those states. By mid-decade, its name was changed to Illinois-Ruan Transport Corporation. The following year, with the acquisition of bankrupt Petroleum Carriers Company, the firm broke into the Minneapolis/St. Paul area. It was authorized to conduct business in parts of Colorado, Minnesota, Montana, Nebraska, and North and South Dakota.[10]

Throughout the 1940s and early 1950s, developing the business was foremost in John's mind. Expansion remained the priority for the balance of the 1950s, but John began devoting greater attention to labor relations. Interest in this area became more urgent in 1950 when two strikes affected the company. In January, terminal operations at Spring Valley, Minnesota, were interrupted by a Teamsters' strike over drivers' wages. The dispute was settled after seven weeks and raised drivers' wages from $1.20 to $1.37 per hour. Several months later, in June, maintenance workers in Des Moines went on strike and returned to work only when they were given the same 13-cent hourly wage increase the Des Moines drivers had already received.[11]

Prior to these strikes, Ruan Transport had been slowly working to create a corporate culture that encouraged loyalty and avoided labor conflict. Although his true feelings were sometimes hidden by his gruff demeanor, John in his own way cared about his employees' welfare. Often when bookkeepers were working late at night at the company's 10th and Cherry headquarters, John gave them money and sent them up the street to the Hotel Fort Des Moines for dinner. Then, when the firm went from this site to East 30th and Scott streets, John quickly solved a problem created by the move. Although the new office was nicer than the previous one, the new location was much less accessible to public transportation than the downtown facility had been. Since few employees owned cars and bus service was generally poor, some office staff now had great difficulty in getting to work. John's answer was a company shuttle service. James Gabriel, a Ruan billing clerk who lived on the west side of Des Moines, was given a company car—a station wagon—to pick up six or seven workers on his morning drive to the office. The station wagon was loaded up at closing time, and Gabriel dropped fellow employees off on his way home. The service proved so popular that a second vehicle and driver were soon added.[12]

Other labor-friendly measures included life and health insurance for employees, with the company paying 30 percent of the premiums. For building esprit de corps at each terminal, there was an annual competition between the facilities for best overall performance as measured by the terminals' safety records, maintenance ratings, problem-free product delivery, and appearance of buildings and personnel. Drivers had the additional incentive of cash bonuses for safe driving, and general office employees were granted a second week of vacation after three years of service.[13]

Management also launched preemptive efforts to head off strikes before they occurred. In late 1950, for instance, Ruan Transport and the Teamsters negotiated a voluntary pay hike. It called for a five-cent per hour wage increase for Iowa drivers a year before their contract expired. The company initiated a new policy regarding drivers' pay as well. Instead of handing out paychecks at the terminals, the firm began mailing them home. The *Des Moines Evening Tribune* explained, "This enables the wives to have at least a watchful eye on the family purse strings, and the system has proved generally popular. A few wives telephoned the offices of the truckers' union to express their gratification, although the idea was Johnny Ruan's own."[14]

Not all of John's focus was on the rank and file. He worked at creating a sense of cohesiveness among the managers as well. Beginning in 1946, he hosted what became an annual managers' retreat at his Clear Lake cottage. Held in the late summer, the three-day event ultimately grew to include up to 200 people and then spilled over into area hotels. But for a good many years, the annual affair was relatively small. It was a time for managers to get better acquainted with each other and John. Activities included boating, fishing, golfing, and poker, with evening feasts often featuring steaks grilled by John himself. Alcohol flowed freely, and these outings occasionally turned raucous. Although they sometimes resembled fraternity parties, these annual affairs allowed managers to blow off steam and provided them with a worthwhile bonding experience.[15]

Meanwhile, management also tried to forge a community within the company by holding holiday gatherings and creating a club honoring employee service. Beginning in 1950, annual Christmas parties for employees and their families were held at all of the company's terminals. Each party featured a visit from Santa with gifts for the children as well as music, entertainment, and food. The Des Moines terminal party often featured KRNT radio personality Bill Riley, who went on to a long television career and for many years hosted the Iowa State Fair Talent Search. In June 1951, the first annual Ruan Five Year Club Banquet was held at the Hotel Fort Des Moines. Established to recognize loyalty to the company, this first meeting was attended by all 57 eligible employees whose experience with the company ranged from the minimum 5 years to Moze Ferris's 16 years of service. The *Ruan Transreporter* referred to the event as a "gala occasion with humor and fun mixed with serious discussion" of how Ruan Transport attained its position as one of the nation's top petroleum carriers. John served as the party's master of ceremonies and entertained the crowd with a performance on the piano. As toastmaster, he handed out years-of-service pins to all present and humorously described each employee's history at the company. Finally, as the evening's keynote speaker, John spoke briefly of the company's history and his vision for its future. In a masterful stroke, he concluded his remarks by instilling a sense of ownership in the crowd: "Our Company is no better than the group that makes it. We, of this Five Year group, are the key people in our organization. If we do a good job, our company will grow. I hope to see you next year at our banquet, plus many more people who qualify for Five Year membership."[16]

Greater focus on employee relations likely aided the company's continuing commitment to safety. By 1952, Ruan Transport was running 240 tractor-trailer tank trucks throughout six midwestern states, and it remained one of the safest tank truck companies on the road. In 1950 and 1951, the company won the Trailmobile Trophy, the National Tank Truck Carriers' highest safety award. The honor was based on the company's "safe operating record and its efforts to promote general public safety." The following two years, Ruan came in a close second to Dan Dugan Transport Company.[17] The company's success in this area won John recognition outside the industry. In 1951, he was selected to chair the Iowa Safety Congress's second annual statewide public safety campaign. The effort included the "most extensive automobile [safety] inspection program in the history of the state."[18]

This emphasis remained a constant, and Ruan Transport continued to win awards for its safety record even as the management team was gradually augmented and reorganized. In 1952, Harold Baker was hired to replace Ray Denkhoff as operations manager. Baker had headed Petroleum Carriers Corporation for Ruan since 1950 and had earlier been the president and general manager for KIOA radio in Des

Moines. Most of his career had been spent with the Great Atlantic and Pacific Tea Company. With Baker now heading operations, Denkhoff was moved to manage the Des Moines terminal. On paper, this change in position looked like a demotion for John's close friend and longtime employee, but in reality it was not. As a result of the firm's rapid expansion, Denkhoff and Rex Fowler, an attorney the company had on retainer, spent a great deal of time seeking additional rights and rate increases from the ICC. Overseeing one terminal instead of all Ruan facilities freed up Denkhoff for this important duty.[19]

With sales becoming more important, John and his vice president Bob Root could no longer make all the calls, and it became clear that a sales manager was needed. In 1953, Gerald "Gus" Geraghty was appointed to the new position. Geraghty had been with Ruan three years before being named to the new position. Prior to coming to the firm, he had worked for Hughes Oil Company in Chicago for 12 years. Also important was the appointment of attorney Henry Fabritz as the manager of the rate and claims department. He succeeded attorney Joe Harrington, who had started with the company in 1950. Harrington had worked on building good public relations with the state legislature and lobbied the lawmakers to revamp state trucking regulations. Once Fabritz came on board, the position's focus changed; now the majority of the company attorney's time was spent dealing with the ICC over issues of rates and extensions of operating authority.[20]

With these administrators in place, John slowly began delegating more authority, but he never relinquished decision-making power, and those who made policy without his awareness or approval were treading on dangerous ground. Harold Baker once made what he thought was a minor decision without consulting John, and it proved to be a serious mistake. During a managers' meeting, a Baker assistant announced the small change in policy. Henceforth, he said, lease operators would be paid a penny more a mile. Caught off guard by the statement, John shouted from where he had been standing at the back of the room, "Wait just a goddamn minute; we're going to have a recess here for about 15 minutes." He then charged up to the podium and angrily told his top people in no uncertain terms, "We're not going to do this. Where in the hell did you guys get this idea?" When the meeting resumed, Baker rose and sheepishly informed the room, "We're very flexible when Mr. Ruan wants to do something so we've changed our minds about the penny a mile." LeRoy Brown remembered the incident: "Ruan put the fear of God in everybody who worked for him. . . . Clearly there wasn't a committee running the place; he was."[21]

John, of course, was overseeing much more than just Ruan Transport. By 1953, his taxicab company owned 40 cabs, up from the 13 when it was purchased five years earlier. This growth had necessitated larger quarters, and early that year, the company moved from its Grand Avenue headquarters to a building at Southwest Sixth and Tuttle streets. The company was still managed by Clayton Ankeny, who had headed the operation ever since John entered the taxi business. In 1954, Ruan Cab purchased Capitol Cab Company (formerly McGrevey Cab). Ruan's acquisition of Capitol left Des Moines with just two taxi companies—Ruan Cab and Yellow Cab.

Meanwhile, Ruan Cab had added a rent-a-car and rent-a-truck service. The rental division maintained two locations, one at the cab company's main office and one at the Des Moines Airport terminal. Soon Ruan Rent-A-Car became part of a national rent-a-car system. In the early 1950s, Roy Fruehauf had introduced John to entrepreneur Warren Avis, who in 1946 had founded Avis Rent-A-Car. John was impressed with Avis and the system he had developed. Avis was expanding his operation nationally by selling franchises. The two soon struck a deal; John bought a franchise, and in 1953, Ruan Rent-A-Car became the Avis outlet for Des Moines.[22]

Although the Ruan cab and rent-a-car unit seemed unrelated to the trucking operation, a system was developed that created economies between the various company components. A range of cars, from entry-level Chevrolets to luxury sedans, was initially purchased for use by the rent-a-car firm. After a certain number of miles, the majority of these vehicles were turned over to Ruan Transport to be used as company cars. Finally, some of these cars were overhauled, painted, and put into service as part of the Ruan Cab fleet. Such recycling of automobiles was right in line with John's attention to costs and the bottom line.[23]

Like the cab company, Ruan Equipment was also growing. As of 1953, its 221 tractors were "rented for 'drive-away' delivery of new and used trailers," with the vast majority of its business coming from Fruehauf. The company was now operating out of four terminals: its general office and terminal at Fort Wayne, its largest terminal at Avon Lake, its facility in Memphis, and the company's smallest station in Los Angeles.[24]

Success in these businesses gave John the wherewithal to put money in a variety of speculative undertakings. Like his father, John was a risk taker, but unlike Doc Ruan, who made financial moves without much forethought, the young trucking magnate carefully scrutinized every investment. Later Ruan executive Larry Miller explained, "He seldom rushes into anything. He really puts an idea through a test before embarking. He's not one bit reckless. He's willing to take a gamble, but it's pretty well thought out and calculated risk-taking that he does . . . He's aggressive, yet conservative."[25]

One of John's earliest moves outside of trucking was at the suggestion of friend Joe Rosenfield. In 1946, the Younkers executive asked John to join him and a couple of other investors—including Bob Root and Ed Buckley, president of Central National Bank—in buying a radio station. John agreed, and the group purchased a station in Marshalltown, Iowa, for $50,000. In a quick turnaround, the station was sold the following year for $75,000, and John realized a profit of nearly $6,000 on a $12,500 investment. Making such easy money whetted the group's appetite for more media investments. Soon John and his friends bought stations in Jamestown, South Dakota, and St. Paul, Minnesota, as well as station KIOA in Des Moines. In 1960, John became involved in an even bigger media investment. Early that year, Rosenfield had received a telephone call from stockbroker George Lyon at Piper Jaffray in Minneapolis. Lyon told Rosenfield that a block of the privately held Boston Herald stock was available. Rosenfield was immediately interested and convinced John to join in the venture. Over the next few years, he and John accumulated additional shares in the firm and became important minority stockholders of the Massachusetts media company.[26]

On these and other investments, John often sought out the advice of accountant Roger Cloutier. The two originally met in 1947 when Cloutier, recently hired by the Bemis accounting firm, accompanied Lester Ream to do some work at the Ruan firm. Gradually, he took over more and more of Ruan Transport's accounting work until John and the company became his client. Conservative in his financial advice, Cloutier generally counseled caution, and he became a reliable sounding board for John to think through possible purchases or ventures. The accountant spent so much time at John's office that at least one new Ruan employee thought Cloutier was a coworker at the trucking firm. Even when not at the Ruan building, Cloutier was still available for consultation, and John often called this trusted adviser at home. While never social friends, the two men were close and remained so through several decades. John's service as a pallbearer at Cloutier's 1991 funeral exemplified their longtime bond.[27]

Cloutier monitored many of John's investments, including the trucker's early involvement in oil properties. In 1951, John accepted an invitation of Roy and Harry Fruehauf to join with them and businessman Howard Hall in the development of oil wells in Oklahoma, Texas, Wyoming, and, to a lesser extent, Indiana and Kentucky. This move was motivated by three factors. First, John was incredibly loyal to his friends, and he had difficulty saying "no" to close associates like Roy Fruehauf. Second, many years before, Doc Ruan had invested in oil wells that turned out to be dry. Not following the doctor into the medical profession, John was likely drawn into the oil business to gain his deceased father's approval and succeed where Doc Ruan had long ago failed. Finally, Cloutier saw tax advantages accruing to John through these investments, and he supported the move.[28]

Early in 1952, Ruan Transport's board of directors authorized John to invest up to $75,000 of company money into the syndicate's oil properties. Over the course of the decade, he continued to pour funds into these projects. Although there were oil strikes and some wells made money, the real advantage to these investments was the tax write-off value. With depletion allowance, drilling and operating expenses, and depreciation, the oil-drilling operations showed losses throughout most of the 1950s, significantly decreasing John's taxable wages over the decade. His first year of involvement in oil properties yielded declared losses in oil drilling of $122,000. This amount outpaced his taxable wages for the year by $46,000.[29]

Somewhat similar to his interest in oil wells was John's 1955 purchase of a picturesque acreage in Booneville, approximately 15 miles southwest of downtown Des Moines. Once again, the 41-year-old businessman was probably measuring himself against his father, who had owned several farms. In addition, John's fond memories of his many fine summers spent on the family farm outside of Beacon might have driven him to find a similar escape outside Des Moines. The property was named Jonbar Ranch, an abbreviation for John and Betty Adams Ruan, and after several additional purchases of surrounding parcels, it eventually totaled nearly 1,200 acres. With its timber, ponds, and the Raccoon River running along the southern boundary, the ranch was enjoyed by the Ruans for hunting, fishing, and one of John's favorite pastimes, tramping about the woods looking for morels, his favorite wild mushrooms.[30]

A discussion of mushrooms, in fact, ultimately led to a helicopter ride out to Jonbar. In the early 1970s, an Enstrom Helicopter representative from Michigan was in Des Moines trying to sell John a helicopter. During their conversation, John mentioned Jonbar and the large numbers of morels growing at the ranch. The salesman said he would like to see these mushrooms and offered John and his friend Howard Gregory a "test drive" in a helicopter he had recently sold to Allied Insurance. The three men flew to John's acreage and landed in an open area on the property known as Indian Hill. John then took the salesman and Gregory into the timber to one of his favorite mushroom haunts. Although the salesman did not sell the helicopter that day, John located plenty of mushrooms, and they headed back to the Des Moines airport with several bags full of the fungi.[31]

Although John certainly appreciated the many recreations afforded by the land, his business sensibility insured that Jonbar was a working ranch operated for profit. Some of the land was planted in corn and soybeans, and for awhile, the ranch maintained a herd of purebred cattle. It was also the site of company picnics in the late 1950s.[32]

In addition to his investments in oil wells and farmland, John quietly went into retail business. In 1950, Russell Settlemyer, Des Moines division manager of Anderson Prichard Oil, approached John with a new idea about selling gasoline. He thought there was a market niche for filling stations offering cheaper gasoline and fewer services. At the time, gas stations around the country provided full service, filling a patron's gas tank, checking the car's oil, and washing the windows. Settlemyer suggested that if fewer services were offered, labor costs would be reduced, and the savings could be passed along to the customers in the form of less-expensive gasoline. The idea made sense to John, and he and Settlemyer joined together as equal partners in the venture. Named R & S Oil Company, the business began in 1951 with a station in Des Moines at Eighth Street and University Avenue and another in Sioux City. While John owned half the operation, he was not an officer of the company, and his participation in the enterprise was kept secret because customers of his petroleum-hauling business might complain about Ruan Transport competing with them in the retail market.[33]

In the mid-1950s, R & S Oil of Waterloo, an associated company of the Des Moines service station operation, was established to retail gasoline in the Northeastern Iowa city. As the business grew, it continued to stress its quality products at inexpensive prices. One R & S advertisement read: "Hi-Octane Regular Gas, Premium Ethyl Gas— Nationally Advertised Oils 'at a savings.'" By the end of 1960, R & S had grown to five outlets: the two original stations, one owned and one leased operation in Waterloo, and a new station in Charles City, a county seat approximately 50 miles northwest of Waterloo. Net profits for the year were $16,500 on revenues of $890,000. By the late 1960s and early 1970s, however, other discount stations had entered the market. This new competition led John and partner Settlemyer to reconsider their situation and eventually close the company after 25 years of business. Ultimately, the two realized large profits on the sale of the defunct firm's real estate properties.[34]

Yet, all these ventures were small compared to a major corporate resurrection John undertook at Roy Fruehauf's behest. In 1953, John's old friend asked him to buy the insolvent Keeshin Freight Lines. Established in 1914, it had become one of the nation's largest motor carriers, operating from the Midwest to the East Coast. By World War II, however, Chicago-based Keeshin was in trouble. Rapid expansion led to financial problems and forced the company into bankruptcy in 1946. After one takeover attempt of Keeshin failed in 1949, Fruehauf became worried. He saw his future riding on the freight carrier's revival. The trailer company was one of Keeshin's major creditors, and Fruehauf became concerned about getting his firm's money back. On the more personal side, he was still battling for outright control of his family firm, and he had borrowed more than a million dollars from the

Teamsters Union to aid in this fight. If Keeshin went out of business, thousands of Teamsters jobs would be lost. It seems likely that the union pressured Fruehauf to save the bankrupt line. In the midst of these troubles, Fruehauf had an idea: he would ask John to acquire Keeshin, restore it to financial health, and pay off its debts.[35]

John's response to his friend's overture about Keeshin came quickly: "No, Roy. I don't know anything about that kind of freight business." But Fruehauf refused to accept that answer. A few days later, he again called John and reminded him that Ruan Equipment was "doing a lot of business with us." The message was clear—John could either take over Keeshin or face losing the account hauling Fruehauf trailers. He had confronted a similar predicament 13 years earlier when Western Grocer had pressured him into opening a grocery store in Corydon by threatening to take its business to another carrier. Now, to keep the Fruehauf business, John agreed to his friend's proposal.[36]

In late 1953, John and M. H. Clarke, a Dayton Rubber Company executive, formed C & R Transportation Corporation to acquire Keeshin Freight Lines. John owned 25 percent of C & R's stock, while Clarke held the remainder. Under the plan, C & R pledged $1.2 million for the rehabilitation of the beleaguered firm. In early 1954, the ICC ruled against the Ruan-Clarke bid for Keeshin because only 100 shares of C & R stock (at a par value of $100 per share) had been issued. In essence, the ICC noted that the two businessmen would be gaining control of the multimillion-dollar property for $10,000. Also bothersome to the regulatory body was the silent participation of Fruehauf Trailer Company. Hearings revealed that Fruehauf was guaranteeing the initial $1.2 million loan to Keeshin, had promised to back another loan of the same amount, and was advancing an additional $900,000 to the venture. The ICC implied that Fruehauf, with such a significant financial stake in the Keeshin resurrection, should be a party in the purchase plan.[37]

With the ICC's critique in mind, John and Fruehauf reworked the offer. John bought out Clarke's stake in C & R, proposed to put $120,000 of his own funds into the company, and agreed to serve as chairman of the board and chief executive officer of the reorganized firm, and Fruehauf Trailer was added as a participant in the application. These changes swayed the ICC, and John won control of Keeshin in the spring of 1954.[38]

Once in charge, John traveled to Keeshin's headquarters and worked at restoring the once prosperous freight carrier. His hands-on management style mandated that he oversee the corporate restoration personally, and he took up residence at the Chicago Athletic Club. For much of the next year, John divided his time about equally between Chicago and Des Moines. John renamed the company General Expressways and began the turnaround by employing techniques that made Ruan Transport successful. His first concern was replacing the firm's worn and outdated equipment. By August 1954, the company took delivery of the first of 200 new Fruehauf trailers, each with 25 percent greater carrying capacity than those being replaced. At the same time, 100 new International tractors were ordered, promising to provide greater hauling power and reduced maintenance costs. Meanwhile, schedules were revised, reducing running time between key points in the system, and plans were laid to improve existing terminals and add new facilities. And as the renewed company was getting back on track, John entertained key people. Just as he continued to do at Ruan Transport, the CEO held parties and get-togethers for current and potential shippers. A great believer in personal contact, John used these gatherings to win new customers.[39]

Shaking up management also aided in the company's revival. While John kept some top people, such as William Drohan, the former executive of Keeshin who was its trustee during bankruptcy, others were replaced. Some of the new managers—such as Earl Wood, named general manager of operations, and Orville Long, who worked for awhile as maintenance supervisor before returning to his former firm—came from Ruan Equipment. Likewise, Ruan Transport loaned managers to General Expressways. LeRoy Brown, for instance, was sent to Chicago to review the freight carrier's keypunch and tabulation operation—by this time called the IBM department. Still others, such as new executive vice president Floyd Shields, who had extensive experience in the transportation field, were brought in from the outside. But new managers alone could not solve the company's problems. The large, unwieldy freight firm covered 17 states and more than 15,000 miles of road. To bring the extensive system under control, a new divisional structure was created. The enterprise was divided into four geographic regions, each headed by an operations manager and a sales manager. These divisional managers reported to the company's general manager of operations and general manager of sales, respectively.[40]

John referred to his first year at General Expressways as a "squaring away" of the organization. By the spring of 1955, the reorganized company had $5 million of new equipment, had paid off its $2.7 million in debts, and was operating at the break-even point for the first time since 1951. *Fortune* magazine was impressed, and it featured John along with the president of North Central Airlines in a story about men who had "revived moribund companies." Roy Fruehauf was also pleased, and he showed his appreciation by expanding Ruan Equipment's Fruehauf business. In addition to the new and used trailers it was transporting for Fruehauf, Ruan Equipment began moving raw materials for the trailer manufacturer in 1956.[41]

By the end of 1956, General Expressways was making money. Operating revenues stood at $11,780,000, while net income was up to $185,000. Returning the business to profitability had not been easy, and from the time he took over the firm, many managers frequently witnessed John's temper. Quick to anger, John's gruff exterior masked a sentimental side he rarely revealed. One December, a couple of days before Christmas, John called a General Expressways manager into his office because he was not satisfied with the way the man's division was being run. John grilled the executive for half an hour, "giving him hell" because he was unable to supply any satisfactory answers. Disgusted, John finally had had enough, and the executive was told to leave. As the man headed out the door, John yelled, "Wait a minute." The manager turned around, expecting more trouble, but to his surprise, John shouted, "Merry Christmas, God damn it!" It was clear John demanded a lot of his managers and told them when they did not meet his expectations. If poor performance continued, the manager in question was generally fired.[42]

One General Expressways executive, however, did not face such a fate and instead was a recipient of John's compassion. Bill Drohan, who led the Keeshin through bankruptcy, remained on as president when the company became General Expressways. Even though the elderly man was "no longer of much value to the company," John "treated him with respect" and kept him in the leadership position. When Drohan's poor health forced him to resign the presidency in early 1958, John named him vice president of public relations, and he was allowed to continue working. He died at a motor freight association meeting the following year.[43]

William Wolfe, executive vice president of Watson Brothers Transportation Company, replaced Drohan as General Expressways president. Highly regarded in the trucking industry, Wolfe began his new job amid a slowing economy. As the country dipped into recession, General Expressways fell deep into the red again, and John wanted out of the freight business. He identified a West Coast carrier as a potential buyer and sent Wolfe to talk with Laurence Cohen, president and majority stockholder of Navajo Freight Lines. When Wolfe could not sell the property, John flew out to Denver himself. At first, he too failed, and Cohen remained uninterested in General Expressways. With its continuing large losses, the freight company required cash advances. These were made by Ruan Equipment, and this troubling situation made John even more determined to unload the Chicago-based operation. Finally, John got Cohen's attention by lowering the asking price, and then he appealed to the prospective buyer's vanity. Before becoming involved in Navajo, Cohen had operated Denver Chicago Trucking Company from coast to coast. If he now bought General Expressways, John reminded him, the resulting firm would have transcontinental rights, making Cohen "the first commodities operator to achieve such a broad grant twice in his career." In April 1960, a deal was cut. Navajo signed an agreement acquiring control of General Expressways, with an option to buy all company stock for $2.2 million in five years. Initially, Navajo bought 55 percent of Expressways preferred stock, with plans to buy the remainder by 1965.[44]

John was finally free of General Expressways, but the deal had cost him dearly. When the transfer was finally completed in 1965, Navajo's final payment covered only about two-thirds of the advances Ruan Equipment made to Expressways, leaving John to write off a million dollars in loans. Roy Fruehauf, who had pressured John into saving the old Keeshin line, provided no help, and five years later, it was mutually agreed that Fruehauf would haul its own material. Ruan Equipment quietly closed its doors and shut down its operations.

As he was abrogating Fruehauf's long contract with John, Bill Grace, the company's new president, gave the trucker a peace offering. In a contrite letter, Grace explained how he felt the trailer company had treated John badly in the Keeshin–General Expressways matter, turning its back instead of absorbing some or all of the bad debt. To assuage his "nagging feelings" and "mixed emotions" about the incident, Grace sent the Ruan CEO a special set of golf clubs made up of gold-plated irons and ivory-inlaid woods. He predicted that sometime in the future, John would say, "Hey man, have you ever seen a set of golf clubs that cost a million bucks? Then take a look at these."[45]

John loved the special clubs. By the time he received them, he had put the Fruehauf-General Expressways matter behind him, and he enjoyed a hearty laugh at Grace's letter and gift. He displayed the clubs in a prominent corner in his office and framed the humorous note from the Fruehauf president.[46]

In the midst of running General Expressways, John started yet another ancillary business to his bulk hauling operation. With the notion of creating savings in insurance costs and actually making a profit, John and a number of owners or representatives of other regional trucking firms began talking in the spring of 1955 about forming an industry-owned insurance company. After several discussions, 14 trucking companies joined together and formed such an insurance service. Not surprisingly, John had called on his friends to join him in the venture, and many of his close associates signed on. Among the group were Dan Dugan (Dugan Tank Lines), Joe Hall (McCoy Trucking), and Birney Baker (Des Moines Transportation). The new business consisted of two related corporations—Transport Indemnity Exchange, the underwriting firm, and Transport Underwriters, the management firm. The founding participants took up 10,000 shares of stock with a par value of $1.00 per share and loaned the management company an amount of money equal to 1.7 percent of each member's 1954 gross earnings. By the time the insurance operation opened that summer, nine additional trucking firms had joined. John was elected president of the management company, and John

Murphy of Gateway Transportation Company of LaCrosse, Wisconsin, was named chairman of the underwriting enterprise.[47]

Transport Indemnity Exchange provided insurance designed specifically for truckers and boasted a 24-hours-a-day claims department to handle claims quickly and effectively. It also created a safety department that held annual conferences, offered driver education courses, and sent safety engineers out to inspect policyholders' terminals. Corporate offices were initially established in the Securities Building in downtown Des Moines, and as had been hoped, the operation was soon showing a profit. Through ten months of 1956, net profits stood at $22,300. That same year, the company was renamed Carriers Insurance Exchange, and by 1960, net profits reached $56,000.[48]

Involved as he was in all these other businesses, John's focus remained on Ruan Transport. As he had done earlier, John expanded the company by taking advantage of the spreading pipeline network, recruiting additional customers, and growing horizontally through the acquisition of other trucking firms. New petroleum pipeline terminals in the region almost always meant more business for his company. In February 1954, for instance, Standard Oil completed a terminal in Ottumwa, and Ruan tank trucks began hauling from this new facility on its opening day. Later that fall, Standard Oil opened another pipeline terminal in Sauk Centre, Minnesota, approximately 120 miles northwest of Minneapolis. With the possibility of extending his carrying trade into new territory, John added a terminal in Sauk Centre as well. With approximately 10 trucks headquartered there, Ruan Transport carried refined petroleum products from the town's pipeline station to other parts of northwestern Minnesota as well as North and South Dakota. Building was also taking place on the Great Lakes Pipe Line, and Ruan grew with it as well. In 1960, it added a terminal just outside of Waterloo, Iowa, 100 miles northeast of Des Moines. Ruan Transport followed suit, opening its new Waterloo-Hudson facility to serve the pipeline outlet.[49]

As Baker supervised the company's operational growth, others in the firm sought new customers. This effort entailed entertaining, investigating new operating rights, and finding additional products that company equipment could carry. Bob Root and Gus Geraghty were largely responsible for hosting customers. These two made frequent use of the company airplane, visiting both existing and potential shippers. In 1957, the company acquired a four-acre island on Brule Lake in northern Minnesota. Soon dubbed "Ruan Isle," the property had several cabins, a main lodge, a boathouse, and a dock. In the summer and fall months, John entertained at the island a couple of times a month, but Root and Geraghty hosted more frequent gatherings at the Brule facility. Part of the camp's allure was its seclusion. Guests were flown to Grand Marais on the northern shore of Lake Superior, where they boarded a pontoon plane that flew 20 miles west to the lake. Since the plane was not allowed to fly over the adjacent federal wilderness area, it landed on the lake. A launch then met the visitors and took them to the island hideaway. Once on Ruan Isle, customers enjoyed fishing, boating, and hearty meals while Root and Geraghty subtly explained the virtues of Ruan Transport.[50]

In the fall, a lot of entertaining took place at University of Iowa football games. Root was in charge of the football outings, and the party often extended well beyond the game itself. During the 1950s, he reserved a train car to take Ruan friends and customers to the Iowa football team's away games. Liquor was generously poured, and these traveling parties often became boisterous affairs. Once, during a return trip from the Iowa–Notre Dame game in South Bend, Indiana, near disaster occurred. John remembered, "We were having a hell of a time. Then all of a sudden, Sid Kent, a Prudential Insurance executive who had had a few beers, became rambunctious and pulled the emergency lanyard, which separated the railroad cars from the engine. It was a wild ride. People were badly shaken up, but luckily no one was hurt." Regardless of this incident, John and his lieutenants continued stressing personal contact as their major strategy for promoting business.[51]

Sometimes this personal contact meant employing experienced oilmen who were well connected in the industry. Prentice Savage was one such hire. Savage had served as the Minneapolis division manager of Texaco for 26 years. Upon retiring from the oil business, Savage was recruited by Indianhead, another trucking firm, but he preferred to join Ruan Transport. Named assistant to the president for special assignments, Savage used his connections to bring in more business, particularly from the Upper Midwest region with which he was familiar. Later, in 1963, he negotiated the sale of the Brule Lake property to the federal government, and it became part of the Superior National Forest.[52]

Besides courting new customers, company officials pursued growth through additional operating rights and carrying new products. Amending or expanding authorities were usually sought after acquisitions put Ruan in new locations. For example, after buying Union Service in 1951, the company requested and received authority to haul from the St. Louis–area refinery to the eastern half of Iowa. In a later instance, when Ruan Transport bought a terminal in LaCrosse, Wisconsin, from Hillside Transit in 1955, attorneys Rex Fowler and Henry Fabritz obtained the rights to carry petroleum products from the new facility to points in Wisconsin, Minnesota, and eastern Iowa. As it gained access to new markets, Ruan Transport also began to broaden the range of cargoes its equipment could handle. By the mid-1950s, top managers considered the possibility of hauling such bulk products as anhydrous ammonia, fertilizer, flour, liquid carbon dioxide, liquefied petroleum gas (LPG), and a variety of other chemicals and resins. While these authorities were being sought from the ICC and/or state agencies, acquisition of other regional trucking firms also extended the array of products the company transported.[53]

Expansion was dictated by John's "belief that our company must continue to grow . . . if we expect to stay in business."[54] Management followed this command with nearly annual acquisitions in the latter 1950s. These purchases were regional, and they filled out the company's coverage of the Midwest. In 1956, Ruan Transport's service in Minnesota and Wisconsin grew considerably with the purchase of Terminal Transport Company in St. Paul, Minnesota, and Superior, Wisconsin. Besides increasing the area and capacity of Ruan's petroleum-carrying business, Terminal Transport also provided the firm with rights to carry vegetable oils and resins, trailers specifically designed to haul these products, and some regional business of Archer-Daniels-Midland (ADM). In its approval of the purchase, the ICC noted that with the new operating rights, Ruan would gain greater efficiencies "from Minnesota points and afford that company an opportunity to effect a closer balance in its primarily one-way operations, particularly in Wisconsin where its origin points have been limited to the Madison area." With the addition of Terminal Transport's equipment, Ruan's trailer fleet now included 337 petroleum tankers, five tanks for carrying asphalt, and two trailers for vegetable oil and resins.[55]

In 1957, the Des Moines trucking line bought James A. Hannah, Incorporated, of Lemont, Illinois, a town in the Chicago metropolitan area. This acquisition gave Ruan Transport greater territory in Illinois and Wisconsin while extending the company into Indiana and Michigan for the first time. In addition to a terminal in Lemont, the acquisition included facilities in Green Bay, Wisconsin, and Princeton, Indiana—the latter subsequently moved to South Bend in 1958. Major clients that came with the Hannah purchase included Pure Oil from its Lemont refinery and, even more important, Texaco from its refinery at Lockport, Illinois.[56]

Ruan Transport looked west in 1958 and bought Transit, Incorporated, based in Omaha, Nebraska. This acquisition added interstate rights in Nebraska, Kansas, and Missouri to the eight states Ruan was already serving—Iowa, Minnesota, Wisconsin, Illinois, Michigan, Indiana, and North and South Dakota. The deal included terminal facilities in Omaha and Hastings, Nebraska, and Sioux City, Iowa. As with the Terminal Transit purchase, Transit's equipment and rights gave Ruan a start in chemical hauling, with several trailers designed for sulfuric acid.[57]

In most of these takeovers, John kept key employees of the acquired companies in their same positions, and sometimes these people rose in the Ruan organization. William Hogarth, for instance, had served as Transit's traffic and sales manager for 10 years prior to the Ruan purchase. Once part of John's company, Hogarth became a sales representative based in Omaha. The following year, he was moved to Des Moines and promoted to traffic manager. In this position, Hogarth oversaw Ruan Transport's rate and tariff matters, areas that had been previously handled by Henry Fabritz. This shifting of workload gave Fabritz much-needed time to focus on further acquisitions.[58]

These corporate additions enlarged Ruan's territory, augmented its petroleum-hauling fleet, and aided the company's efforts to diversify the goods it handled. By the end of the decade, in fact, growth in chemicals and special products being hauled led to the creation of a new managerial position overseeing the transit of these goods. Don Fiedler, who had been with Ruan since 1954, was named to head the newly formed special products division.[59] Of all the new commodities carried, however, the most important was cement. In the wake of the Interstate Highway Act of 1956 that initiated construction of the massive national highway system, executives at Ruan Transport saw great potential in hauling cement. The company's first steps were in Des Moines in the late 1950s. Initially, Root and Geraghty made calls on local cement operators and assured John "that when cement was hauled in Des Moines by truck, Ruan would be trucking it." Yet when Schwerman Trucking of Milwaukee, Wisconsin, broke into the city and began moving cement for two local plants, it was clear that the two managers had failed in their pledge. Disgusted, John relieved them of cement sales and took it over himself.[60]

Supremely confident in his own people skills and the product he had to sell, John approached the cement business differently than his managers had. Rather than sell local plants, John traveled to the headquarters of various cement companies. The strategy quickly paid off; in 1959, he had contracts with a Missouri Portland plant in Sugar Creek (Kansas City) and in two southeastern Kansas sites—at Chanute with Ash Grove Lime and Portland Cement and at Fredonia with General Portland. The following year, he cut a third deal in the same region by signing an agreement with Universal Atlas Cement to haul its product out of Independence, Kansas. Small terminals were soon erected on land rented from the cement facilities, and Ruan trucks began moving both bag (on flatbed trailers) and bulk (in tank trailers) cement from these locations.[61]

Shortly after moving into cement transport, John realized he needed a manager solely devoted to the growing cement business. He tapped Bob Seeley, who had been with Ruan Equipment since 1946 and its general manager since 1953, for the new position of vice president–cement transport division. Besides overseeing sales and operations of the new division, Seeley worked closely with Ruan maintenance superintendent Bill Giles and Fruehauf in building equipment for hauling the new product. For bulk cement, Ruan employed specially designed tank trailers that used compressed air for blowing cement in and out of the tank. This new technology significantly sped up delivery time. Equally important for efficiency's sake, these tanks could be cleaned in a matter of hours and used to haul petroleum products. In a region where cement hauling was seasonal, these dual-purpose tanks provided versatility and allowed for year-round utilization. Another advance resulting from the long-standing Ruan-Fruehauf relationship (which continued, although it was strained after the General Expressways fiasco) was the development of an aluminum cement tank. Since these tanks were lighter than the steel ones, more cement could be carried while still meeting the weight requirements. Since this resulted in greater operating revenue, the company went to an all-aluminum cement tanker fleet by 1961.[62]

Actually, developing or exploiting new technology and the obsession with reducing equipment weight had been important factors in the company's success throughout the 1950s. John saw it as a simple equation: "Every 100 pounds we pulled out of the tractor-trailer combinations could be converted to more gallons of product and more profit."[63] Early in the decade, he and his team began to work with the Bernstein brothers; their brother-in-law, Leon Alexander, who had joined them at Independent Metal Products; and Lou Thomas, the Fruehauf engineer based there; to develop lighter petroleum tanks. Meanwhile, the Aluminum Corporation of America was working on additional uses for its product. As the firm developed a stronger aluminum alloy, Airco patented a new, short-arc-welding technique that was believed to be stronger than traditional welding methods. Both these companies approached the Bernsteins about building tankers with the new alloy and welding process. With the possibility of saving up to 40 percent in tanker shell weight, John jumped at the opportunity.[64]

The first few aluminum tankers taken by Ruan were originally painted to look like the steel tanks already in use. The camouflage was used for two reasons. First, it kept competitors in the dark about the new transports. Second, since the ICC had not yet developed any standards for this type of aluminum or the welding process used in these tanks, it kept the regulatory agency out of the process. When these original tanks apparently functioned flawlessly, Ruan Transport ordered several hundred to replace its entire petroleum tank fleet. By

late 1955, however, the company began to experience "leaks and structural failures" with some of its new aluminum tankers. The following
year, Ruan had completed its conversion to an all-aluminum petroleum tank fleet and became the first oil transporter to do so. Problems
with the new tanks continued, however, and in 1958, Ruan's Bill Giles
wrote a detailed study of the tank failures the company was experiencing. Armed with the Giles report and tank trailer warranties, John went
to Fruehauf, which had purchased Independent Metal by 1955, and
the tanks were repaired or replaced. Once its design was corrected, the
aluminum tank proved an important advance in Ruan equipment.[65]

Other improvements resulting from Ruan's partnerships with vendors included the development of aluminum asphalt tanks, stainless
steel tanks for hauling acids, cast-aluminum spoke wheels, and a tire
recapping system. One of the more important developments that
addressed John's desire to lessen equipment weight came through
Ruan's work with Firestone. Together, the trucking firm and the tire
manufacturer enhanced tubeless tires to the point that Ruan Transport's entire fleet was outfitted with these tires in 1956. Since blowouts
and flats with these tires were much less likely, safety was enhanced.
Such improved performance made spare tires largely unnecessary, and
the company removed spare tires and the spare tire racks from its trailers and the jacks from all its tractors. The resulting weight savings of
approximately 175 to 200 pounds per tractor-trailer unit meant better
performance, less wear and tear on equipment, and greater payload
capacity.[66]

In most cases, the use of these technological advances held costs
down and gave Ruan a competitive advantage over rival trucking firms.
Combined with its ability to meet the growing demand for moving
petroleum products and its diversification into other bulk cargoes, the
company's upward march continued. In 1960, Ruan Transport and its
subsidiary companies enjoyed operating revenues of $14.4 million and
net income of $540,000.[67]

Ruan's rise in the transportation business gave John both the
opportunity and the responsibility to take a leadership role in the
industry. In the late 1940s, John had begun serving in various administrative positions in national trade associations. Early in the 1950s, he

remained a conference vice president of the American Trucking Associations, stayed on as treasurer of the Iowa Motor Truck Association, and was tapped as first vice president of the National Tank Truck Carriers (NTTC) conference. In 1953, John was elected to the NTTC's presidency. In his presidential address, entitled "Improvement Must Come from Within," John suggested that tank truckers could be successful by focusing on safety, service, and efficiency. Most in the audience listened closely, because they realized John knew of what he spoke: he was offering his colleagues some of the secrets for Ruan Transport's achievements.[68]

John's leadership abilities were soon recognized more widely. In 1958, he was appointed to Iowa Power and Light's board of directors. Two years later, he was invited to join the board of Bankers Trust Company. Already acquainted with a number of Des Moines's prominent figures, John was now sitting and conversing with the city's most powerful men. Connections made here and the ties to both Iowa Power and Bankers Trust would prove very important to John in the upcoming decades. Meanwhile, John also became associated with Northwestern University's Transportation Center. Established in 1954 to "develop a broad program of education, research, and other professional services for the industry," the center advisory committee included leaders from the nation's leading airlines, auto manufacturers, oil companies, railroads, tire companies, and trucking firms. In 1958, John's rising standing in the business world, coupled with a budding interest in public service, led to his selection to the Transportation Center's advisory board. Over the years, John would make substantial contributions to the center and bring in additional sums as an aggressive fund-raiser for the institution.[69]

These obligations on top of John's demanding work schedule allowed little time for family and less for socializing, which left Betty largely responsible for Johnny and Jayne. Like most other women of her social position, she stayed at home to raise the children and run the household. Slightly whimsical, Betty loved playing with the children, while John was a more remote and formal figure. He was a strict disciplinarian who liked order and demanded that everything be kept in its proper place. Toys, for instance, were not supposed to be out of the children's rooms. Betty's sister, Evelyn Benson, recalled that when John was at work, "Betty and Johnny would play, and they'd haul all his toys out of his room. They'd be spread all over the place. But when they'd hear [John's] car coming up the drive, they'd hustle around and get the toys back [to Johnny's room]."[70]

Since John "was always busy and not home much," young Johnny's time with his father was frequently spent at Ruan Transport. Before John remarried, he would sometimes send driver Hap Tulk to pick up Johnny and bring him down to the office for a few hours. Later, after his son was seven or eight, John brought him to the office on Saturdays. There Johnny enjoyed roaming the building. He spent hours down in maintenance watching the trucks being serviced and often carrying a rag in his pocket that he used to shine tractors. He also visited John's secretary, Peggy Kempster, in her office, where, under her supervision, he enjoyed tallying billing figures on the adding machine.[71]

As Johnny grew older, it became clear he was not his father. Early on, he participated in sports as John had, but he was not as competitive as his father. Johnny played Little League with friends Jim Cooney and Kingsley Macomber. Known as a good sprinter, he also excelled at track, but his interest in interscholastic sports soon waned, and his involvement ended before high school. Not surprisingly, Johnny also lacked his father's superhuman drive. As an adult, he later reflected, "I realized my father lived to work, and I decided I didn't want to do that."[72] With these very different personalities, the two did not always understand each other, but they did share some special times together hunting and fishing. Some of these outings took place at Jonbar, while more extended trips employed the company plane, taking John and Johnny on excursions to Canada or weekend jaunts to Ruan Isle on Brule Lake.[73]

If John had thoughts of grooming Johnny to head the company someday, it was not yet evident. Nevertheless, father and son apparently shared an assumption that Johnny would one day work at Ruan Transport. Whatever his future plans, Johnny received a first-class education. After going to local neighborhood schools—Greenwood Elementary and Callanan Junior High—he and his socially prominent friends looked to attend boarding school. Culver Military Academy of Indiana was selected because both the Bendixens and the Macombers, family friends of the Ruans, had long-standing relationships with the school. In the fall of 1958, sophomores Johnny Ruan, Devere Bendixen, and Kingsley Macomber together headed off to Culver. Once at the military academy, Johnny's extracurricular activities focused on joining the Black Horse Troop and riding horses several times a week. When not on horseback, Johnny could ordinarily be found playing cards, usually bridge, at the student union. Possibly most memorable of his Culver experiences, however, was when his father sent the company plane to bring Johnny and his friends home for vacation. Although Culver boasted students from many privileged families, few, if any others, were flown home from school. Culver had its own airstrip, and before landing, Ruan pilot Jerry Ware buzzed the campus three or four times to signal his arrival. After seeing the maneuver, Johnny, Kingsley, and Devere headed to the plane for the flight to Des Moines.[74]

Four years younger than Johnny, John's daughter Jayne was a bubbly, happy, and unassuming child. She had the artistic bent of her mother but the fierce competitiveness, steely reserve, and directness of her father. Early in her life, Jayne's playmates consisted of daughters from other upper-class, south-of-Grand families; some of her best friends were the Macomber twins, Elise and Cathy, and Susan Hobson. After John bought the ranch in 1955, however, Jayne started riding horses, and her life changed. About 1957, she and other neighborhood girls, including Elizabeth and Katy O'Reilly, Jane Prescott, and Charlotte Robson, joined the Raccoon Valley Pony Club, the local affiliate of the United States Pony Club. Others, such as Barbie Weeks, Harriet "Rusty" Hubbell, Marion Blount, and Maggi Moss, became members a couple of years later. With club members riding their horses six or even seven days a week, it soon became clear that winter riding accommodations were needed. Several fathers stepped forward and built a riding arena for their equestrian daughters. On land purchased by Sam Blount, Jim Hubbell and John erected a year-round, indoor riding arena. Riding now took up most of the young women's spare time, and some of them—Jayne among them—took their riding very seriously. A talented horsewoman, Jayne became interested in hunters and jumpers and began to win local competitions. Before long, riding and competing in horse shows were her twin passions, and it was here that father and daughter connected. Busy though he was, John made time to see Jayne ride, and he rarely missed any of her events. Likewise, John soon contributed to her success by providing Jayne with exceptional horses.[75]

Betty, meanwhile, busied herself in a variety of activities. When not with the children, driving in car pools, or participating in the PTA, she was involved in organizations such as the Junior League. Betty was also devoted to many charitable causes and frequently worked on campaigns for both the March of Dimes and the United Way. Yet for Betty and some of her friends, the hectic pace of raising children, attending club meetings, and doing volunteer work left little time for simply chatting about their everyday lives. Like many others in the 1950s, these women were joiners, and their solution to the lack of time and place to banter led to the formation of the "Do Nothing Club." The brainchild of Betty Ruan, Helen Cooney, and Nellie Weeks, the club met once a month to provide these society women with a chance to "do nothing" except talk to friends. Over lunch and cocktails, members discussed their children, griped about current problems, or shared their hopes and dreams. Sometimes, when meetings dragged on into the early evening, husbands joined their wives and the entire group went out to dinner. The club met regularly through the mid-1950s. Along with the three founders, it included Margaret Ann Bannister, Arabella Bendixen, Mattie Locke Brammer, Zita Hitchcock, Elise "Squeak" Macomber, Patty Neal, Virginia Pearsall, Peggy Percival, and Betty Sears.[76]

What Betty most desired, however, was to spend more time with her husband. To that end, she tried taking up two of his hobbies— hunting and fishing—hoping she and John could enjoy them together. Betty liked the latter activity, and as she had anticipated, it provided another pastime she and her husband could share. Hunting did not work out so well. Although she liked target shooting and, according to John, "became quite a good shot," Betty quickly realized she "couldn't bear to shoot any living thing." Instead of hunting, she thought, the two could enjoy shooting at clay pigeons at Jonbar. In 1962, *International Trail* magazine ran a story on Betty (because she drove the company's four-wheel-drive International Scout) and featured a photograph of her, shotgun in hand, practicing her marksmanship. Although John and Betty occasionally engaged in these outdoor activities together, such instances were rare.[77]

Also rare were extended family vacations. During the 1950s, the Ruans took a couple of road trips out west. In the summer of 1952, for instance, John purchased a Cadillac limousine, loaded up Betty, Johnny, and Jayne, and headed out to Yellowstone National Park. Not surprisingly, upon the family's return, the limousine was turned over to Ruan Cab Company and put into service. In another drive westward, John took Betty and Jayne to Vancouver, British Columbia, to pick up Johnny, who had taken a trip to Alaska with Devere Bendixen and Arabella Thompson, Devere's aunt. Usually, however, since John did not like being away from work so long, family outings generally consisted of picnics at Jonbar or weekend escapes. A summertime vacation ritual palatable to John had been established soon after Jayne was born. Shortly after Memorial Day, Betty and the kids migrated north to the family cottage at Clear Lake. There they summered, returning to Des Moines after Labor Day. John stayed behind to work but visited his family on weekends. In establishing this practice, John was repeating his childhood experiences. During his years in Beacon, John, Rachel, and Arthur passed the summers at the family farm outside of town, while Doc Ruan, who was busy tending to his patients, joined the family on weekends.[78]

Besides his wife and children, John's mother, Rachel, as well as his brother, Arthur, and his family (including wife Dorothy and their daughter Ina Rae Ruan and son John Lee Ruan) remained in town. Over the years, Arthur had served Ruan Transport in various capacities, worked as a lease operator for the company, and tried several ventures, including a greenhouse and florist shop, on his own. Fiercely independent, Arthur had difficulty working for others, especially for his younger brother. Regardless of a tension that existed between them, John had often loaned or given Arthur start-up money for various businesses. When they did not live up to Arthur's expectations, he pushed on to other ideas but invariably blamed John for his predicament. As their strained relationship worsened, John decided Arthur might do better out of Des Moines and on his own. When Rachel began complaining of arthritis pain, John saw an opportunity for change. Using their mother's malady as the pretext, John urged Arthur to pull up stakes and take Rachel to a dry climate, which might provide relief for her arthritis. At loose ends at that time, Arthur agreed. In 1953, the family relocated to southern California because of its weather and because Dorothy's parents lived there. John lined up a job for Arthur at a local Fruehauf plant and picked out a house for them in Monrovia, a northeastern Los Angeles suburb about 15 miles from downtown.[79]

Sending Arthur to the West Coast did not improve John's relationship with his brother, but at least it put distance between the two. Unhappy with the Fruehauf job, Arthur left in search of something else. During the next few years, he undertook several different jobs and businesses, but nothing seemed to work for Arthur. Twice, for instance, he tried running a restaurant, but, according to Dorothy, he was not a good businessman and neither attempt was successful. John, meanwhile, was concerned about his niece and nephew's future, and he put Arthur on the payroll of Terminal and Supply Company and later Ruan Equipment to provide money for the children and insurance for Arthur. News of the monthly stipend came in a sternly worded letter from John: "It has been my intention to continue the salary from Ruan Equipment and let it accrue to your benefit for eventual retirement and I don't want it dissipated or spent except in the case of education for the children."[80]

Toward the end of the 1950s, Arthur became convinced that buying a tractor-trailer was the answer to his problems. John disagreed, and Dorothy was opposed as well. So Arthur put the idea on hold and continued to search for his place in the world. At about the same time, Rachel decided that southern California was not for her. Bothered by the smog and homesick for Iowa, she returned to Des Moines in 1958. Arthur and his family, however, stayed in Monrovia.

By the time Rachel returned to Des Moines, John's family had undergone two major changes. In April 1957, Betty gave birth to the couple's third child, Thomas Heyliger Ruan. Johnny immediately saw humor in the birth of his younger brother. "You know," he told his parents, "I'll be in college before this kid even starts school."[81] Everyone laughed at the teenager's exclamation, but he was exactly right. Fourteen years his junior, Thomas was a year old when Johnny headed off to Culver Military Academy and only four when his big brother went away to college. Likewise, 10 years separated Thomas from his sister. Busy with her friends and activities in Pony Club, Jayne had little time for her baby brother. Unfortunately, the arrival of Thomas was not the biggest adjustment the family would face. Shortly after the baby was born, Betty began noticing numbness in her hands. Then one night she "couldn't see anymore." The blindness lasted only an hour but led to the doctor and a battery of tests. Although multiple sclerosis (MS) was eventually diagnosed, neither the doctors nor John told Betty, thinking it would be kinder to spare her the bad news. As her symptoms continued and she began to receive informational mail about MS treatments, however, she grew suspicious, but John remained mum on the subject. Finally, after reading a newspaper article about MS, Betty showed John the story and asked if she had the disease. "Yes," he said simply, "You do."[82]

The news of Betty's multiple sclerosis was difficult for John. With his many successes in business, he was used to winning, but doctors told him there was no cure for MS. He first tried shielding Betty by keeping her in the dark about the disease. When he finally admitted it to her, there was nothing else he could do. Betty, however, handled MS with grace and strength. "If I'd been a mess," she recalled, "they [my family] would have been a mess, too." Therefore, as much as possible, Betty did not change her routine. Over the following decade, her health would deteriorate, but by 1960, MS had not significantly altered Betty's life.[83]

As the 1950s gave way to a new decade, John's businesses and career were moving ahead full throttle. With his voracious appetite for work and a personal charm he could turn on at will, he pushed forward and the companies flourished. Good fortune and good people certainly played a role, but at the center of the success was John's dynamic leadership and vision. His achievements led to a growing recognition both inside and outside the trucking industry, and the resulting connections laid the foundation for future opportunities.

5 Expanding Outward and Upward

During a visit to Des Moines in 1964, Fruehauf executive vice president Fred Neumann asked John when he planned on taking Ruan Transport national. The firm's rapid expansion made this seem like the next logical step, but John's answer caught Neumann off guard. "Never," he quickly replied. Although the firm did eventually go national, John's explanation for his answer suggested a changing focus: "The union labor problems on the East Coast, West Coast, and Gulf Coast are too much for an Iowa boy. I'm going to stay home and rebuild the town."[1]

John's trucking operations grew through the 1960s and into the early 1970s and were the foundation for his widening empire, but he devoted an ever-increasing amount of time and energy to projects outside his original business and inside Des Moines. As always, his people skills and the relationships he established were critical to his success. Looking back over his career, John often explained his rise by expounding, "It's not what you know, it's who you know."[2] Of course the adage was too simplistic and failed to identify many of his other important attributes, but it had a particular resonance for John. He was simply a master in dealing with people. His strong personality gave him a commanding presence, and the jovial manner he affected in public drew people to him. Among an ever-increasing circle of friends and acquaintances, John extracted favors, received tips, and conducted business deals. Mel Straub, a Des Moines business owner and longtime chairman of the Central Iowa MS Chapter, believed "John made wiser use of relationships than anyone I have ever known."[3]

These connections and the way John used them carried him far. From 1961 through 1975, contacts led John into the banking business and fostered his role in the renewal of downtown Des Moines. One of the first major moves in the capital city's redevelopment was his $26 million Ruan Center. When completed in 1975, the 36-story tower was the tallest building in Iowa. Even as John's priorities shifted, however, there was no doubt that he remained in control of the trucking company. It was John who negotiated the acquisitions, John who decided to take the firm into the truck-leasing business, and John who seemingly had his finger in all its operations. Over the years, he became famous for the "flurry of notes" he personally drafted and sent to the appropriate people. These memos reminded "everyone that the boss is on the job thinking about something."[4]

Even though his company grew dramatically, John found ways to remain abreast of the operation. A former Ruan employee later told a *Des Moines Register* reporter how John used information to manage his firm and keep his staff on its toes: "John always arises early. He can be on the phone before employees are out of bed. It might be 6 o'clock on Sunday morning when he calls a terminal manager in say, Denver." After identifying himself, he asks, "Why has trailer No. 709-4 been out in your back lot for the past six days?" The stunned manager "doesn't even know it's there. But he knows that somehow or another, John knows. And he is on the defensive from the start. He knows he had better come up with some answers fast."[5]

With John apparently watching over the smallest details of his trucking firm, the 1960s began much like the 1950s for Ruan Transport. The company expanded through growth and acquisition, pioneered or employed the latest technology and innovations in the industry, and broadened the range of products it carried. This expansion and diversification led to other changes, such as an organizational restructuring and a move to a larger corporate headquarters.

After buying a couple of smaller trucking companies, including Indiana Tank Lines, John signed a major deal in November 1961. He paid Denver Chicago Trucking $1.8 million for D–C Transport, its liquid products–hauling division.[6] The acquisition gave Ruan 15 new terminals spread across Colorado, Idaho, Nebraska, South Dakota, Utah, and Wyoming and more than 300 additional trucks and trailers. From these new locations Ruan would carry commodities such as petroleum and various petroleum products, acids, chemicals, molasses, concrete aggregates, and vegetable oils throughout this western region. After the purchase, Ruan Transport was moving products in 30 states.[7]

One of the most interesting new hauling authorities with this agreement was the right to haul missile fuel from Denver, Colorado;

Baltimore, Maryland; Lake Charles, Louisiana; and Saltville, Virginia to Cape Canaveral, Florida; Vandenberg Air Force Base in California; and other missile research and testing centers in Arizona, Arkansas, Colorado, Kansas, New York, and Tennessee. Given the heightened cold war tensions of the time, much of this operation took place under the veil of secrecy. Schedules and routes of Ruan drivers carrying missile fuel were classified and under the auspices of the U.S. military. Even before the deal was consummated, Ruan engineer Bill Giles was working with the Fruehauf Corporation on stainless steel tanks specially designed for hydrazine missile fuel. Giles remembered, "We ultimately determined that the tank needed to be built with 1/8-inch thick stainless steel, but because of the highly explosive nature of the fuel, we built the tanks with 3/16-inch stainless so we could sleep nights." It was Ruan-hauled fuel, in fact, that powered NASA's Gemini space program from 1964 to 1967.[8]

As the purchase of D-C Transport was in the works, John and his top managers were thinking about how the acquisition might fit in the company's organizational structure. They feared that the centralized departmental management system that had been successful when Ruan Transport's region was relatively compact would become ineffective with the enlarged firm's greater size and span. In its place, a more decentralized, divisional structure based largely on geographic area was tried. With the exception of its cement operation, which remained a separate entity, the company was divided into three regions. An operations manager and sales manager oversaw each division and reported to Harold Baker, vice president in charge of operations, and Bob Root, executive vice president in charge of sales. When the acquisition was finally approved in the spring of 1962, the former D-C Transport became the basis of the new Ruan western region, with headquarters in Denver. Ray Denkhoff, John's trusted old friend and longtime employee, was named operations manager of the new division. The central region's main office was in Des Moines and included terminals in eastern Nebraska, Minnesota, Iowa, and western portions of Wisconsin, while the eastern region was run out of Chicago and comprised company facilities in Illinois, Indiana, and parts of Wisconsin.[9]

The new organizational alignment made sense in light of the increasing size and scope of the firm's trucking business, but it soon became apparent that a few alterations were necessary before achieving John's goals to improve "our operating results and prepare the company for further growth in the future."[10] Rapid expansion of the cement division put immediate pressure on the system. When Ruan's cement operation was small, largely located in southeastern Kansas, maintaining it as a separate business unit worked well. But with new cement terminals added in more distant locations, problems arose. In 1961, John finally opened a cement terminal at Northwestern States Portland Cement Company in Mason City. A couple of years earlier, James H. Windsor, president of Equitable of Iowa, had introduced him to Jack MacNider, president of the cement firm. John developed a close relationship with MacNider, and later in the 1960s, he joined the Northwestern States board of directors. Meanwhile, John also began hauling cement out of a Missouri Portland plant in Memphis, Tennessee, and opened a terminal for Monarch Cement in Humboldt, Kansas, its fourth in this southeastern section of the state.[11]

The growing distance of the terminals from each other and differences in local issues and regulations affecting each area made administering the cement division difficult. John and his top managers solved these problems by eliminating the cement operations as a separate division and integrating its various terminals within the company's central or eastern regions, depending on their respective locations. At the same time, they dealt with turf battles that had erupted between the sales managers and operations managers atop each of the three regions by placing a single administrator over each geographic area.[12]

Because of the ongoing interstate highway construction boom, Ruan's cement business continued growing. Additional terminals were added as demand dictated, and they were usually located near interstate construction. In late 1963, for example, Ruan built a new cement terminal at a Missouri Portland Cement facility in the southern Illinois town of Joppa. Bob Stachovic, the Joppa terminal manager, explained why the site was selected: "We can foresee at least 10 to 15 good years in the cement hauling business in this immediate area, primarily because of the heavy amount of construction of interstate highways." Sure enough, most of this facility's cement deliveries went to nearby contractors working on Interstate Highways 57 and 24.[13]

Since this segment of Ruan Transport's business was becoming more important, Bill Giles devoted additional attention to it. Early on, he wondered if the company's "key-stop" principle, the innovation that allowed Ruan to deliver petroleum products around the clock, even at unattended plants, could be applied to cement transport. Cement delivery differed from that of petroleum because cement was largely hauled to temporary locations where highway construction was under way. As he had in the past, Giles worked on the problem with his counterparts at Fruehauf. Together, the two firms soon developed the 4,100-cubic-foot portable cement storage tank trailer. Trucked to job sites, these tanks augmented the stationary vertical cement storage bins erected by the contractors. First used in Missouri with Koss Brothers Construction's work on Interstate 70, the portable tanks provided Ruan with "key-stop" access and proved immediately popular with customers. Each storage tank held six truckloads of cement and could be filled "at any hour of the day or night when there is no interference with the contractor's equipment or operations." Besides staying out of the builders' way, the system also "provided them with a backlog of cement on the job to meet peak demand periods."[14]

In addition to developing innovative tanks, Ruan moved from gas-powered to diesel-powered tractors. The company had begun to experiment with such engines in 1958 by purchasing 15 tractors equipped with six-cylinder Detroit Diesel engines. Although it was believed that the maintenance costs of these engines were higher than comparable gasoline ones, they were much more powerful and got better mileage. During the first few years of the 1960s, the company exchanged 200 gasoline-powered tractors for the new International tractors with diesel engines. These units performed even better than expected and proved much more reliable than predicted. So satisfied with the new diesel tractors, Ruan Transport replaced its entire fleet in 1964 with a $7-million purchase of 364 International series 400 V-8–powered diesel truck tractors in conventional and over-the-cab models.[15]

By that year, Ruan had 1,600 employees and 2,300 pieces of equipment operating out of 47 strategically placed terminals. With 50 types of specialized trailers, its new International tractors hauled more than 200 wet and dry bulk products—including acids; caustic sodas; dry cement; food products, such as flour, molasses, and sugar; fertilizers; liquefied petroleum gas (LPG); missile fuel; petroleum and petroleum products; and weed killers. Company drivers logged more than 135 million miles annually, delivering these goods to a variety of customers in 31 states. This dramatic increase in the range of products handled was the result of management's strategy to broaden its market and lessen its reliance on petroleum-based liquids. By the late 1960s, this effort appeared successful. In 1957, well over 90 percent of company revenue came from the moving of various petroleum commodities, but by 1967, petroleum hauling accounted for only 54 percent of gross revenues. Cement now made up 20 percent, asphalt and fertilizer comprised 17 percent, and the remaining 9 percent was lumped together in the category of "special products."[16]

Besides hauling a greater variety of goods, John was also branching out into another aspect of trucking. Early in the 1960s, he became increasingly interested in the leasing side of the industry. John had garnered some experience in this field with Ruan Equipment, but almost all that company's work was with Fruehauf. Firms such as Ryder were already involved in this business, but John decided there was an opportunity for such an enterprise in the midwestern market. In late 1962, John formed Ruan Leasing, which, along with Ruan Truck Rentals, would specialize "in putting first-rate transportation equipment in the hands of users without the high capital investment of ownership."[17]

The new leasing division was headed by 29-year-old Larry Miller. A Clear Lake native, Miller was raised down the street from John's lakeside cottage, and as a youngster, he mowed the large lawn at the Ruan property. Miller had later gone on to the University of Iowa and then became a fighter pilot with the U.S. Marines. Following his military service, he joined Iowa Warehouse and Iowa Truck Leasing Company in Waterloo, where he advanced rapidly. Whenever John was at Clear Lake, he often visited with Larry's parents, Lloyd and Oneida Miller, and regularly inquired about their son. One day during the summer of 1962, Lloyd told John that Larry was discouraged because while he was interested in expanding his company's leasing operation, the owner was not. John briefly thought about Larry, remembering that he always liked the young man's initiative and straightforward, direct manner. The two had similar personalities, and John must have seen a lot of himself in the young man. He then told Lloyd that he was thinking about setting up a leasing business, and he wanted to talk to Larry about it. John and Larry met several times that summer and fall of 1962 and finally, John was convinced: he established Ruan Leasing and hired Larry to run it.[18]

Originally sharing space with Ruan Cab Company at the Sixth and Tuttle facility, Ruan Leasing commenced business in 1963. It planned on providing "all types of trucks on a full service lease basis" through the company's extensive networks of terminals spread across the central United States. John had always used superior service as a means of winning and holding customers, and his venture into leasing was no different. Rather than providing merely trucks, Ruan offered a large package of services. Miller went after customers by explaining that instead of tying up their money in trucks, they could put it to more productive use in plant expansion, marketing, or research and development. When a company came to Ruan Leasing, managers drafted a plan to fulfill the customer's needs. Then engineer Bill Giles and his staff selected and designed the most efficient trucks for the particular job. With their experience in the field, they were able to standardize many of the components, and because of Ruan's buying power and long relationship with vendors, the firm could hold down costs.[19]

Once the trucks or tractors were delivered, Ruan Leasing lettered and painted the equipment to the customer's specifications and insured the vehicles through Carriers Insurance. Complete maintenance, fuel, oil, and truck washing were supplied through Ruan terminals or several hundred contracted truck centers. In the event of a breakdown or accident, emergency service was available at these same locations, and repairs could usually be done immediately. If special parts or a mechanic with particular training were required, Ruan had them ferried via company plane. And if the company was unable to get a customer's truck back on the road in a reasonable amount of time, Ruan rental units were available for emergency use. In essence, Ruan Leasing provided everything its clients needed except supplying the drivers and dispatching the trucks.[20]

With the smart and aggressive Miller at its helm, the leasing business took off. Much like John, the new manager was a "commanding figure" who "had a presence."[21] His determination and charisma motivated his staff and won over customers. Under his close supervision and John's oversight, Ruan found a ready market for its full-service truck leasing throughout the central United States. In Iowa, for instance, early clients included beverage distributor Fred Nesbit, who opted for a fleet of straight trucks, while freight carrier Bos Lines and food distributor Grocer Wholesaler, Inc., chose tractor-trailer combinations. Growth for the Ruan company was rapid; by 1965, it was the leading truck-leasing operation in the Midwest. The increasing business pleased John but did not really surprise him. He explained, "We find that when the facts are properly presented to a prospective customer . . . such as our ability to engineer vehicles for his exact requirements, to buy them and maintain them for less than he may be able to, and to guarantee his transportation costs week after week without unexpected expenses or losses cropping up . . . he often realizes that leasing can, indeed, be best suited to his transportation requirements."[22]

As the corporation grew, the company's 30th Street location became cramped, and because the firm's general offices were situated above the terminal's maintenance shop, noise and garage odors from below often made the workplace unbearable. Given these circumstances, John decided to separate the offices from the terminal and began looking for additional space. When Standard Oil of Indiana's district office building at Keosauqua Way and Third Street in downtown Des Moines became available in 1962, John bought it for his new corporate headquarters. The pre–World War II structure required extensive updating, however. John had been impressed with the recently remodeled downtown Iowa Power and Light Building and asked Harold Baker to find out who had designed it. Baker put his boss in contact with Ken Kendall of Griffith Kendall, a local architectural firm responsible for the renovation, and Kendall soon won the contract with a proposal that pleased John. Plans called for a sleek, ultramodern exterior surrounded by trees and an adjacent garden. When the work on the three-story, 30,000-square-foot edifice was completed in the spring of 1964, Ruan Transport and Leasing moved into the basement and first floor, Carriers Insurance occupied the third floor, and the second floor was originally reserved for outside tenants.[23]

If the building's modern exterior suggested a forward-looking company, so too did Ruan's new logo, which by 1965 was adorning company trucks. For several years, Larry Miller had pushed for a new company symbol that would grab people's attention. John finally agreed, and Bill Fultz of Graphic Corporation was given the job. He came up with an eye-catching emblem consisting of a red, lowercase "r" that was slightly slanted to the right. Under the arch of the letter was a solid black dot. The "Rolling r," as the clean, contemporary design was sometimes called, seemed to indicate motion, and Fultz saw it as a stylized depiction of the front end of a tractor cab over the wheel. Upside down, John said it looked like a boot kicking a ball, another reference to motion and action.[24]

With its new logo and corporate headquarters, Ruan looked like a firm on the move. Gross revenues of its transport division, which rose from $17.4 million in 1963 to $21.1 million in 1967, seemed to support this notion. The problem, however, was that costs were increasing faster than revenues. Rising costs had already chipped away at profits in 1960, 1961, and 1962, and John worried that the continuing trend could wipe out the company. In a December 1962 memo to all company personnel, he bluntly spelled out his plans to reverse the situation: "We are going to reduce our expenses, we are going to remain competitive, and we are going to stay in business. As head of the company that has been 30 years in the making, I don't propose to admit that I, or the people that I have surrounded myself with, can't measure up to today's competitive environment. The economies that we are faced with making will not be to everyone's liking and all of us will be affected in one manner or another. However, a real tightening of the belt must be made and it is in the best interest of every employee in this company that we do so and as quickly as possible."[25]

While his company's gross revenues were increasing, net profits were somewhat erratic. Closely watching costs in 1963, Ruan Transport and its subsidiaries netted $527,000 out of gross revenues of $19.9 million. Yet rising costs remained a concern. By 1967, Ruan Transport Corporation's revenues were up to $28 million, but net income fell to $404,000. Some subsidiaries such as leasing, which earned $508,000, performed very well, but overall net income was down 20 percent from the 1963 mark. Over the next few years, growth was rapid, costs were controlled, and profits went up. In 1973, for instance, total revenues reached $63.3 million, while net profits rose to $2.9 million. Much of this expansion was fostered by truck leasing, which accounted for half of that year's profits. Carriers Insurance, meanwhile, was also growing. John now served as this company's president, and its net income more than doubled from 1963 to 1967.[26]

With his companies on the rise, John's stature in the area's business community continued upward. In 1963, he was appointed to Equitable of Iowa's board of trustees. Drake University soon followed, electing John to its board as well. Already a director of two other Des Moines–based companies, John's latest memberships signaled his arrival among the city's leading power brokers. Here John made new contacts and cemented old ones. The relationships he made and nurtured on these various boards often came in handy and sometimes led to opportunities he would not otherwise have encountered. Bankers Trust was one such case.[27]

Bankers Trust was a privately held Des Moines financial institution founded in 1917. By the time John joined the board in 1960, it was owned by a small group of investors led by the Hubbell family. With $90 million in assets, Bankers Trust was the city's third largest bank, behind Iowa–Des Moines National Bank and Central National Bank. In recent years, however, it had slipped farther behind its two larger rivals, and profits had lagged as well. After a merger attempt with Central National failed, several board members thought John's bold leadership was what the bank needed. In July 1964, bank directors James Windsor, president of Equitable of Iowa; Joe Rosenfield, John's old friend and chairman of the Younkers board; Sam McGinn, then president of Tangney-McGinn Hotels; and recently retired John Shuler, president of Shuler Coal Company; met with John at his new office building at Third and Keosauqua. There they reviewed the bank's problems and asked John if he would consider buying a majority interest in the bank.[28]

John initially was not interested, largely because he knew nothing about running a bank. He believed, however, that recently hired bank president Robert Sterling was capable of revitalizing the bank, and

Windsor and the others continued to press John throughout that summer and fall. With his resistance flagging, John told his fellow directors he "wouldn't want to buy it unless I could get 51 percent [of the stock], so that I had absolute control." When they assured him that was possible, John went ahead with the acquisition. His initial purchase included the stock of McGinn and Shuler as well as the Hubbell holdings. By the end of December 1964, John owned 26,145 shares of the stock, or 44 percent of the company. Four years later, John increased his stake to 48,350 shares, or 80.6 percent of the bank's 60,000 shares of outstanding stock.[29]

Once in charge, John's hands-on style became immediately apparent. He revamped the bank's organization to ensure he was included in all major decisions. This change was accomplished through the creation of an executive committee. Chaired by John, the committee met biweekly and consisted of bank president Sterling, another bank officer, and three members of the board of directors. At the same time, John appointed several new directors, including his close friend Bob Root. Other ideas initiated by the aggressive chairman were clearly taken from his successes in trucking. With a focus on the customer, John emphasized the basics, such as the necessity of staffing the bank with friendly, knowledgeable tellers. He also called for improving service by extending banking hours to include Saturdays, building better drive-up teller access at the downtown office, and adding branch offices.[30]

John moved on his plans immediately. Land was soon purchased in northwest Des Moines, and in 1967, a new Bankers Trust branch opened on Merle Hay Road, across the street from the city's largest shopping center. The next year, the company leased space on the northeast corner of Sixth Street and Grand Avenue, and in fall of 1970, a new downtown drive-in banking facility opened. With six service lanes and access to both Sixth and Grand, the bank also offered a walk-in lobby. The bank was set amid a parklike courtyard replete with benches and a fountain. A Bankers Trust advertisement for the new downtown location promised "fast, efficient" service from the "same friendly folks" customers had come to expect at its other branches. About the new facility and grounds it proclaimed: "Sure, it's a restful

oasis in the middle of downtown hustle and bustle—but more important, it has all the equipment and personnel to handle your banking
quickly and efficiently." Designed by Griffith Kendall, both new banking buildings included beautiful landscaping, and because they
replaced older, run-down structures, they were welcome additions to
their respective neighborhoods. More important to John, they raised
the bank's visibility and brought in more business.[31]

Then the consummate salesman made use of his many connections
in the trucking industry and began to recruit new bank customers personally. Shortly after taking control, John started writing to the many
corporate executives he counted as friends. His letter to Fruehauf president Bill Grace was representative. After explaining that Bankers Trust
was ready to extend Fruehauf a $1 million line of credit, John noted,
"We may be small town, but I am sure you will agree, we ain't timid.
When you are ready for this money, let me know and I'll bring it in
and personally give it to you."[32]

John also used his growing connection with Iowa State University
(ISU) for the bank's benefit. A booster and financial supporter of ISU
athletics, he and Bob Hicklin, a Detroit Diesel dealer in Des Moines,
began to hold annual corn roasts as fund-raisers for the school's sports
program in the mid-1960s. During one of the parties, John became
acquainted with Johnny Majors, Iowa State's football coach. After several more conversations with the coach, John lined him up for a bank
promotion. In the fall of 1971, Bankers Trust offered miniature footballs to those who opened new accounts of $25 or more, and over the
course of the campaign, Majors was on hand at the Merle Hay office
signing the footballs and being photographed. Pleased with the results,
a bank manager wrote John that during the promotion, Bankers Trust
gained "332 new savings accounts for $23,750!"[33]

When coupled with Sterling's no-nonsense style, these various
strategies worked well. By 1970, the bank's assets were up to $153 mil-
lion, while net income had nearly doubled, rising to $1.1 million from
$584,000 in 1964. The upward trend continued, and by 1975 assets
topped $250 million, a 179 percent increase since John had obtained
control a decade earlier. Such growth lagged behind that of the city's
largest bank, Iowa–Des Moines National Bank, which saw its assets

increase 233 percent over the same period, but easily surpassed number two Central National's asset growth of 92 percent.[34] John's self-confidence and his talent for using personal contacts were major reasons for his success in trucking and now in the banking business. These traits also led to his socializing with labor leaders such as Teamsters president Jimmy Hoffa and his chief lieutenant and successor, Frank Fitzsimmons.

John had his first experiences with the Teamsters years earlier while negotiating a labor contract. When talks stalled in late 1949 and into early 1950, two mysterious explosions occurred at Ruan terminals at Clear Lake, Iowa, and Spring Valley, Minnesota. Although there was no proof that the Teamsters were involved, John took these incidents as messages, and the sticking points in the labor negotiations were soon ironed out.[35]

As his trucking firm grew, John thought he could lessen the chances of strikes against the company by building friendships with labor kingpins. He therefore decided to "make it my business to know Hoffa."[36] As head of the International Brotherhood of Teamsters from 1957 to 1971, Hoffa wielded tremendous power, and John believed having a personal relationship with him could be very helpful. John visited with the Teamsters president often and later remembered, "I grew to know Hoffa quite well, and we were friends, as much as you could be friends being on opposite sides of the fence."[37] John also kept in close touch with Fitzsimmons, sometimes playing golf with him in Florida or California. This relationship was one of the motivating factors in John's purchase of a home in southern California at La Costa—a first-class resort community featuring a golf course, country club, hotel, and spa—located 30 miles north of San Diego. He originally heard of the complex from friend and developer Bill Knapp, who already had a home there and urged John to buy one as well. After he discovered that Fitzsimmons frequently golfed at La Costa, John followed Knapp's advice, and in 1970, he bought a condominium overlooking the golf course.[38]

Although John did not frequent La Costa often, the condominium was used whenever he was in southern California and could line up a round of golf with Fitzsimmons. Clearly, John was aware that some of the Teamsters had connections with the criminal world, and he recalled "playing golf a couple of times with a couple of guys who were supposed to be pretty unsavory characters. I wouldn't have picked either one of those fellows [to join the foursome]. But they were nice enough guys." Later in the fall of 1970, the labor leader began the annual Frank Fitzsimmons Invitational Golf Tournament at La Costa to raise money for the Little City Foundation, which supported a residential facility for mentally disabled children in Illinois. John and his old friend John Murphy, owner of Gateway Transportation and cofounder of Carriers Insurance, served on the tournament's executive committee and participated in the yearly event through the 1970s.[39]

Unlike the La Costa home, John's Clear Lake cottage was used frequently for business. Here he regularly entertained customers and suppliers, often barbecuing steaks personally on a large, custom-built grill in the house. Hoffa and Fitzsimmons were among the many guests who enjoyed John's culinary skills. Ruan Transport's annual managers retreat remained at Clear Lake, and after he gained control of Bankers Trust, John held its yearly board meeting at the lakeside site as well. Once, during one of his large weekend gatherings at Clear Lake, the city's power went out. Most people would either wait for the electricity to be restored or inquire at the local utility company, but not John. As was his custom, he relied on a personal contact. Having served on the Iowa Power and Light Board since the late 1950s, he had become good friends with several executives of the firm. After a few minutes without electricity, John called Ralph Schlenker, an Iowa Power vice president, at his home in Indianola, 135 miles south of Clear Lake, for help. Amazingly, the tactic worked. Schlenker knew people at the Mason City power company, and after several phone calls, he located someone who soon corrected the problem and restored electricity to Clear Lake.[40]

The Clear Lake property also remained the summer destination for the Ruan family. Even after Johnny went to Culver Military Academy, he made the annual summer trek with his mother and siblings to the cottage. But Johnny's time at the lake was not all vacation. As it became clearer that he would eventually take a position at one of his father's companies, Johnny spent much of his summer learning aspects of the trucking business by working at Ruan Transport's Clear Lake terminal.

While at Culver, Johnny benefited from the perks of an elite preparatory school. One of the opportunities was riding with the school's Black Horse Troop in the 1961 presidential inaugural parade in Washington, D.C. John and Betty were in the nation's capital that brisk January morning to see their high school senior ride with his Des Moines friend and classmate Devere Bendixen and the rest of the company down Pennsylvania Avenue. Given John's frequent business trips, he missed many family events, and Johnny must have appreciated his father's attendance at this special occasion. "In his own way," Johnny later reflected, "Father was certainly devoted to his family, but he was devoted, first and foremost, to his business, which he loved."[41] In this revealing statement, Johnny captured a critical aspect of his father. John loved his family and cared deeply about Betty and the children, but he was truly captivated by the business world. Always looking for new products to sell or new ways to "make a buck," John was driven to take advantage of every opportunity he perceived. This all-encompassing commitment left little time for the children or Betty. Often, in fact, when he had something to say to Johnny, Jayne, or Thomas, he communicated with them the way he often did employees at work: he sent them memos. These letters covered a variety of topics and ranged from praise for jobs well done to notes that reproved poor behavior or performance. Unfortunately, this correspondence had the unintended consequence of widening rather than lessening the gulf between John and his children.[42]

Instead of literally being there for his family, John expressed his affection by giving his children and wife the material advantages provided by his wealth. To Johnny, that meant a top-notch, private education and the eventual opportunity to one day head his father's firm. Following his graduation from Culver, Johnny went off to Northwestern University. Although very bright, Johnny by his own later admission was an undisciplined student who did not always apply himself to his college courses the way his workaholic father did in business. This basic difference in their personalities created a chasm between the two that would take time to bridge.[43]

During Johnny's years away at high school and then college, Jayne's interest in the horse world grew. She remained part of the Raccoon Valley Pony Club and continued to do well in jumping competitions.

Even her summers at Clear Lake did not take Jayne away from her horses; Betty made arrangements to board some of her daughter's animals at a neighbor's stable near the family cottage. As she matured, Jayne seemed more and more like her father. Outgoing at times, she could also be somewhat shy, and she shared with John a competitive focus and determination. These similarities led to a closer relationship between father and daughter than that shared by John and Johnny, and it was the competitive horse circuit that tightened their connection.[44]

When he could clear his schedule, John enjoyed watching Jayne in various equestrian events around the country. He often arrived at the arena with buckets of fried chicken, which he freely distributed to friends in the stands. But he provided more than moral support; John continued to buy Jayne outstanding mounts, and in the mid-1960s, he built Jonbar Stables just north of Waterworks Park in Des Moines. The stables used the same name already employed at John's ranch west of the city and were overseen by Don Snellings, a first-class trainer brought in from Virginia. With Jonbar, described in an advertisement as "Iowa's Newest and finest Stabling and Year-Round Training Facilities for Hunters and Jumpers," John supported his daughter's interest in competition.[45] As in most of his other endeavors, he also tried to make money with the business by buying, selling, and boarding horses as well as training other riders. Backed by Jonbar and under Snellings's direction, Jayne began to win more prestigious events. One of these victories came at the Chicago International, where in 1967 on Honey Bee, Jayne won the Pussiance Class with a jump of 6 feet, 4 inches.[46]

With riding dominating her life, Jayne decided on a college with a strong equestrian program. She and her good friend Elise Macomber eventually chose Stephens College, a private women's school in Columbia, Missouri. Besides having a good academic reputation, Stephens boasted its own stables and equestrian facilities spread over 18 acres as well as one of the nation's oldest riding clubs.[47] Although away at school, Jayne remained active on the horse circuit, frequently traveling to shows and competitions on weekends. Unlike Johnny, who did not see his parents often while he was away at school, Jayne saw John and Betty frequently at various equestrian events throughout her college years.[48]

Too young to attend most of Jayne's horse shows, Thomas Ruan initially stayed at home under the care of either mom Betty or the Ruan maid, Darlene Willis. Later he traveled to many of these equestrian events, but because of the age difference between Thomas and his older brother and sister, he grew up without much interaction or support from his siblings. John too was detached from his youngest son because of his heavy travel schedule and dedication to his companies. The only time Thomas regularly saw his father was at the dinner table. No matter how busy John became, when he was in town, he usually made it home for dinner. Most evenings, the meal was followed by some brief conversation, after which young Thomas was hustled off to bed around 7:30 P.M. Then John and Betty enjoyed some television together before retiring.[49]

Betty prized these moments with John; in fact, she loved any instant she could steal away with her husband. Much to her delight, she and John began taking more frequent vacations together in the early 1960s. Good friends Hud and Nellie Weeks and Howard and Bea Gregory often accompanied the Ruans on these trips. On an almost annual basis, the three couples climbed aboard John's twin-engine Beechcraft G18 airplane, and with Howard Gregory at the controls, they headed for tropical destinations in either Mexico or the Bahamas. These excursions were boisterous affairs, filled with daytime fishing and hijinks followed by dinner, dancing, and drinking. During one stay in the Bahamas, Hud repeatedly explained to the group the importance of using the best Bacardi rum when making tropical libations. He also claimed that he could easily distinguish Bacardi from lesser-quality rums. John soon tired of Hud's airs, and once back in Des Moines, he conspired with Nellie to test Hud's palate. One day he called Nellie, and upon hearing that her husband was at work, John headed over to the Weeks' house with a bottle of the cheapest rum he could find. In a fraternity-like prank, he emptied Hud's expensive bottle of Bacardi rum down the sink and refilled the container with the cut-rate liquor. A week passed and Hud never mentioned the rum. Soon thereafter, the Weeks had the Ruans and Gregorys over for dinner, and John finally told Hud about the rum. Everyone laughed but Hud, who promised to return the practical joke in the future. "Ruan," he pledged, "I'm going to get you."[50]

Besides savoring these rollicking trips and get-togethers, John and Betty were also planning a spectacular dream home to be built at their Jonbar Ranch. Pleased with the way the renovation of the new Ruan office at Third and Keo was progressing, John took architect Ken Kendall to his acreage west of Des Moines and asked him to draft plans for a rambling house that matched the beautiful rolling landscape. Blueprints called for a huge manor with an indoor pool and a separate apartment for John's mother, Rachel. Plans for the house were laid out on a coffee table in the den of the Ruans' current 34th Street home, where John and Betty were constantly tinkering with them. The grand home, however, was never built. Two events pushed back the groundbreaking, and a third eventually killed the project altogether.[51]

Plans were originally put on hold when John learned that the proposed route for Interstate 80 ran through his property. After much wrangling, the highway was eventually located north of the Ruan land, but by the time it was settled, John's mother was ill, and one of the reasons for the impressive structure was to move Rachel out to the ranch as well.[52]

John and his protective mother had always been close, but Rachel grew even more devoted to her youngest son in 1962, when a trucking accident killed her only other child. John's older brother, Arthur, had been in southern California for several years, but he never found a suitable job. After working for Ruan Equipment and Fruehauf as well as trying his hand at several other businesses, Arthur decided the life of a trucker on the open road best fit his independent nature. After much discussion, he finally convinced his wife, Dorothy, as well, and in 1960, he bought a truck. Trucking seemed like a good choice for Arthur, but two years later, tragedy struck. During a run in northern California, Arthur was in the passenger seat while his partner drove. When a tire blew out, the driver lost control, and the truck went off the highway into the adjacent culvert. Arthur was thrown from the cab, and his back was broken. Paralyzed from the neck down, he was rushed to the hospital, but doctors could not repair the damage. John flew out to see Arthur, who lingered for a week before dying in February 1962. The two men had had a difficult relationship over the years because Arthur had trouble dealing with his younger brother's great success while never quite finding his own. Unfortunately, they did not settle their differences, but John still struggled with this tragic and unexpected death. As he had done twice before, he stoically worked through the loss by putting in even greater hours at his companies. Rachel, meanwhile, dealt with the loss of Arthur by clinging ever more closely to John.[53]

Except for her few years in southern California, Rachel had never lived far from John. Her apartments at the Commodore Hotel and later at 3660 Grand were within a few blocks of his 34th Street house. This proximity made her weekly Sunday dinner visits to John's a quick and easy trip. It was a year or so after Arthur's death that John and Betty began talking about building out at Jonbar. If the plans went forward, Rachel would be even closer to John—a few steps down the hall in the new home rather than a few blocks away. But in early 1965, Rachel became ill and never recovered. She died that March, and John buried his mother next to his father in Oskaloosa. The death of his mother meant another change in the house plans, but more significantly, building the new place seemed less important to John, and the project was put on a back burner.[54]

By the time John became interested in the ranch house again, another problem intervened, and this one ultimately put an end to the idea. Even though she had been diagnosed with MS in the late 1950s, Betty's life did not change significantly over the next few years. She remained active in clubs and organizations and had a busy social calendar. Yet, late in the 1960s, the debilitating disease began to take a greater toll on her. It became more difficult for Betty to get around, and she began to cut back on her various activities. Soon, she was no longer able to drive and needed a full-time caregiver. This decline in her health also meant more frequent visits to doctors and hospitals. With the prospect of losing even more independence, Betty became less enamored with the idea of moving away from the close proximity of friends and family. Likewise, with Betty requiring greater medical attention, John did not wish to relocate farther from doctors and hospitals. By the early 1970s, therefore, John and Betty permanently shelved plans for the Jonbar Ranch home.[55]

Dropping this project did not stop the Ruans from looking for another house, however. Instead of building at the ranch, the couple started looking for a winter vacation home in a warm climate. They first considered Scottsdale, Arizona, and in the early 1970s, the family spent a Christmas holiday there looking at prospective property. Although they liked Arizona, John was ambivalent because he did not know anyone in the area. Meanwhile, James W. Hubbell Jr., who had become well acquainted with John on the Equitable of Iowa board, suggested that John consider the Lost Tree Village development in North Palm Beach, Florida. The Hubbells as well as several other wealthy Des Moines families had homes there. Intrigued, John flew down to investigate the gated community in 1972, and liking what he saw, he soon bought a small home there.[56]

By the time John bought the Florida property, traveling had become much easier for him. Four years earlier, he had upgraded his twin-engine Beechcraft G18 to a Learjet. John had been interested in buying a Lear for quite awhile but thought the plane too expensive. Dale Walker, a Lear salesman who had been working with John for several months, enlisted Howard Gregory, who had sold John several previous planes, to help him with the sale. Negotiations continued, but $3,500 separated John's offer from the purchase price of $750,000. Late one night in the summer 1968, Gregory finally closed the deal while out drinking with John. On a napkin he wrote: "I owe you $3,500 if at the end of three months you are not satisfied with the airplane." He signed the note and slid it and the purchase order across the table to his friend. John read the napkin, folded it, and signed the order.[57]

He had purchased a Learjet 24 that could carry up to six passengers in addition to its crew of two. It had a range of 1,800 miles and cruised at 540 miles per hour. Like four of his previous aircraft, John named the plane after his wife; hence the Learjet was *My Betty V.* Although it was intended for John's frequent business travel, he also thought the plane could bring in additional revenue. That fall, John established Ruan Aviation Corporation, Iowa's first jet charter service. In his words, the new company would "help meet the growing need for fast, unscheduled jet transportation to any destination in the Western Hemisphere." He added, "It's another transportation service as far as we are concerned. Lots of people have a need for this type of service." Jerry Ware, the Ruan pilot of 12 years, would fly the plane, with Gregory's Des Moines Flying Service providing additional crew members as well as flight scheduling and aircraft maintenance. Much as John had believed, Ruan Aviation soon had customers drawn by the convenience and speed with which it could get patrons to their destinations.[58]

The creation of Ruan Aviation and using the jet beyond its original purpose of his corporate travel was right in character for John; he did not like a piece of equipment sitting idle when it could be making money for him. On the other hand, the private planes had become important sales tools for John. He recalled, "Having a plane, particularly a jet, impressed people. My planes brought in a lot of business, and they more than paid for themselves over the years."[59] Clearly there were times when these two ideas conflicted. After several instances when John could not have the aircraft because someone else was already using it, Ruan Aviation's mission was reconsidered. It remained intact as a corporate entity, but its charter service was basically dropped, and from then on, *My Betty V* and its successors could be ready for John at a moment's notice. Sometimes the freedom and access the Lear provided benefited John's friends as well.[60]

Always loyal and generous with his friends, John made his plane available to them in times of need. One day, for instance, he was talking to a glum Howard Gregory. Gregory was ill and unhappy about the prospects of an upcoming business trip that involved a layover because commercial airlines did not provide direct flights to his destination. John excused himself from the conversation and made a phone call. Upon returning, he told Gregory the Lear would be ready to take him on his business call. Later, on the request of W. T. Dahl, an old friend and founder of the Des Moines grocery chain Dahl's Food Marts, John sent the plane down to Naples, Florida, to bring him and his frail wife back home to Des Moines.[61]

He also put his plane at the disposal of people in need. Two particular cases stand out. In 1979, an eight-year-old Laotian girl who had only recently arrived in Boone, 30 miles northwest of Des Moines, was diagnosed with a rare bone disease that would have been fatal without an urgent bone marrow transfusion. Iowa Methodist Medical Center officials arranged for her to be treated at the Fred Hutchinson Cancer

Center in Seattle, Washington, a leading facility in such diseases. Since John had used his plane to transport sick children before, he was contacted this time. Without hesitation he agreed, and young Bouangeun Dinthongsai was rushed to Seattle. Originally given only a slight chance of recovery, the little girl pulled through in what some observers termed as "miraculous." Two years later, another emergency arose, and Senator Roger Jepsen asked John for help. Fifteen-year-old Jane Hughes of Council Bluffs was visiting relatives in Boston when she became seriously ill. Doctors suggested she return to Iowa for treatment, but because of her family's "financial difficulties and the air traffic controllers strike," she could not get a commercial flight back to Iowa. Doctors contacted Jepsen, and he sought help from several Iowa companies. John responded to the request first, dispatching his jet to Boston to pick up Hughes and her family and bring them back to Iowa.[62]

Of course, most of the time, John used the plane for business. Pilot Jerry Ware explained, "John Ruan is on top of everything [in his businesses] and goes wherever anything is happening. We may fly three or four days in a row, rest up a couple of days, and then fly another four-day stretch. We're on a day-to-day scheduling basis because he wants the airplane when he needs it. That's the only way he can stay on top of his operations."[63] In the early 1970s, John employed the plane in two important endeavors: lining up a major tenant for his planned office tower and raising money for his friend Richard Nixon, the incumbent president seeking reelection.

By the late 1960s, growth at Bankers Trust suggested that it would soon require additional office space. John therefore asked architect Ken Kendall to make some preliminary drawings of an office building for which money was no object. Even though downtown Des Moines had been in a long period of decline, he believed the business district was ready to bounce back, and if he erected a new building, it would be downtown. With that in mind, John and bank president Bob Sterling began acquiring downtown property for a possible building site. In 1969, Bankers Trust bought the last piece it needed, the 66-year-old Chamberlain Hotel on the northeast corner of Seventh and Locust streets. Now Kendall gave this project greater priority. He and John met frequently, discussing the design and size of the building. At one point, the two were considering a 50-story structure, but John was not sure he could lease all the office space such a tower would afford. That, he realized, was his next challenge—finding tenants for his high-rise. Here again, John's salesmanship and personal contacts were critical.[64]

One of these associates was Bill Guy, president of Blue Cross–Blue Shield of Iowa. The two had become acquainted in the mid-1960s, and by 1969, John thought highly enough of Guy that he had him elected to the Bankers Trust Board. The following year, there was a rumor circulating in business circles that Blue Cross–Blue Shield had outgrown its current facilities and was looking to consolidate its operations in one building. After a Bankers Trust Board meeting, John asked Guy if the story was true. When he answered yes, John immediately set about wooing the potential tenant. After telling him, "I might just put up a damn building," John asked Guy to keep this option in mind.[65]

As John and architect Kendall continued to confer about the tower, John kept a close eye on the progress of Guy's search for new office space. In late 1970, Guy chartered John's jet, and he and several of his executives flew around the country examining buildings that other Blue Cross–Blue Shield organizations were using. The following year, John stepped up the pressure, applying all his skills to winning a long-term lease from the insurer. Part of his ploy included showing Guy the advantages of renting space in a modern office tower. He and Sterling, therefore, asked Kendall which North American cities had the most impressive skyscrapers comparable to the one John was planning. The architect identified Montreal and Toronto, and John told him to have drawings and a model of the proposed building ready for a potential tenant. He then invited Guy on a quick inspection trip of these buildings. After Guy accepted the invitation, Sterling and Kendall joined the two men, and the group headed north in John's plane.[66]

Impressed with his royal treatment and John's determined efforts, Guy liked the buildings he visited as well as Kendall's plans and model. Following the exhaustive day of travel, he and John ended up at the bar in Montreal's Queen Elizabeth Hotel. After much conversation and several drinks, Guy leaned over and told his host, "Anyone who wants this [Blue Cross–Blue Shield as tenants in his building] as bad as you ought to have it."[67] There was a catch, however. Although Guy liked everything he saw and believed John's tower would work well for the insurer, he was soon leaving his position for a job with California's Blue Cross–Blue Shield. He felt that his successor in Iowa should make the decision about where to locate the offices. John had not won over the tenant, but he clearly had his foot in the door.[68]

Plans for the building moved forward. At the end of 1971, Kendall went to Chicago and met with Larry Halprin of Morris Construction. The firm had done many tall office structures around the country, and it was interested in building John's. Halprin suggested using reinforced concrete for the tower, and Morris's cost estimate was based on using this material. On his way back to Des Moines, Kendall started thinking about a building he had always admired—the Deere & Company's Administrative Center in Moline, Illinois. Eero Saarinen was the architect of this striking structure, and the material employed was COR-TEN steel, a product that required no maintenance. Once home, Kendall contacted Pittsburgh–Des Moines Steel Company and local contractor Arthur H. Neumann & Brothers (renamed simply Neumann Brothers in 1976) for cost estimates of doing the building in COR-TEN steel. Combined, the firms' estimates were less than Morris's, and Kendall went to John with the news. A man who always closely monitored costs, John liked what he had heard, and he gave Kendall and Walter and Gordon Neumann a week to put together a firm proposal.[69]

The three met with John on a Sunday morning at the Ruan office building. After listening intently, John was ready to give the Neumann brothers the contract, but he wanted something in return. He told them, "You can build the building on two conditions: First, your firm will move its offices into the new building, and second, you will start banking with Bankers Trust." When the Neumanns realized John would not budge, they agreed, and all four headed to John's house for a drink to celebrate. The deal was win-win for John. He had hired a local contractor, taken the cheaper bid, gone with a cost-efficient exterior, gained a tenant, and obtained a new commercial bank account.[70]

In October 1971, the *Des Moines Tribune* reported that John Ruan and Bankers Trust were considering a "major downtown office development," and early the following year, John finally reached an agreement with David Neugent, the new president of Blue Cross–Blue

Shield, winning the insurer as his major tenant. That December, when plans for the office complex were announced, John already had 80 percent of the building leased. Blue Cross–Blue Shield would take 14 floors, Bankers Trust would occupy 7 floors in the tower and an adjoining two-story glass-enclosed pavilion, and the Ruan companies were slated for 4 floors. At 36 stories, the tower would be tallest in Iowa, nearly double the size of the Equitable Building, at the time the tallest building in Des Moines, and 11 stories higher than Iowa–Des Moines National Bank's Financial Center already under construction. Situated on property bounded by Grand and Sixth avenues and Locust and Seventh streets, the facility would occupy all but the northeast corner of the block where the Liberty Building stood.[71]

In addition, plans called for a landscaped plaza and fountains adjacent to the bank pavilion and south of the Liberty Building. A 120-car parking garage would be built below the huge office complex, and John proposed installing a private club atop the tower. Several months before the project was announced, Kendall and John were discussing a name for the building. After talking about the prominent role the structure would play in the downtown's redevelopment, the architect compared the complex to a famous edifice on the East Coast. "In New York," he said, "They have the Rockefeller Center. In Des Moines, we should have the Ruan Center." John smiled and readily agreed. The man who had seen his name on thousands of tractors and trailers would soon see it gracing the state's tallest building.[72]

When it became clear that the building project required more oversight than John could muster, he launched a search for a new bank president. This move would free Sterling from supervising Bankers Trust's day-to-day operations, and more of his time could be devoted to the Ruan Center and future projects. In June 1973, John hired 46-year-old Tom Wright, who had been the executive vice president of First National Bank in Jackson, Mississippi. With Wright now serving as president, Sterling moved up to chairman of the board and became John's chief spokesman.[73]

Several months earlier, in March, groundbreaking ceremonies for the Ruan Center took place, and central Iowans were transfixed by the rapidly changing landscape of the capital city. In the shadows of the

Financial Center—under construction one block south at Seventh and Walnut streets—the Ruan Center's structural steel skeleton began to rise. While the Financial Center was temporarily the city's tallest, its reinforced concrete-and-glass exterior was fairly typical and did not capture people's attention the way the steel skin that was soon applied to the Ruan Center did. Kendall had sold John on using COR-TEN steel plate to sheath the building. This special material required no painting or maintenance. When installed, the steel was gray in color, but once exposed to the elements, it would "weather" to a rusty hue and later to a dark brown. As the color changed, a permanent protective coat developed on the building's outer skin. Developed by U.S. Steel in the 1950s, COR-TEN was first used in heavy industry and later in bridges. More than 500 buildings across the United States had used this specialized product, but when the Ruan Center was completed, it became the tallest COR-TEN steel structure west of the Mississippi River. Although praised by many in the building industry as a "model for future high rise construction," the Ruan Center's striking appearance also led to derision. Some referred to it as "Bankers Rust" or "the towering rust bucket," while others simply called it the city's "ugliest building."[74]

Still, John liked what he saw, and as his tower headed skyward, he continued to line up tenants. When the last beam of the steel frame was hoisted into place in March 1974, a "topping" ceremony was held, complete with dignitaries, including Governor Robert Ray and Senator Dick Clark. Hosting the affair, John did not miss the opportunity to promote his building. He half-jokingly told the audience, "From a crowd of this size, there must be someone looking for [office] space, so you can see me at the bar later. This is bargain day."[75]

Whether or not he leased space that day, John was highly successful at filling his building before it was completed. John's many connections certainly played a role in this achievement. Two new tenants were drawn from companies John knew well because of his service of their boards. In May 1974, John was appointed to Northwestern Bell's board of directors, and he started working the group immediately. Two months later, the telephone company agreed to establish its Des Moines Briefing Center in the Ruan building. A year later, John won a bigger client when Iowa Power and Light leased two floors.[76]

For the top two floors, John had targeted the Des Moines Club. Established in 1909, it was the city's oldest private men's club and had been located at Eighth and Locust streets. A longtime member, John himself pitched the idea of moving the organization to the 33rd and 34th floors of the Ruan Center in a formal presentation to the Des Moines Club. Club members voted in favor of the move, but a substantial opposition retained an attorney to fight the relocation. As only John could do, he worked behind the scenes smoothing over problems and cutting deals. Ultimately, he bought the club's old building and its furnishings, gave the club a loan to facilitate the move, and offered the group an attractive lease. In the end, John won, and he and the club president, attorney Hedo Zacherle, signed the agreement in November 1974.[77]

In March 1975, firms such as Blue Cross–Blue Shield started to move into their new quarters at the Ruan Center. Amazingly, when John moved into his office on the 32nd floor that fall, he had already leased 95 percent of the facility's space. In October, several open houses showcased the impressive structure. The invitations correctly boasted, "The Ruan Center dramatically changes the Des Moines skyline, while adding substantially to the renaissance of the downtown business district."[78]

But John was not one to rest on his laurels, and after the whirl of parties and celebrations, he was busy at work in his simply appointed, functional office suite. Few adornments in the office meant that the items John displayed stood out. One was an oil painting entitled *Old Shoes* by his daughter that hung on the walnut-paneled wall behind John's desk, while in the adjoining room, a model of the Ruan Center sat on a coffee table. From his suite, John had a spectacular view: he looked out over the Iowa capitol, and on clear days, it was estimated one could see as far as 50 miles away. Yet John rarely appreciated the sights from his windows, and although he was clearly proud of his $26 million complex, he was already looking elsewhere. On the significance of the Ruan Center and the Financial Center, John said, "I now believe the two new high-rise office buildings . . . have demonstrated the desire of the business community to redevelop downtown Des Moines and that the next ten years will see even greater activity."[79] The next few years proved John correct, but he fulfilled much of his own prophecy with several of his own downtown projects.

Many people would have been entirely consumed by the construction of a major building like the Ruan Center, but not John. Even as plans were being developed for the structure, he was actively engaged in another large undertaking. His prominence in trucking—he was currently serving as secretary of the American Trucking Associations—and his connection with Richard Nixon, which dated back to World War II, led John into the political fund-raising arena. Maurice Stans, Nixon's campaign finance chairman, called John in 1972 and asked him for a campaign contribution. More important, Stans asked the trucker to solicit additional funds from others in the industry. John readily agreed and set up a number of meetings throughout the country with leading truckers. With his full business schedule, his Lear again came in handy, shuttling him efficiently in and out of Des Moines to these various gatherings.[80]

Most leading trucking executives wanted Nixon reelected, and with John's cajoling, many contributed generously. All told, the truckers raised over $600,000, which was the "largest single-industry gift for the Nixon reelection effort, overshadowing the huge flow of money [$427,500] from milk producers." John's share of the donation was $50,000. Such large contributions to political campaigns were often given in hopes of getting something in return, and that appeared to be the case here. John and the others seemed to have ulterior motives, and these became public, largely because of the Watergate investigation.[81]

A week before the election, Clark Mollenhoff of the *Des Moines Register* reported that John's $50,000 contribution to the Nixon campaign came while Ruan Transport was awaiting a ruling from the Interstate Commerce Commission (ICC) on the firm's recent acquisition of another trucking business. Earlier that year, in March, an ICC hearing examiner had turned down Ruan's application to obtain control of Eldon Miller, Inc., an Iowa truck line with operating rights in nine states. In response, John asked an ICC panel to overturn the examiner's decision. While awaiting its judgment, he became actively involved in raising money for Nixon's reelection.[82]

After Nixon won the election, John enjoyed the spoils of victory. Attending the inauguration, he watched proudly as the band from his alma mater, North High School, performed in the parade. In fact, he had made its participation possible by providing bus transportation to and from Washington, D.C., for the 115-member band.[83] Soon thereafter, John was invited to a White House reception. After waiting in line to greet the president, John remembered, Nixon approached him and said, "Where the heck have you been? I've been looking for you ever since we started." He then thanked John for his support. In March, John was back at the White House for a stag dinner. He was seated between Henry Ford Jr., and Harvey Firestone Jr. As the evening began, John recalled, each person introduced himself. John rose and said, "I'm John Ruan, a trucker from Des Moines, Iowa." Ford immediately stood up and asked, "Mr. President, you certainly aren't going to allow any Teamsters in here, are you?" Before Nixon could say anything, Firestone interjected, "What John didn't say was that he has over 10,000 trucks!"[84]

These occasions and others at the White House likely occurred because of John's success at fund-raising, but this presidential access did not sway the ICC in his favor. In October 1973, the full commission voted down Ruan's acquisition of Eldon Miller, Inc. The company was ordered to divest itself of the 45 percent stock interest in the truck line it had acquired in 1967 and drop its option of purchasing the remaining 55 percent of the firm. This adverse ruling was not his only problem, however. As the Watergate investigation widened, John's fund-raising efforts were scrutinized.[85]

Among other things, Watergate prosecutors were examining accusations that Maury Stans employed high-pressure tactics in soliciting campaign donations, which led to questions about the truckers' generous gift to the Nixon campaign. In the fall of 1973, investigators from the Senate Watergate Committee traveled to Des Moines to interview John. They were especially interested in whether or not promises of political favors were made in exchange for contributions. Certainly John hoped for a favorable ruling from the ICC, but he stressed that Stans never mentioned Ruan Transport's pending ICC case when he asked for campaign contributions.[86] John told the *Washington Star-News* that the fund drive was not aimed at influencing government policy but solely "to defeat the other candidate." More generally, the committee was interested in the relationship of the truckers' large donation and their concurrent fight against an administration-backed bill in Congress that would have relaxed the ICC's regulation of rates and created greater competition in the trucking industry. John acknowledged that the proposed changes in trucking regulations were discussed at the fund-raising meetings, but such ideas, he explained, would have been raised at any gathering of trucking executives. Emerson Swan, president of Red Ball Motor Freight in Dallas, who personally contributed $25,000 to the campaign, said there was never any mention of getting political favors for donations. He jokingly added, "If we got something for that money, I'd like to start collecting."[87]

The Senate Watergate Committee ultimately agreed with John. It found no illegality in the truckers' donations and abandoned its inquiry. Interestingly, however, after the truckers made their large contribution to the Nixon campaign, the federal Department of Transportation (DOT) "quietly dropped its proposal to revamp the [trucking] industry." The "deregulation" plan would have "allowed freer entry into the business by new [trucking] firms, and it would have permitted rates to respond to competitive pressures, thus encouraging price-cutting." Viewed as a serious threat by most truckers, the industry had been fighting the plan since its inception in 1971 and, along with railroad and barge interests, had launched a public relations drive to derail the DOT bill and replace it with one of their own. Whether the strong opposition of the transportation interests or the truckers' large donation finally led to bill's demise is difficult to determine, but for John and his friends in the industry, it did not really matter. The bill had "evaporated," and that was an important victory.[88]

Occupied though he was with fund-raising, planning the Ruan Center, and closely supervising his companies, John remained on the lookout for additional moneymaking opportunities. Thriving in the world of commerce, he often acted on the advice of close associates. Through two old friends, John became involved with three companies in the early 1970s.

One was the Boston Herald-Traveler, a company he and Joe Rosenfield had been interested in since 1960. Although its newspapers were losing money, its television station, WHDH, was very profitable. But by 1964, Rosenfield and John as well as Sidney Brody, a shareholder from Los Angeles, were growing increasingly concerned about the newspapers' losses. Their worries were heightened by the company's ongoing struggle to keep its television station. Three other media concerns had applied for the license from the Federal Communications Commission (FCC).[89] With their consent, Brody nominated his two Iowa associates for membership on the company's board. Although they received 30 percent of the vote, they fell short of being elected.[90]

They remained concerned and continued plotting. If they could get control of the company, John and Rosenfield were considering selling off the newspaper and concentrating on the television station. Several more efforts at getting board representation failed, but John, whose stock interest in the company eventually climbed to 5.6 percent, kept a close eye on the WHDH-TV situation. In 1969, the FCC ruled against the Boston Herald-Traveler Corporation and removed its television license, giving it to Boston Broadcasters Incorporated (BBI). Although the decision was appealed, the ruling stood, and in March 1972, BBI took control. A CBS affiliate, WHDH-TV went off the air and was replaced by the new ABC station, WCVB-TV. In the midst of the battle over WHDH-TV, the Hearst newspaper group expressed interest in merging its *Record American* with the *Boston Herald-Traveler*. At about the same time, John became part of a proxy fight. He won and finally attained a seat on the company board. After it was clear that the television license was lost, plans to merge the paper with the Hearst operation went forward. Hearst paid $8.6 million for the Herald-Traveler's physical plant, land, and circulation, and its new *Boston Herald American* resulted.[91]

Without its television station or newspaper, the much smaller company was renamed WHDH Corporation. What remained were two radio properties—a moderately profitable AM station and a less successful FM station. Rosenfield thought the only way to salvage their situation was to find a buyer for the company. John and several other board members agreed. By 1973, John Blair and Company, a firm that sold time for television and radio stations, and a minority stockholder of WHDH as well, stepped up and bought out the other shareholders for $10.1 million, or $33 a share. Although this investment had not gone as John had hoped or planned, the hours he and Rosenfield devoted to the Boston venture paid off handsomely.[92]

At about the same time, John put money in another enterprise, and this investment soon became lucrative. Here again, tips and advice from friends proved valuable. In 1970, Joe Rosenfield told John about a new company in California called Intel. Through his Grinnell College connections, Rosenfield knew Robert Noyce, one of the company founders and a fellow graduate of Grinnell. Noyce and partner Gordon Moore had established the firm in 1968 and soon pioneered the development of computer chips. Their breakthrough came in 1971 with the creation of the world's first microprocessor. After further refinement, Intel's microprocessor chips were operating machines such as cash registers, and in 1978 IBM chose the Intel 8088 computer chip for its line of personal computers. Its chip quickly became an industry standard, and the company went on to dominate the microprocessor market.[93]

The Intel Corporation went public with its first stock offering in the fall of 1971. Rosenfield recommended that John buy some shares, but he disregarded the suggestion and all but forgot about the West Coast firm. Months later in the spring, John heard someone mention Intel in passing. The reference jogged his memory, and he soon called Rosenfield. His friend acknowledged that Intel was a good investment but wondered why John had not bought shares earlier. This time, John followed the suggestion and was immediately on the phone with Stan Madson, his stockbroker at William Blair and Company in Chicago, buying his first shares of Intel.[94]

Further purchases ensued until Intel's rising stock price led John to sell all but 6,900 shares in 1982. He realized a $100,000 profit. Instead of congratulating his friend on the financial gain, however, Rosenfield scolded John for selling Intel and told him he should buy some more. Again, he followed the advice and bought more shares of Intel. He kept on buying over the years, and after these additional purchases and dozens of stock splits, John's Intel holdings in 2001 amounted to roughly four million shares.[95]

Besides Intel, Rosenfield sold John on another rewarding investment. James Hoak Jr. and James Cownie had put together a small cable television venture initially called Des Moines Cable Company. They incorporated the firm in 1970 and soon sought investors in the Des Moines business community. Rosenfield jumped in and encouraged his friend to do the same. John followed the advice and made a small investment. The following year, the company offered its stock to the public and obtained its first cable franchise. By 1973, it won the Des Moines franchise and was on its way to becoming one of the nation's top 50 cable providers. As the company grew beyond central Iowa, it went through several name changes, finally settling on Heritage Communications, Incorporated. Early in this period of growth, Heritage wanted to retire some of its bank debt, but unfavorable market conditions led to a postponement of another stock offering. Instead, Hoak asked John if he might be interested in buying 50,000 additional shares of the company. John saw great potential for the company and agreed to the purchase, paying $300,000 for the stock. This acquisition took his interest in the company to 11.7 percent, and he was soon thereafter named to its board of directors.[96]

John held on to his Heritage shares, and his strategy of buy and hold proved wise. In the 1980s, Heritage Communications became part of the consolidation of the cable industry. Tele-Communications Inc. (TCI) bought Heritage in 1987 for $887 million, bringing shareholders $34 a share in cash and stock. Ten years later, AT&T acquired TCI, and the value of John's early investments in Heritage soared to nearly $20 million.[97]

By 1975, the 61-year-old businessman's fortunes were on the rise. His companies were expanding and his major outside investments were also growing. As if symbolic of his position, the Ruan Center now dominated the Des Moines skyline. Yet there were no indications that John was ready to slow—he loved the game of business too much. Nor did he seem affected by the trappings of wealth and power. "I'm just John Ruan," he once said. "I go along and conduct my business every day. If I see something that intrigues me, then I put my effort into it."[98] With this straightforward attitude, John continued to work. Personal problems and business setbacks occurred, but neither deterred him from his life's pleasure of selling products and ideas or of initiating projects he believed were important.

6 The Man with the Midas Touch

By the mid-1970s, John could survey downtown Des Moines from his office high above the city in the recently completed Ruan Center. Along with the builders of the Financial Center, he had ignited the redevelopment of the city's core, but much remained to be done. Years of urban flight, neglect, and decay had taken their toll on the capital. Business executives and community leaders now agreed on the necessity of rebuilding the downtown but disagreed on what was required, where new facilities should be located, and how they were to be financed. From 1975 to 1982, John was in the middle of the fray. Embroiled in controversy from the start, he was a major proponent of the skywalk system and headed up a group of investors that built the 33-story Marriott Hotel across from the Ruan Center. Closely tied to the Marriott's success was a new parking garage that John demanded immediately south of the hotel. Before the hotel was finished, he moved on to another project, erecting the 14-story Carriers Building adjacent to his office tower. And as this structure was nearing completion, John became the leading voice for construction of a downtown convention center.

Once introduced as "the man with the Midas touch," John was living up to the description: when it came to downtown development, everything he touched seemed to turn to gold.[1] The many victories he enjoyed were not without hard-fought battles, yet John had the wherewithal to see them through. He possessed a combination of traits that set him apart from most city and business leaders. While others envisioned promising projects, few had the inner drive and the fortitude to shepherd such plans from the drawing board to reality. John did both, and he did it again and again in the late 1970s and early 1980s. As the downtown renewal proceeded, *Des Moines Register* columnist and later editor James Flansburg jokingly suggested a way of speeding up the urban renaissance: "What downtown Des Moines needs is three more John Ruans. It would end up looking like downtown Minneapolis."[2]

Committed to a new downtown, John remained involved in the oversight of his other businesses. The trucking operations enjoyed successes. The recession of the late 1970s and then deregulation cut into Ruan Transport's revenues, but rapid expansion in the company's leasing division more than offset this decline. Carriers Insurance seemed stable, and Bankers Trust continued to grow.

As his Ruan Center was going up, John became widely viewed as a person who could get things done. Some in the media touted this new building as his crowning achievement. *Modern Bulk Transporter*, a trucking trade publication, ran a story under the headline, "Ruan Center . . . Caps Career of John Ruan."[3] The Ruan Center was only the beginning, though, and Des Moines businessmen recognized it as such. They saw John as an ascending leader, and his peers elected him president of the Greater Des Moines Committee in November 1974. Originally incorporated by past presidents of the city's chamber of commerce in 1907, the elite group's stated purpose was to "encourage, promote, develop, and protect commercial, manufacturing, and other business interests in the city of Des Moines and the state of Iowa."[4] From John's perspective, the group "was pretty much an advisory committee" that could "help make things happen if they're so inclined." Under his leadership for two consecutive years, that was exactly what happened. From there, he became even more involved in the future of downtown development.[5]

Since the late 1960s, Des Moines business leaders and politicians had been imagining a revitalized downtown area. Early moves in this direction started with the completion of several new structures, such as the United Central Bank office facility, the Federal Office Building, and the J. C. Penney store. In 1972, plans for both the Ruan Center and the Financial Center jump-started the renewal efforts, but that same year, officials closed the dilapidated KRNT Theater, the downtown's 3,000-seat auditorium, because of a badly leaking roof. Realizing the importance of the theater and wishing to maintain the momentum of downtown redevelopment, the Greater Des Moines Committee took action. Led by then president James W. Hubbell Jr., it hired New York architectural firm Charles Luckman Associates to develop plans for a "hotel-theater-convention center" complex to be located between Grand Avenue and Walnut Street, and Second Avenue and Fourth Street. The proposal suggested a 2,500-seat performing arts theater, a 300-room hotel, a convention center, and a large, open plaza area. Funding for the projects was to come from a $22-million issue of urban renewal bonds, but a majority of the city council refused to approve the move without a referendum first being held. Mayor Dick Olson and James W. Hubbell Jr., chairman of the Equitable of Iowa Companies, led the charge, and the bond issue was put before the city voters in September 1973.[6]

Although 54 percent of Des Moines voters supported the bond issue, it fell short of the 60 percent majority required. Public financing was unavailable, but under Mayor Olson's leadership, the city agreed to donate the land for the theater project if the facility could be built with private money. Two prominent downtown businessmen—David Kruidenier, CEO of the Des Moines Register and Tribune Company (R&T), and John Fitzgibbon, president of Iowa–Des Moines National Bank—took up the challenge of raising the needed funds from the private sector. With amazing speed and efficiency, they succeeded, amassing more than $9 million over three months in 1975. Although John had reservations about the theater's location, he finally contributed $50,000 for the cause through Bankers Trust. Near this planned civic center, "the cultural anchor of the new downtown," many hoped that a hotel and parking ramp would eventually follow. Kruidenier, who would also serve as chairman of the civic center's board of directors, was among this group.[7]

Most members of the business community embraced the idea of the civic center, but there was debate about where a downtown hotel should be located. Discussions of the hotel and its possible sites were hot topics at Greater Des Moines Committee meetings. John soon became the leading figure of the five-member subcommittee established to investigate the issue. He worked closely with Charles Duchen, the president of Younkers, and James Hubbell Jr. on the matter. In fact, John started to meet with Duchen once or twice a week for early-morning breakfast discussions at the downtown Younkers Tea Room. Once convinced there was enough support for the project, John consulted with financial adviser Roger Cloutier, who put him together with attorney Edgar Hansell. A specialist in issuing securities, Hansell created a partnership structure for the undertaking. At the same time, John had architect Ken Kendall prepare drawings for a large hotel across Seventh Street immediately west of the Ruan Center. In October 1976, he unveiled plans for a 20-story hotel. This was the opening volley in what became a long and contentious struggle over the facility.[8]

Not only was the hotel project controversial, but the necessary parking garage and skywalk connections were divisive topics as well. These issues were not new to John, but the degree of acrimony surrounding the fight to win the structures was something he had not experienced before. While in the planning stages for the Ruan Center, it was determined that additional parking beyond the projected spaces underneath the building would be required. John worked closely with the Des Moines city manager, and after several months of fairly routine discussions with the city council and the Des Moines Plan and Zoning Commission, he thought he had the situation under control. The council was ready to approve the $4.3 million Grand Avenue Garage. There was a last-minute attempt by Kruidenier and leaders in the Des Moines Chamber of Commerce to have the parking facility built underground, but John and city officials argued that changing the garage plans at this late stage would be very expensive and delay the project for an unacceptable period. The council agreed, and it voted unanimously in favor of the ramp. John won what was a minor confrontation with Kruidenier, but it set the stage for a much greater battle over the hotel project.[9]

The Grand Avenue Garage was designed by Kendall and constructed immediately north and west of John's new building.[10] As the five-story structure, which spanned Seventh Street between Grand Avenue and High Street, was being completed, it was connected to the nearly finished Ruan Center by a skywalk in late 1974. Paid for by Bankers Trust, the skywalk was an elevated, climate-controlled, glass-enclosed bridge that provided public access from the parking ramp across Grand Avenue to the second floor of the Ruan Center. It was the city's third such walkway, following by a couple of years the skywalk connecting the J. C. Penney department store to the Fifth Avenue

Garage and the one linking Bankers Life with its annex. None of these skywalks caused much commotion, but when asked if there were too many, Plan and Zoning Commission member Mark Engelbrecht knowingly said, "The important thing is to pay attention to what the strong visual corridors in the city are. In my mind, that is Locust Street. When we start throwing them up across Locust, that's one too many."[11]

Soon after the hotel project was announced, John and others on the Greater Des Moines Committee as well as city leaders began seriously considering a skywalk system for downtown Des Moines. In the late 1960s, Dick Olson, then a member of the city council, started investigating the possibilities of such a network, but little had been done until 1976, when several people took up the idea in earnest. They began by visiting cities that already possessed skywalks. Leading figures, such as Olson (by now mayor), Bankers Life president Robert Houser, and James Hubbell Jr., traveled to Minneapolis, St. Paul, and Cincinnati. John, of course, used his own plane and took close friend and ally Charles Duchen, city manager Richard Wilkey, and others on his skywalk inspection tours. It quickly became clear that a system combining the best aspects of the private one in Minneapolis and the public one in St. Paul was in order. The major drawback to the Minneapolis system was that it ran through retail and commercial buildings, which meant that when one store on the system closed, access to the walkway was compromised. John and the others immediately recognized this flaw and worked to avoid the same problem in Des Moines. The skywalks in St. Paul had been constructed with public money, including large amounts of federal dollars from Housing and Urban Development (HUD) programs. Such funds were no longer available, and a fully public skywalk was not an option for Des Moines.[12]

Both business and city leaders, therefore, looked to build a hybrid skywalk, combining the best aspects of each system in the Twin Cities. The city hired the Minneapolis-based architectural firm Barton Aschman Associates to consider design and structural standards for the proposed system, and the mayor formed the "skywalk committee" to develop plans for the overall network. The committee was comprised of city administrators and representatives from the downtown businesses affected by the planned walkway. Leading figures included city attorney Phil Riley, city bonding attorney Ken Haynie, and Jim Thompson from the Traffic and Transportation Department. Because the first "spine" of the skywalk would basically impact only Ruan and Equitable of Iowa interests, Edgar Hansell, attorney for the Ruan companies, and Russell Schrage, who sat in the Equitable, were also on the committee.[13]

From 1978 to 1980, the group decided on a combined public and private skywalk system. John, however, saw problems with the proposed arrangement and had his own idea of how the city and private sector should cooperate. As Michael Hayes, who joined the city attorney's office in early 1980, was preparing the skywalk agreement, John summoned the entire skywalk committee to the Ruan boardroom for a discussion. In no uncertain terms, John made his position clear. Slamming his fist on the table, he argued that the only way to get the skywalks up and running was for the city to fund the project and the private sector to build and manage it. Riley calmly replied that legally, the city could not just turn public funds over to private interests, but it could use money for the public benefit. Viewed as "elevated sidewalks," the proposed skywalks would certainly provide a public benefit, and Riley was interested in further discussion of a cooperative arrangement with downtown businesses. John did not win this argument. Ultimately, like the network in St. Paul, the Des Moines plan set unified standards for the height, width, and hours of all skywalks. The city agreed to fund skywalks that ran across streets and alleys. For interior walkways and for connecting to the system, however, Des Moines followed the Minneapolis notion of having the affected businesses foot the bill. Public easements through the private buildings had to be granted, but, within reason, the business owners could determine where the skywalk easements were located. Maintenance, heating and cooling, and eventually security costs were borne by the private sector.[14]

While the skywalks were first being discussed, the *Des Moines Register* recognized John's growing influence in the city. In the fall of 1976, the newspaper ran a series called "The Powers that Be," a multipart story about the power structure in Des Moines. To determine the city's most influential figures, the *Des Moines Register* asked a series of questions to a panel of the area's top business and civic leaders. Few were surprised when John Ruan topped the list, but interestingly, he also ranked first in two other categories: those whose "power was on the rise" and those "who craved more power." When told of his number one ranking, John said, "I've never thought about it [power]. It's my opinion that anybody who's busy doesn't have time to stop and think about such things."[15] Much more important to him was translating his standing into action. At the time, he was very much interested in directing the hotel project to completion.

The proposed hotel was badly needed in downtown, and after the civic center, it was a top priority among most members of the Greater Des Moines Committee. Under John's plan, the newly created City Center Corporation, which was to be made up of local investors, would own the hotel. Others could buy limited partnerships in the project or purchase debenture notes. Management, however, was to be provided by a national hotel chain. For the hotel to be successful, John called on the city to build a 600-car parking ramp south of the hotel on Locust Street between Seventh and Eighth streets. The garage was to be located on the site of the Younkers Parkade and, John suggested, could be connected to the hotel, the Register Building, and the Ruan Center with skywalks.[16]

Along with John, early City Center investors included Younkers, F. M. Hubbell, Son and Co., Iowa Power and Light, and Iowa Realty. Regardless of these and several other shareholders, the project was immediately dubbed the "Ruan Hotel," and John was rightly perceived as the major force behind the scheme. He was, in fact, president of City Center Corporation and initially controlled 60 percent of its stock. Several years before, when John first became concerned about the central business district's decline, he had had a "beautiful scale model of the downtown built." He and close associates used to sit over the model and, as if playing a game of Monopoly, they planned and plotted the direction of redevelopment by "demolishing" a miniature structure here and adding a toy building there. Now the stakes were real, and much like the game, opponents had their own ideas, which often ran counter to John's.[17]

With his hotel plan now public, John went to work. He looked to Bankers Life to carry a mortgage in the $10 million range and sought the remaining funds from wealthy individuals and companies in Des Moines. Initially, the business community lined up behind John. Robb Kelley, president of Employers Mutual, expressed the general view: "Anybody against this is against progress." Another saw investing in the hotel as "my civic duty." According to the *Des Moines Register*, many were supportive largely because "Ruan, a major business power" was pushing the project. In the meantime, the Des Moines Development Corporation (DMDC), the financial arm of the Des Moines Chamber of Commerce, had taken options to purchase the properties on the proposed hotel site. At the same time, some did not like the way John "steamrolled" the project, and there was disagreement over the location of the hotel and the accompanying parking ramp.[18] Yet even those who opposed the site acknowledged John's powers of achieving his goals: "Wherever Ruan wants it, that's where it will probably be."[19]

Led by editorials in the morning *Des Moines Register* and the evening *Des Moines Tribune*, some began calling for a different hotel site, one closer to the new theater complex and not, as the *Tribune* noted, in the "middle of 8-5 buildings in the 'business core.'"[20] Their preferred location was the so-called Ward block between Locust and Walnut streets and Fourth and Fifth streets. Situated on this land, immediately west of the planned civic center plaza area, were an empty Montgomery Ward Building, the soon-to-be-vacated Valley National Bank Building, a furniture store, and an abandoned parking structure. Others opposed building a parking ramp at Seventh and Locust because, as the *Tribune* explained, it would "add to downtown traffic jams and displace existing businesses." Since the city might not build two parking facilities, the hotel ramp could threaten construction of a civic center parking garage, a project supported by the newspapers and important to the theater.[21]

In April 1977, Des Moines Development Corporation exercised its options to purchase two properties on the hotel site and reached verbal agreements to acquire the other two buildings there. Interestingly, one of the properties being sold to DMDC was the Royal Union Building, owned by the R&T. While continuing to oppose the venture editorially, the newspaper company pledged $350,000 toward John's hotel project in September.[22] If these disparate actions were not confusing enough, when a Canadian development firm expressed interest in building an office-retail–hotel complex near the new civic center, Kruidenier and the *Register* and *Tribune* threw their wholehearted support behind the rival project.[23]

John persevered, and as he approached finalizing the hotel's financing, the Des Moines City Council responded to his request for an informal vote on the parking garage. On February 6, 1978, it unanimously endorsed the construction of the facility at Seventh and Locust streets. Five days later, John held a press conference. Flanked by Duchen and Hubbell, the other leading spokesmen for the City Center Corporation, he announced that the group was ready to go ahead with the hotel. Referring to it as "the greatest thing to happen to Des Moines in the last 50 years," John described the hotel—now thirty stories with 425 rooms—that would be built across from the Ruan Center. The structure was to have several restaurants and bars, a roof garden with a swimming pool, and a dramatic two-story ballroom over Locust Street linking the hotel with the new parking garage. Included with the hotel plans was a three-block skywalk running south down the west side of Seventh Street, connecting the Grand Avenue Garage to the hotel, the new Locust parking ramp, Younkers, and the Mulberry Street Parking Garage.[24]

As with many of his other business deals, John had relied on his numerous connections to line up hotel investors. He finagled financial support from many of the city's leading individuals and businesses. Friends who contributed included Bob Brown, a local automobile dealer; W. T. Dahl, owner of Dahl's Food Marts; Robert Hicklin, president of Hicklin GM Power Company; James Hoak of St. Regis Paper Company; Paul Manning, the person who sold John his first truck back in 1932; and Jack Pester, chairman of Pester (Oil) Corporation. Major corporate support came from companies where John served on the board of directors or knew key executives. As already noted, F. M. Hubbell, Son and Co., Iowa Power and Light, Iowa Realty, and Younkers were among investors, while those taking out limited partnerships and/or debenture notes included American Federal Savings and Loan, American Republic Insurance Company, Brenton Brothers, Inc., Employers Mutual Casualty Company, Equitable of Iowa, General Growth Properties, Meredith Corporation, Mid-America Group, National By-Products, and Northwestern Bell Telephone.[25]

With the necessary funding assured and plans ready, everything seemed in place for the hotel, but more opposition soon surfaced. City manager Richard Wilkey came out against building either of the parking garages—the hotel's ramp at Seventh and Locust or the proposed civic center garage—with public money because the cost would require the city to cut other programs. The *Tribune* applauded Wilkey's position and ran the results of a poll, which indicated that 70 percent of Des Moines residents opposed using property taxes to pay for downtown parking garages.[26] Then a group of private citizens called the Association of Community Organizations for Reform Now (ACORN) pledged to use "whatever legal means necessary" to prevent the use of taxpayer monies on downtown parking facilities. In response, Dwight Swanson, head of Iowa Power and Light Company and president of the Des Moines Chamber of Commerce, said the city should "proceed without delay" on the hotel parking garage and that the recent opposition was a "severe setback" to city renewal. Robert Houser, president and chairman of Bankers Life, which was providing roughly one-third of the hotel's financing, was more blunt: "The hotel will not be built if the parking ramp isn't."[27]

That spring, even as John announced that the Marriott chain would manage the downtown hotel and join the venture as a limited partner, the R&T took up another line of attack. The *Tribune* referred to the planned two-story ballroom extending over Locust Street as an "aesthetic disaster" because it would block the view of the capitol. It called for a redesign of the hotel, which included the facility within the main structure. If John would not voluntarily make the change, it argued that the city council should block the offensive span.[28]

With the parking ramp and ballroom still matters of contention, John remained confident, and in July 1978, demolition of the buildings on the northwest corner of Seventh and Locust to make way for new hotel began. The city council remained committed to building the parking structure, and late that same month, it voted 5 to 2 in favor of issuing bonds for its construction. The council later approved using property taxes to pay off part of the bonds being used for the project. The R&T kept arguing for locating the ramp elsewhere, and ACORN filed a lawsuit—which it won in June 1979—to prevent the city council from using property tax dollars to pay off a portion of the garage bonds. In September 1978, John put one of these issues to rest. He announced that the hotel design would be altered to accommodate the ballroom, thus addressing one of the R&T's complaints. This move was in line with James Hubbell Jr.'s view of John. "He is not uncompromising," said Hubbell, "but he has definite views of what his objectives are and it takes quite a bit of argument to persuade him otherwise." One area where John remained steadfast was the location of the parking ramp.[29]

Regardless of the continuing controversy over the garage, groundbreaking ceremonies for the hotel went forward in October 1978, exactly two years after the project was originally proposed. John opened the event by telling the assembled crowd, "It's not the easiest chore that I ever undertook, and I'm glad we've reached the point where we're going to break a little ground." He then joined Governor Robert Ray, Chamber of Commerce president Dwight Swanson, Mayor Dick Olson, Bankers Trust chairman Robert Sterling, Reverend Louis Valbracht, and his strong supporters on the Des Moines City Council, George Nahas, Russell LaVine, and Robert Scott, in ceremoniously turning the ground with silver shovels.[30]

John hired Neumann Brothers, Inc., the same firm that built the Ruan Center, as the hotel's general contractor, and excavation began in December. Amazingly, yet another problem surfaced. Including the ballroom in the hotel's main structure required a six-foot-wide, two-story extension over the Locust Street sidewalk. Much as former Des Moines Plan and Zoning Commission member Mark Engelbrecht had suggested, structures on Locust Street that impaired the view of the capitol could prove problematic. Robert Mickle, the city planning director, rejected the planned hotel overhang for exactly this reason. He also worried about setting a precedent and suggested that if the city were going to allow such a structure, a policy should be developed. Mickle's decision could be overturned by a favorable vote by the Des

Moines Plan and Zoning Commission followed by similar support from the city council. Architect Kendall and attorney Hansell took the hotel's case to the zoning commission. Kendall made it clear that the additional space was critical and the impact of losing it would be "substantial." Hansell then asked commission members to do what he had done earlier that day: "Walk down Locust Street and turn around and see what six feet is going to do to us . . . I think your fears will be soothed, and you'll see that it won't be a problem. The six foot overhang is critical to us, and I think you'll find it won't be a visual impairment." He also noted that the Register and Tribune Building had a 12-foot overhang running along both Locust and Eighth streets.[31]

Despite the R&T's backing of Mickle's position, John and hotel investors won the battle when both the zoning commission and the city council supported the hotel's overhang. Since the encroachment hung over public property, the City Center Corporation had to purchase the air rights over the sidewalks from the city. After successfully fighting off this challenge, the only remaining hurdle was settling the parking garage issue. The matter was made all the more difficult when ACORN filed new lawsuits against the city's involvement in the parking ramp. In essence, the citizen organization alleged that the garage was "too expensive and being built at public expense for a private hotel developer."[32]

With no end to the parking standoff in sight, Equitable of Iowa's executive vice president, Luther Hill Jr., considered other options. Equitable saw the Locust Street garage as crucial for two reasons. First, like most investors in the hotel, it believed the parking structure was necessary for the Marriott's success. Second, it had recently purchased Younkers, and the retailer's flagship store, immediately south of the proposed garage, would clearly benefit from the facility. With much at stake, Hill broached the idea of building the ramp. James Hubbell Jr., the company chairman, thought the project worthwhile, and John, not surprisingly, was very supportive. In July 1979, the Equitable announced its intention to put up the Seventh and Locust Street parking garage privately. Mayor Olson praised the move as ending a long "nightmare" and continued, "I don't think there has been an issue in my 12 years [in city government] that has divided the community more than this one." The plan called for the city to issue $6.5 million in industrial revenue bonds, which the Equitable would pay off. The other $2 million needed would come from Equitable and Younkers. When completed, the garage included 18,500 square feet of first-floor retail space as well as a second-floor retail area tied to the skywalk that ran through the facility. Hailing the Equitable's move as "welcomed news," the *Des Moines Register* congratulated the company for "break[ing] the impasse" and dropped its opposition to the garage. ACORN responded in a similar manner, abandoning its lawsuits. Another major barrier to the hotel had been overcome.[33]

With the parking garage headache behind him, John watched the hotel construction go forward. Along the way, plans had been altered and the building's costs had risen well beyond the early estimate of $20 million. Originally, an exhibit hall for convention purposes was slotted for a portion of the parking structure, but John had backed away from the idea because of pressure from some city council members and the mayor. Instead, the exhibit space was inserted in a reworked hotel configuration. Another modification included the addition of two floors of luxury apartments on top of the Marriott. These changes, combined with delays and inflation, increased the hotel costs to more than $31 million.[34]

By 1980, the skywalk issue returned to the front burner. When planning the skywalk system, city engineers followed the Minneapolis model, with skywalk bridges crossing streets at midblock. This meant that the north-south walkway from Grand Avenue to Locust Street would be laid out over the alley between the Marriott and the R&T Building. John and his architect, however, had envisioned the skywalk running along the east side of the hotel over the Seventh Street sidewalk. They successfully argued that the alley skywalk was not feasible because the link to the Marriott would have to go through structurally necessary wall. In the end, the skywalk went where John had wanted it all along, but this created a problem of connecting the R&T to the system. Eventually, a deal was brokered. City Center Corporation, the Hubbell interests, and the R&T contributed $25,000 each to the city's skywalk fund. In return, the city agreed to make an exception to its rule allowing only one skywalk bridge per block and build a link over

Locust Street connecting the Register Building to the new parking garage and the skywalk system.[35]

Nothing about the hotel project had been easy, but as the festivities for the ceremonial "last bucket" of cement being delivered to the top of the building neared, an unexpected danger arose: John received a bomb threat against both the hotel and the Ruan Center. A bomb squad and specially trained bomb-sniffing dogs (brought in from Kansas City, Missouri) went through both buildings but found no evidence of explosives. Amid tight security, the hotel ceremony went forward on September 3, 1980. Mayor Pete Crivaro and city council members praised John for his leadership of the hotel project. Having grown accustomed to criticism surrounding the hotel, John joked, "There are a lot of kind words here. All of a sudden I'm almost believing them myself."[36]

Several months later, in January 1981, the hotel finally opened. The 33-story, 416-room tower featured a four-story lobby graced with tall trees, polished wood, and marble. Dining options included the sophisticated Quenelle's restaurant or the more casual Allie's. Evening entertainment of music and dancing was available at the lively Gambit's, or a quiet drink could be enjoyed at either the Lobby Bar or the more intimate Skywalk Lounge. Standard rooms ranged in price from $45 to $75 per night, depending on their size, floor location, and number of beds, while several suites sat on the 31st floor. The Presidential Suite was the most opulent. It featured two bedrooms, two bathrooms, a bar, and two parlors and was $500 per night. For parties, conferences, or conventions, the hotel had the Hall of Cities Ballroom and the Iowa Ballroom, two facilities that could serve large gatherings or be divided into smaller meeting rooms, as well as the huge Exhibit Hall and two additional meeting rooms. Together, these rooms offered over 25,000 square feet of meeting space.[37]

Grand opening ceremonies were held January 28 on the new Marriott's third floor. Hotel general manager Peter Hubschmitt decided to add some local color to the festivities as a nod to the state's strong ties to agriculture. Those in attendance saw a ribbon-cutting ceremony—usually performed with scissors—carried out by two giant John Deere tractors facing in opposite directions. One end of the ribbon was attached to each piece of equipment, and as the tractors moved apart, it snapped, officially opening the Marriott Hotel. Likewise, the company's tradition of "throwing away the key" when the doors of a new hotel were opened—symbolizing that the facility would never close—was altered to honor Iowa's agrarian connections. A special three-foot key made of sweet corn and molasses was split in two, half given to a Duroc Hampshire hog and the other half to a Red Angus steer. The crowd cheered as the hog quickly devoured its share and laughed as the steer ignored its portion. Hubschmitt hoped the ceremony might attract the attention of the large numbers of Iowans involved in agriculture or agriculture-related industries and ultimately lead to their patronage. Meanwhile, he summed up the good feelings about the building, calling the Des Moines facility "a real jewel in the Marriott chain."[38]

The evening before, John held a smaller, lavish party for investors and other prominent figures in Des Moines. The 400 who attended the formal affair were treated to a sumptuous dinner and entertained by the music of Pete Fountain. Many speeches paid tribute to John, but he clearly took the most pleasure from Michael Gartner's light-hearted presentation and gift. The R&T president and editor said, "I want to welcome you as a neighbor on this nice block in downtown Des Moines. As you know, John, we've tried to be good neighbors through this whole project. And, just as a reminder of all this, I've gone through our files and pulled all the nice, neighborly things we've had to say about you and this hotel project, and I present them to you here tonight, John, as a lasting reminder that David [Kruidenier] and I have been with you all the way." Mounted on a plaque was a collection of "the most blistering anti-hotel editorials" the newspapers had run over the past several years. They appeared under the headline, "John, We Were With You All The Way." In the middle of the memento was a Frank Miller cartoon featuring an editor and a soldier on the roof of the 13-story R&T Building. The two were standing behind a cannon aimed at the rising Marriott Hotel. The caption read, "When they start on the 14th floor FIRE!"[39]

Much as John had hoped and expected, inquiries about booking conventions in the new hotel came immediately, and the salesman in

John could not resist recruiting conventioneers himself. He used his contacts and influence to bring in conference reservations. Initially John turned to fellow truckers, and before the hotel opened, he had won over the American Trucking Associations. It reserved Des Moines Marriott space for a 1983 Private Carriers Conference. While this was certainly in character for John, so was his need for new challenges.[40]

Well before the hotel was completed, John stepped into another controversy with, as he put it in January 1979, "another project that's going to keep me busy." That November, he announced plans for another multistory office building, but the idea immediately raised eyebrows. The new building was to be located where the 88-year-old Bankers Trust Building and its newer addition stood on the northwest corner of and Sixth and Locust streets. Original plans for the Ruan Center had called for leveling these buildings and laying out a plaza area, but the proposal had been thwarted by the local Foundation for Historic Conservation, which had succeeded in getting the old structure listed on the National Register of Historic Places. Instead of the courtyard, the Ruan firm tried to find a buyer interested in restoring the vacated, deteriorating, historic structure. No one was forthcoming, and John considered other options. Consultants had told him that renovating the old Bankers Trust Building was "prohibitive cost-wise and convenience-wise." Meanwhile, projections for his companies suggested they would soon outgrow their current quarters, and with the Ruan Center full, there was no room for expansion. At the same time, some current tenants in his building wanted additional office space. These factors led to the idea of the second office structure.[41]

Besides the issue of the Bankers Trust Building's listing on the National Register of Historic Places, some people raised objections to the new Ruan building because of another downtown project. Redevelopment of the Ward block immediately west of Nollen Plaza had been deemed the "number one priority" of the city and Des Moines Development Corporation. John was one of the 18 local chief executive officers who made up the DMDC and was well aware of these plans. He also knew that the group had purchased this property and was hoping to sell it to a developer who would put in an office and retail complex. The problem was that demand for downtown office space was limited, and many were afraid that John's new building would saturate the market, making developers less interested in the Ward block.[42] City manager Wilkey was among this group. The *Tribune* also had concerns. It chided John for being "so secretive about his plans" and "wished he had coordinated his activity with the other Des Moines businessmen he serves with on the Des Moines Development Corporation."[43]

Despite the opposition, John forged ahead. Actually, compared to resistance he faced with the hotel, the problems associated with this proposal were minor. Former city bonding attorney Kenneth Haynie remembered John's resoluteness: "When he believed in something and thought he was right, he focused all his energy on completing the project."[44] Friends and allies saw this as determination, while opponents and detractors considered it bullheadedness. Regardless, from John's perspective, the issues were usually straightforward. In this case, the old Bankers Trust structure was run-down and unusable. Since the new building was principally designed for the expanding needs of his companies and those of other Ruan Center tenants, John did not think it would affect plans for the Ward block.[45]

John and assistant Bob Sterling first worked on having the Bankers Trust Building removed from the National Register of Historic Places. Although such status did not prohibit destruction of the building, it did mean that John would face costly restrictions, such as the inability to deduct demolition expenses from the taxes. They succeeded in getting it delisted on a technicality. According to the *Des Moines Register*, "The error came when the state preservation office failed to notify the owners until after the state review committee had considered the nomination."[46]

After that, opposition soon faded away. Des Moines Chamber of Commerce president A. Arthur Davis's glowing comments about the new Ruan building reflected the attitude: "The project fits nicely into existing downtown plans. We welcome it as a further commitment to the core area of Des Moines. When a local firm continues to make investments in its own city, it really mirrors the confidence it has in the community."[47] Razing the old Bankers Trust Building commenced in early 1980, and construction went forward. Sterling and later John Ruan III oversaw the rising structure, which went up without much fanfare. Although there was a small topping ceremony, John III referred to the facility as "just another office building." Named the Carriers Building because it became the insurer's headquarters, the 14-story tower was designed by Ken Kendall and featured the same COR-TEN steel exterior as the larger Ruan Center. It opened in 1982 and was soon connected to the skywalk system.[48]

Yet John was already on to something else. Well before the Carriers Building was completed, he became the city's leading proponent of a conveniently located downtown convention center. There had been discussions about building a convention center in downtown Des Moines, but the facility always had a lower priority than the Civic Center or a new hotel. Now that these were completed, the issue of the convention center resurfaced. Originally, city officials thought expanding Veterans Auditorium, several blocks north and east of the central business district, could fulfill convention needs. In 1979, the Greater Des Moines Chamber of Commerce publicly opposed this plan and instead suggested the city build a new downtown convention center connected to the skywalks and closer to restaurants, hotels, and shops. City and chamber officials hired a consultant to study the convention center issue, but the city council, having gone through great controversy with the Marriott Hotel, was moving very slowly on the matter. Many in the business community grew impatient, and in early 1981, John decided it was time for action.[49]

Once again, architect Kendall was called in and prepared drawings of the proposed convention center. John then shopped the idea around town, talking to city leaders and business executives. The projected location ran along the west side of Fifth Avenue from Keosauqua Way, crossed Grand Avenue with a skywalk, and continued all the way south to Locust Street. When the first part of the consultant's report suggested that "demand for additional convention facilities is not overwhelming," city manager Wilkey opposed building a new center as well as a large renovation of Veterans Auditorium. Wilkey's resistance did not surprise John, but the R&T's position did. The papers, which had fought him on almost all his activities, came out in favor of a downtown convention center.[50]

By late spring 1981, John decided to apply pressure to the city council. He sent out a Mailgram urging the 40 investors in the Marriott Hotel to attend the city council's June 1 meeting and support the proposed downtown convention center. The tactic worked. The large turnout of prominent businessmen backing the new center, coupled with the Des Moines Development Corporation's offer to "loan money to the city or buy buildings on land considered for the convention center," led to the council's call for preliminary planning of the downtown facility.[51]

John's aggressive salesmanship set the process in motion, and he kept lobbying for the convention center. In August, he addressed the Des Moines Pioneer Club and stressed the importance of the complex for future development: "The convention center is a building block in the future of downtown. It's a very important building block. If we have more people downtown, it just follows we need more services of all types, and these things will support new construction." With his persistent promotion and steady R&T editorial support, plans for the project soon gelled. The eventual design was not as large as John had envisioned, and the building did not extend past Grand Avenue. Still, under John's leadership, the business community pushed the city to build the downtown Des Moines Convention Center, which ultimately opened in 1986. Subsequently taken over by the county, the facility today is known as the Polk County Convention Complex.[52]

This work capped a decade of devotion to redeveloping downtown Des Moines. In the spring of 1981, John's efforts were recognized when a city council–appointed committee named him Des Moines's 1980 Citizen of the Year. At the award presentation in the summer of 1981, Joe Rosenfield explained why his good friend was being honored: "John Ruan has had more impact on downtown [Des Moines] than any other individual who has ever lived." The dinner party and roast took place at the Marriott Hotel, with 450 guests each paying $18 for evening affair. This price led banker John Chrystal to joke, "John Ruan is the only person I know who could be honored and make a profit at the same time." Most of the speakers followed in this vein, with a number poking fun at John's reputation for toughness. Mayor Crivaro, for instance, said, "I found him to be a man who favors law and order as long as he lays down the law and gives the orders." Bill Callahan, a retired International Harvester executive, noted that having a heart of gold was a requirement for the award.

Then he quipped, "I'm not sure about the color of John's heart, but of its metallic hardness I am certain." John thoroughly enjoyed the evening and rolled with the good-natured punches. His closing remarks indicated that the award and accompanying keepsake touched him: "I feel more humility at this point than anytime I can remember. This plaque is not costly but priceless. It can't be bought; it can only be obtained as a gift. It's a gift from people . . . most of whom I don't know. This makes it all the more precious."[53]

His focus on downtown bore fruit: Des Moines was in the midst of a renaissance, and John was receiving credit for his pivotal role in revitalizing the city. There were costs, however. His dedication to downtown came at the expense of his family and businesses. Because of his habit of long hours at work, time away from his wife and children was nothing new, but time away from his trucking-based empire was.

Two of John's three children had come of age prior to his involvement downtown and were now young adults, starting families of their own. Thomas, the youngest, grew to adulthood in the 1970s. John III had thoroughly enjoyed life at Northwestern, and like many college students, he was not fully devoted to his coursework. This upset John, especially when it resulted in John III needing an extra semester of classes to graduate. It also reinforced the basic difference between the two. John had built his business through great acumen and extraordinarily long hours. He loved working and had always focused all his energy on whatever project was at hand. Although he partook of such diversions as golf, hunting, or mushrooming, he was "not a man for hobbies."[54] John III, on the other hand, had a variety of interests and was not driven to work constantly as his father always had. Clearly, the two were sometimes poles apart, but on the issue of John III joining the family company, they were in complete agreement. Once back home, John III began in the leasing division under Larry Miller. That only lasted for several months because John III was soon drafted into the U.S. Navy. After basic training, John III was assigned to the Naval Construction Battalion (the Seabees) and stationed at a base in Rhode Island. Honorably discharged in 1968, he went back to his position in operations at Ruan Leasing, moving up to administrative manager over the next couple of years. He also had become acquainted with the young woman he would eventually marry.[55]

Shortly after his return to Des Moines, some friends suggested that John III might hit it off with Janis Arnold, then a fashion coordinator at Younkers. Not currently seeing anyone, John III took their advice and asked Janis out. After dating for two years, the couple married in September 1970. They were wed in a small ceremony in Des Moines at Plymouth Congregational Church, followed by a large reception at the city's exclusive Wakonda Club.[56]

John III progressed up the corporate ladder, but his immediate future was not clear. John had not thought much about succession, although most believed Larry Miller would eventually run the trucking firm. It was clear, though, that John's growing downtown activity meant he had less time for the trucking operation. To assure continued strong leadership, he reorganized top management in 1973. The aging Bob Root was named chairman of Ruan Transport, and 40-year-old Larry Miller was promoted to Root's former position of executive vice president. In this slot, Miller basically became the company's chief operating officer. Tough and smart, he had built the leasing company, and he looked to John as a mentor and father figure. At the same time, John III was promoted to vice president of operations. Being the owner's son was a blessing as much as a curse, and John III struggled to prove himself to his father. Not surprisingly, these efforts invariably led to conflicts with Larry Miller. A growing rivalry eventually developed between the two men, and John dealt with the problematic situation by easing his son out of the trucking company and into the Ruan Center organization. By the late 1970s, John III was president of the Ruan Center Corporation, which occupied most of his time, as well as senior vice president of finance and planning at Ruan Transport and Ruan Leasing. An additional move further separated him from Miller; in 1982, John III was named president of Carriers Insurance Company.[57]

While John was working out the role his son would play in the company, several new members of the Ruan family were born. John III and Janis had a son, John IV, in June 1973, followed by a daughter, Rachel, in 1978. John IV was not the first grandchild, however. Janis and her sister-in-law, Jayne Ruan Fletcher, were pregnant at the same time, and Jayne had a son, Jonathan Ruan Fletcher, two weeks before his cousin was born.[58]

Following her graduation from Stephens College in 1969, Jayne came back to Iowa and took a job at Younkers in the marketing department. That summer, she went on a blind date with Gary Fletcher, a son of Jonathan Fletcher, a prominent Des Moines banker. The two dated casually because Jayne was still heavily involved in horse competitions. In fact, after roughly a year at Younkers, Jayne quit to run Jonbar Stables and spend even more time with her horses. The relationship between Jayne and Gary ultimately turned serious, and the two were married at Plymouth Congregational Church in May 1971. Soon thereafter, Gary joined his wife in managing the stables.[59]

When Jayne became pregnant in the late summer of 1972, she and her husband stopped running the stables, and he returned to his family's American Federal Savings and Loan. After son Jonathan Fletcher was born the following May, Jayne gave up competitive riding altogether and became a "very devoted mother." Two years later, in January 1975, Jayne had a second son, Gary Stephen Fletcher II. The two young children kept her busy, but Jayne quickly returned to her active lifestyle. One afternoon that spring, while she and Gary were playing tennis, Jayne had trouble seeing the ball. Her blurred vision continued, and she went to her doctor. Following tests and visits to several specialists, Jayne received a dreadful diagnosis: she was suffering from multiple sclerosis, the same disease that had stricken her mother. Jayne broke the bad news to her father. The information hit him hard, but it devastated Betty. She remembered, "That was harder than finding out I had it. When John came home and told me . . . I thought I was going to die." Although she had no control over it and was not diagnosed with MS for more than a decade after Jayne was born, Betty blamed herself for passing the disease on to her daughter.[60]

John dealt with the tragedy by taking action. For the past couple of years, he had participated in the local MS chapter's charity golf classic. Sponsored by Eddie Webster's Restaurants, the outing raised funds for the national MS Society. Proceeds from the first golf exhibition in 1973, for instance, amounted to $14,000 for the national organization. After the second annual exhibition, however, the restaurant company was bought out, and its new owner informed Mel Straub, the director of the Central Iowa Chapter of the Multiple Sclerosis Society, that it would no longer sponsor the event. In the fall of 1974, Straub called Larry Miller and asked if he thought John could take over the charitable event. Miller connected Straub with John, and the trucking magnate soon signed on as the golf exhibition's major sponsor. Several months later, after Jayne had been diagnosed with the crippling disease, John stepped up his efforts for the MS affair.[61]

With his forceful, "I'm in this, dammit, and you need to be too" approach, he finagled sponsorships for each of the exhibition's 18 holes from friends and business associates.[62] The upcoming event was renamed the John Ruan MS Golf Exhibition, and organizers landed golf legend Arnold Palmer for the August 1975 occasion. Given his personal connections to the disease, John wanted all the money raised to go for the fight against MS, so he agreed to cover all the exhibition's expenses. As anticipated, Palmer was a big draw. On a hot, humid Sunday afternoon, a crowd of 5,000 came to the Wakonda Club and watched Palmer shoot a round-leading, one-under-par 71. John's 18-year-old son, Thomas, and local golfer Bill Warner shared the honors of carrying Palmer's golf bag that afternoon.[63]

The one-day event raised over $40,000 for the MS Society, more than the two previous golf exhibitions combined. And that was only the beginning. John continued to work closely with Mel Straub, and his annual golf outing grew bigger and bigger, attracting such high-profile golfers as Jack Nicklaus, Tom Watson, Johnny Miller, Lee Trevino, and the always entertaining Chi Chi Rodriguez. As the proceeds from the annual event mounted, John became interested in keeping the money in the area rather than sending it to the national organization. With Straub's help, John organized the John Ruan MS Charity, which could designate where all its funds were sent. Contributions were channeled to the MS Re-evaluative Clinic at Iowa Methodist Medical Center in Des Moines, supported the Central Iowa MS chapter, and purchased necessary equipment and supplies for local MS patients. In 1982, it donated $223,000, "the largest single grant every earmarked for MS research in the 36-year history of the MS Society," to fund a three-year test of a regimen that could lessen the effects of MS. The trial took place at Rush-Presbyterian–St. Luke's Medical Center in Chicago. Large donations continued over the next few years, and by 1988, the Ruan MS Charity had donated more than $500,000 toward the fight against the neurological disease.[64]

As he did with everything he took up, John became engrossed in the fight against MS, especially because the disease had hit home twice. Jayne, meanwhile, went about her daily life, and while the disease was in its early stages, it did not immediately affect her routine. In 1976, she took over the editorship of the Ruan in-house magazine, now called *Remark*. The position was perfect for Jayne—it kept her active, engaged her creative side, and because most of the work could be done from her home, it did not take her away from her small children. About the same time, Gary also joined the Ruan companies, working in sales and marketing. He and Jayne remained with Ruan until the mid-1980s. By then, Jayne's health had deteriorated to the point where she could no longer do the job, and with John's financial assistance, Gary established his own marketing firm called Fletcher Communications.[65]

When Jayne and John III began raising children of their own, Thomas was in high school. He grew up under John's long shadow, watching his father accomplish great things but not seeing him much. After graduating in 1975 from Theodore Roosevelt High School in Des Moines, Thomas enrolled at Iowa State University in Ames. Here, too, he felt John's reach. A donor in the Cardinal and Gold Scholarship program, John served on the Iowa State Foundation's board of governors and was an important leader in the effort that resulted in the university's new football stadium. That fall, the Iowa State Alumni Association recognized John's many contributions by naming him Cy's Favorite Alum. The honor was given annually to the "Iowa Stater who has shown outstanding devotion to the university and especially to the athletic department and program." The award meant a lot to John, and the "Cy's Favorite Alum" banner he received was soon added to the few mementos he proudly displayed in his office. Well aware of his father's close ties to the institution, Thomas tried Iowa State for a short time but soon decided college life was not for him. Independent like his father, he tried several jobs at Ruan but never found his niche. By 1980, he was considering a career in commercial aviation and took a job at Des Moines Flying Service, where he eventually took flying lessons. He soon headed down to Florida, where he briefly continued his pursuit of a pilot's license. Before moving back to Des Moines, he married, and although the marriage did not last very long, Thomas and wife Margery Lynn had two sons, the last of John's grandchildren, Thomas Adams Ruan and Philip Arthur Ruan.[66]

As the Ruan children matured and eventually left home, Betty's health continued to decline. The debilitating effects of MS were more and more apparent, and routine tasks became complicated. Her muscles weakened, holding things grew difficult, and an inability to coordinate leg movements meant that she often fell, once breaking her elbow on the kitchen floor. Given her situation, Betty required additional care within the home. At first, housekeeper Darlene Willis assumed these duties, but when she left for another job in the late 1970s, a full-time companion was needed. Several people filled the position over the next few years until June 1986, when Elizabeth (Betty) J. Lester was hired. Having the same nickname as Betty Ruan soon caused some confusion, so John started calling the new member of the household B. J., for Betty Jean. The name stuck, and B. J. remained on the job until 2002.[67]

Betty's decreasing mobility led her to cut back on social activities, but she religiously maintained her seasonal travel ritual. Now accompanied by her attendant, she headed up to the Clear Lake cottage for the summer and stayed in North Palm Beach during the winter. In fact, John and Betty increased their commitment to Florida in 1980 when they built a larger house just down the street from their original home in the Lost Tree development. Designed by Ken Kendall, the elegant Mediterranean-style home sat on a private beach. The single-story structure was laid out around a courtyard, which included a swimming pool and overlooked the Atlantic Ocean.[68]

Much as Betty stuck to her yearly schedule, so too did John. Sixty-six years old in 1980, John remained totally immersed in the world of work. As he had always done, John was regularly at the Ruan Center by 5:30 A.M., but as his wife's MS worsened, he often drove home to get Betty lunch and then returned to the office until 5:30 or 6:00 P.M. He still spent Saturday and Sunday at the office except when Betty was away at one of their vacation homes, where, via his Learjet in winter or car in summer, he would join her on weekends.

Daily operations of his trucking companies were now overseen by the capable Larry Miller, but John kept an eye on both transport and leasing through weekly meetings with top managers, often over early-morning breakfasts. All major decisions—such as acquisitions of other firms or major equipment purchases—remained in his hands. Through the 1970s, evidence suggested the new managerial arrangement was working. The company was growing and making money. In 1975, revenues of the transport division alone were $49.9 million, with a net profit of $1.9 million. Leasing's revenues and profits, meanwhile, were about half the size of the transport unit. Three years later, transport's revenues were up to $69.3 million while profits stayed at the $1.9 million mark. At the same time, revenues at leasing doubled, reaching $51.9 million, with net profits of $1.5 million. Given the current environment, company managers were optimistic about the future and forecasted continued expansion for both divisions. The industry, however, was about to undergo radical change.[69] Deregulation, which had been discussed since the early 1970s, was looming. It became reality when the United States Congress passed the Motor Carrier Act (MCA) of 1980.

This legislation eased restrictions on market entry and lifted the limit on the number of carriers that could serve a particular area. Those wishing to enter interstate trucking now needed "only prove useful public purpose" rather than the much more difficult standard of "public convenience and necessity." Furthermore, the ICC's role in setting rates was relaxed, and carriers were now free to negotiate rates with individual shippers. Thus "carriers that were previously restricted to the commodities, service areas, and routes for which they held certificates are [now] permitted to compete in any market and price according to what the market will bear." Under these rules, many new trucking firms entered the business, and price wars began.[70]

The MCA and poor economic conditions of the early 1980s hurt many in the industry. Indeed, preexisting carriers such as Ruan were at a disadvantage compared to the firms born after interstate deregulation. Many of these new carriers were nonunion and thus were not hamstrung with costly union contracts. With lower overhead, they could charge lower rates, and they lured market share away from the traditional carriers. Adding to industry woes, the Employee Retirement Income Security Act (ERISA) and the Multiemployer Pension Plan Amendments Act (MEPPA) created complications for trucking firms participating in Teamsters pension plans. The laws placed potentially heavy liabilities on carriers if they dropped out of multiemployer pension plans, preventing them from leaving the business (and the pension) except by a strictly controlled gradual pullout or completely liquidating. Similarly, as industry expert Michael Belzer explained, "Potential buy-outs were discouraged because buyers would have to assume a carrier's pension liability, further reducing a carrier's market value. While existing carriers, whose employees generally participated in multi-employer defined benefit plans, had significant withdrawal liability, new entering carriers had no pension liability, as they had no existing pension plans."[71]

Many in the industry saw deregulation as a threat, and their inability to deal with the new situation led to a number of business failures. From 1980 to 1983, 305 carriers declared bankruptcy. Others, remembered Scott Weiser, president of the Iowa Motor Truck Association, saw opportunities, and Ruan was among this latter group.[72] One of the major reasons John's trucking operations had grown and remained profitable over the years was his call for innovative techniques and new technologies. Such an emphasis gave Ruan an edge over the competition. Once again, he would rely on fresh ideas for success.

A three-pronged strategy was developed. After discussions with Larry Miller and other key executives, John realized that Ruan Transport could not compete with nonunion carriers in many of its markets, and with his support, the company began a gradual withdrawal from the petroleum-hauling business. Petroleum hauling had made up the majority of the company's business, and from the late 1950s through the 1970s, Ruan was the nation's largest hauler of petroleum. Over the next few years, the company pulled back in what Bill Giles, former Ruan vice president of research and engineering, called a "strategic withdrawal" from this operation. Since the company's obligations to the Teamsters' multiemployer pension plan were based on its size, gradually shrinking its bulk hauling business—which was permitted under MEPPA—decreased the company's pension liability. As expected, this contraction resulted in lower revenues, but the company hoped to make up some of this decline with the second part of Ruan's overall strategy—giving a greater emphasis to contract carriage. Early deals in contract carriage were struck with companies such as Super Valu (groceries), Toro (outdoor equipment), Clorox (cleaning products), and Farmland Industries (dressed meat). The new business picked up some of the slack, but the planned contraction, coupled with rate-cutting competition and the ongoing recession, led to falling revenues. From a 1979 mark of $69 million, revenues dropped to $63.8 in 1980 and $61.1 in 1981. Net profits, meanwhile, went up, then down, moving from $1.9 to $2.6 million before falling to $420,000.[73]

Shrinking bulk hauling where Ruan could no longer compete profitably and building contract carriage were the first two parts of rethinking its truck business. The third element consisted of shifting company energy and resources to the expanding and very profitable leasing side of the operation. The idea was to sell its expertise in trucking to shippers, and one of the first aspects of this renewed focus was the development of a better truck. Given the high interest rates and inflation of the period, it was hoped that a longer-lasting, more reliable truck could be built that would be cheaper to maintain and operate. Such a truck could give Ruan an edge over the competition when shippers were considering their leasing options. Ken Penaluna, vice president of purchasing, was put in charge of the "super" truck project. He brought together a group of 31 vendors with the mission of creating components with superior performance standards that could be applied to either a standard International or Freightliner tractor. While the "super" truck was in the works, Larry Miller decided that with a captivating name, the new truck could differentiate Ruan in the marketplace and be a great sales tool. Jeffrey Barber and his small marketing firm called Energy were given the task. When it became clear that the truck would be a major advance, Barber proposed the name "MEGA Truck."[74]

Ruan managers liked the sound of it, and the prefix *mega* would serve as an important label for several new products and services offered by the company throughout the 1980s and 1990s. One that had an immediate impact was the MEGA Task Force. It consisted of the vendors Penaluna had assembled for creating the advanced truck. From that point forward, this group of representatives from various truck component manufacturers met once a year and worked on various problems the Ruan fleet was experiencing. In essence, Ruan was having industry experts troubleshoot their equipment difficulties, and meeting annually over the next 20 years, the task force saved the company time and money.[75]

MEGA Truck debuted in November 1981. Outfitted with the latest technology, it was designed to travel a million miles without requiring major repairs. Among its advances were a self-lubricating system, sensors that monitored and adjusted air pressure in its tires, and a reservoir that gradually dripped fresh oil into the oil compartment while old oil was slowly bled into the fuel and burned off. This continuous replenishment essentially eliminated the need for periodic oil changes. Although a MEGA Truck would cost more than the standard model, the extra cost would be more than recovered over its longer life. Larry Miller explained, "The additional life built in MEGA Truck is really a hedge against inflation. In effect we are buying more miles in the future at today's prices." Among the initial six MEGA Trucks built, four were sent to leasing customers, and Ruan used the other two black MEGAs for promotional purposes at truck shows. As had been hoped, the new truck proved highly reliable and durable, and by the end of 1982, more than 100 MEGAs were in service. More important, however, was the positive buzz it created.[76]

Much smaller than industry-leading Ryder, Ruan Leasing found that MEGA Truck gave it tremendous publicity and succeeded in setting the company apart from its competition. It built on Ruan Transport's long reputation for developing leading-edge technology in its tractors and trailers and aggressively applied it to leasing operation. Now relying more heavily on leasing for expansion, the division did not disappoint. It overtook the transport unit in size—in terms of revenue—in 1981 and continued as a growing profit center for the firm.[77]

As the trucking companies were being reconfigured, Carriers Insurance also seemed to be performing well. By the time John III was named president of the insurer in March 1982, John controlled 84 percent of the company. It continued to specialize in insuring large truck operations, and with a net income that ranged between $2 and $4 million from 1980 to 1982, it looked financially solid. These appearances notwithstanding, the firm was in trouble, but the problems did not immediately surface.[78]

Bankers Trust, meanwhile, another important element of John's business empire, had experienced rapid growth, and when he hired Tom Wright as president in 1973, continued expansion was mandated. But Wright's "easygoing manner accented by a Mississippi drawl" was not a good match for John. Most critical, bank performance under the new president was poor. Net income fell from $1.6 million in 1973 to $803,000 in 1977, while return on equity decreased from 11.25 percent to 4.39 percent. Problems worsened after January 1977, when Sterling retired as chairman. John stepped into the chairmanship and began making the "major [bank] decisions, sometimes second-guessing Wright." Relations between the two men grew more strained over the next few months, and in September, Wright was ousted in favor of 44-year-old Herman Kilpper, then executive vice president in charge of operations and investments at rival Iowa–Des Moines National Bank.[79] "Everything happened so fast," Kilpper remembered. "Iowa–Des Moines's board accepted my resignation and I left the meeting, hustling up the street for a Bankers Trust board meeting where I was introduced as the company's new president."[80]

An accountant by training, Kilpper was well regarded in banking circles, and much as John had hoped, the new president was assertive and innovative. Through aggressive sales, Kilpper rapidly increased the bank's loan portfolio. He also expanded the bank's operations, soon establishing an investment department that specialized in the tax-free securities market. Such activist leadership was the kind John appreciated, and after being on the job just 16 months, net income was up to $2.1 million.[81]

Even as John was overseeing these varied interests, he remained involved in Republican politics. Despite the problems he encountered after raising money for Richard Nixon, John continued to work for the party, and by 1976, he was a member of the Republican National Committee's Finance Executive Committee. That year he cohosted several fund-raisers for President Gerald Ford's unsuccessful reelection bid. Later, as the 1980 Iowa caucuses approached, John backed former

Texas governor John Connally's bid for the presidency and served as the candidate's state finance chairman. Particularly appealing to John were Connally's ideas of downsizing the federal government while maintaining the ICC's regulation of the trucking industry. George Bush went on to win the Iowa caucuses, but as the Republican National Convention neared, it became clear that Ronald Reagan would be the party's presidential nominee. That spring, John threw his support behind Reagan, whom he had first met during the candidate's stint in Des Moines as a WHO radio announcer in the 1930s. Reagan went on to the White House, and John had an amiable relationship with the president, but over the next few years, he developed an even closer rapport with then vice president and later president George Bush.[82]

By 1982, it was time for John to take stock of his many accomplishments. That year was a milestone for John: July 4 marked his 50th year in the trucking business, and for a brief moment, he looked backward instead of forward. The journey from his one-truck beginnings, he said, "had been rough, but exciting and rewarding." The occasion was marked with a company party at Adventureland, a Des Moines amusement park. With the theme "50 Years and Rollin'," the event recognized John's achievements. His trucking business now included more than 6,000 units operating across the United States, while Carriers was one of the "nation's largest writers of transportation insurance." With assets of over $700 million, Bankers Trust was the state's largest locally owned bank and was headquartered in one of his two major downtown buildings. A third significant downtown structure, the Marriott Hotel, had been John's project from the beginning, and he was its general partner and majority owner. Smaller businesses had been established or acquired as well. These included the Des Moines Avis Car Rental franchise, Capitol Cab, and as of 1981, Yellow Cab, and ancillary operations that largely served his trucking companies, including three Bandag tire-recapping franchises and American Diesel, which rebuilt tractor components. Beyond his own companies, John was an important advocate for the industry and a leading figure in both state and national trucking organizations.[83]

Recognition extended beyond internal accolades. In December 1982, his peers of the Greater Des Moines Committee elected John to its Iowa Business Hall of Fame. The honor was given annually to

Iowans who "made outstanding contributions to the development and enhancement of Iowa's business climate." The tribute put John among select company: previous Hall of Fame inductees included Frederick M. Hubbell, Joe Rosenfield, and Henry A. Wallace. In accepting the honor, John noted that past winners were usually retired, and he joked that the award was the organization's way of sending him a message to retire. No one was surprised when the still hard-charging entrepreneur told the crowd he had "no such plans."[84]

John appeared to be at the top of his game. His trucking operations were rapidly adjusting to the new deregulated climate, and his other companies seemed strong. At the same time, his downtown activities were widely recognized. His rusty steel Ruan Center and then the concrete Marriott Hotel gave Des Moines a skyline and encouraged other development in the area, while the growing skywalk system offered pleasant, climate-controlled connections to the central business district. But that was not all. He rounded out his decade of revitalizing the city center by putting up the Carriers Building and leading the charge for the new convention center.

Davenport, Iowa, mayor Thomas Wright said, "It's true Des Moines has done a better job [in redevelopment] than we have, but they have a John Ruan." Chuck Offenburger, the *Des Moines Register's* "Iowa Boy" columnist, wrote in the same vein, calling John "the father of the renaissance in downtown Des Moines." And a letter to John from two "ordinary citizens" thanked him for his "enormous effort" in making "the downtown area of our city come alive again." It ended by thanking John for his "wonderful efforts to breathe life back into an area that was very close to being 'terminal.'"[85]

Yet clouds were on the horizon. Over the coming decade, business problems and personal tragedy would suggest that John was a mere mortal. The mythic golden touch of King Midas that John seemed to possess would not last in the long run.

John Ruan (far right) at an Air Force demonstration. Others from left to right: a U.S. military official; Bob Root, Ruan Transport vice president; Walter Carey, trucking executive; and Jimmy Hoffa, Teamster official, 1955. Courtesy of John Ruan.

Betty Ruan and youngest son Thomas, with daughter Jayne in the background, at Ruan Isle on Brule Lake in northern Minnesota, 1961. Courtesy of John Ruan.

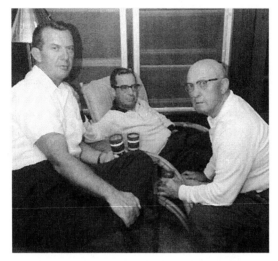

Ruan managers, from left to right: Joe Johnson, Harold Baker, and Prent Savage at the Ruan Clear Lake cottage, 1961. Courtesy of John Ruan.

Several members of the Raccoon Valley Pony Club, from left to right: Kathy Bader, Maggi Moss, Michael Matthews (a district commissioner of the club), Betsy Harwick, Jane Prescott, Jayne Ruan, Katy O'Reilly, and Rusty Hubbell, 1963. Courtesy of Maggi Moss.

John talking to Bill Callahan of the International Harvester Motor Truck Division, 1963. Courtesy of John Ruan.

John and John III hunting at Fountain Grove, Missouri, 1965. Courtesy of John Ruan.

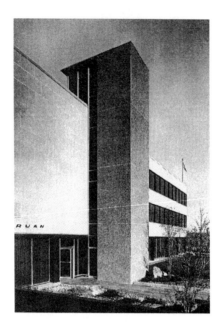

New Ruan headquarters
at Third Street and
Keosauqua Way in
Des Moines, 1964.
Courtesy of John Ruan.

Open House announcing the introduction of Ruan Aviation,
1968. Standing in front of John's first Learjet, *My Betty V*, are
from left to right: Ruan pilot, Jerry Ware; Howard Gregory;
and John Ruan. Courtesy of John Ruan.

John III, John IV,
and John Ruan visiting
the Ruan Center under
construction, 1973.
Courtesy of
John Ruan.

John and Betty Ruan talking with golf pro Arnold Palmer
during his visit to Des Moines for the first John Ruan MS Golf
Exhibition, 1975. Courtesy of John Ruan.

Marriott, Hotel 1981.
Note the skywalk under
construction in the
foreground. Courtesy
of John Ruan.

Plaque presented to
John by Michael Gartner
at the Marriott Hotel's
completion, 1981.
Courtesy of John Ruan.

Downtown Des Moines in the mid-1980s. The skyline is dominated by, from left to right, the Marriott Hotel, the Ruan Center, the Hub Tower, and the Financial Center. Courtesy of John Ruan.

MEGA Trucks 1982. Courtesy of John Ruan.

Ruan Transportation president Larry Miller discussing the company's new MEGA Safe Program. Photo by Ann Klose. Copyright 1986, The Des Moines Register and Tribune Company. Reprinted with permission.

The Ruan home in North Palm Beach, Florida. Courtesy of John Ruan.

The proposed Iowa world trade center, 1984.
Courtesy of John Ruan.

John singing for
friends, ca. 1996.
Courtesy of
John Ruan.

171

John and John III, 1998.
Photo by Sher Stoneman.
Copyright 1998, The Des
Moines Register and
Tribune Company.
Reprinted with
permission.

John standing next to a recasting of *The Boy Scout* statue that he
had erected in honor of Joe Rosenfield, 2001, at Camp Mitigwa.
Courtesy of Ely Brewer.

Iowa State Capitol adorned with banners for World Food Prize festivities, 2001. Courtesy of World Food Prize.

John Ruan's grandchildren, 2002. From left to right: Jonathan Fletcher, John Ruan IV, Rachel Ruan, Stephen Fletcher, Adam Ruan, and Philip Ruan. Courtesy of John Ruan III.

173

Friend Ralph Schlenker and former first lady Barbara
Bush look on as her pet dog Sadie gives John a kiss at
the Bush property in Kennebunkport, Maine, 2001.
Courtesy of the Mayo Foundation. Reprinted with
permission of Chris Smith, Ocean Exposure,
Kennebunkport, ME.

John Ruan addressing the crowd after receiving Iowa Award, 2001.
From left to right: Betty Ruan, former governor Robert Ray, John Ruan,
Lt. Governor Sally Pederson, and Governor Tom Vilsack. Photo by Bob
Nandell. Copyright 2001, The Des Moines Register and Tribune Company.
Reprinted with permission.

7 Chinks in the Armor

At the invitation of a Des Moines teacher, John once spoke to a group of eighth graders during the middle school's Leadership Week. In his speech, he emphasized his long-held belief in the value of hard work. "If you want to be successful," he told the students, "forget about the 40-hour a week thing. Work extra and give all you've got."[1] From the odd jobs of his Beacon childhood to running large enterprises late in the century, John's legendary work ethic had paid off handsomely. By the 1980s, however, hard work was not always enough. New ventures and successes on several fronts were overshadowed by business troubles, failure to win a world trade center in Des Moines, and the collapse of Carriers Insurance. Characteristically, though, he weathered those storms and looked to other projects. Another blow in the summer of 1992 would not be so easily surmounted.

Riding high from victories of the preceding years, John fully expected continued triumphs in the 1980s. His trucking company certainly gave him reason to be optimistic. After initially struggling with the impact of deregulation, Ruan Transport was reinvented over the course of the 1980s, becoming a larger and more profitable operation. The first signs of retooling had been introduced at the outset of the decade with MEGA Truck and MEGA Task Force. Jeff Barber, the marketer who came up with the MEGA label, was soon thereafter hired as Ruan's director of corporate communications, and originally a large part of his job was selling the MEGA name. MEGA rapidly generated a lot of publicity, and the company built on this momentum by introducing a host of new products and services bearing the prefix. While these were being launched, company managers introduced the ideas of W. Edwards Deming and his Total Quality Management (TQM) throughout the firm. Together these new programs retrofit a company that had originally been honed for success in a regulated market, adapting it to the now highly competitive world of deregulation.[2]

Larry Miller remained the driving force behind the revitalization of the trucking group, while John supervised the transformation.

Through the 1980s, new MEGA offerings established Ruan as a forward-looking company. With MEGA Truck, "the maximum reliability vehicle," being adopted by more Ruan customers, the company followed up with MEGA Max, a specially designed trailer offering "maximum cubic capacity for low density freight." Much like the MEGA Truck, the trailer performed effectively, but more important was the image being created. In a market that offered customers many shipping options, Ruan started standing out from its competition as the MEGA Company.[3]

In 1985, the MEGA tag was applied not only to hardware but also to software. That fall, John unveiled "an array of computerized information services designed to help operate truck fleets more efficiently." With computers and software, the system could provide truckers with a wide range of valuable information. It could direct them to the cheapest fuel, help them find the nearest repair center, or provide drivers with the shortest route to their destination. In addition, a component of the system could be installed in a cab, allowing drivers to record the expenses and miles usually stored in a logbook. Customers had the option of leasing only the information system and applying it to their own fleet or ordering it as part of a package using Ruan trucks. Miller believed the typical customer would be someone who leased a Ruan truck and added the information service as "an option, just like you'd add air conditioning." The company marketed the new logistics package by loading the equipment on MEGA One, a brightly painted red semitrailer, which showcased the system across the nation on a 32-city tour.[4]

MEGA One represented a significant shift for the company; Ruan began selling its experience in transportation to customers rather than merely providing them with trucks. Richard Fischer, a Merrill Lynch vice president who followed trucking companies, explained the Ruan strategy: "They're taking their expertise to other companies and saying, 'hey, you don't have the expertise, and we do. Buy it from us.'" Now, in addition to hauling goods or leasing vehicles, the firm also offered an array of services such as providing drivers, training drivers and managers, locating parts and repair facilities, and supplying fuel. Miller observed, "I may put a driver in a truck; I may put fuel in, or the customer might do that. I might sell them a fuel routing system or a parts locating service. . . . They can buy as much or as little as they want."[5]

With the company moving in this new direction, two important changes took place. The first was a new corporate name to reflect the firm's broader focus. In the spring of 1986, officials rolled out a refashioned moniker: Ruan Transportation Management Systems (RTMS), which combined Ruan Transport and Ruan Leasing. Under this new umbrella, RTMS offered full-service leasing, alternative contract carriage, a national rental fleet, contract maintenance, driver leasing, administrative services, and truck sales.[6] The second important change was the promotion of Larry Miller. He had been largely running both Transport and Leasing for several years and was growing increasingly frustrated that his title of executive vice president was not commensurate with his leadership role. But John, as founder and owner, had served as the company's only president, and he was not interested in relinquishing that title. Miller forced the issue in 1986, threatening to quit and take top executives with him if he was not granted the presidency. John finally relented, and in June, Miller became president of RTMS, while John remained chairman of the board and chief executive officer. Other managers were also promoted. Most important, Gary Alvord, vice president and general manager of leasing, was named senior vice president of the truck group. Asked if the changes meant that John was cutting back in his work schedule, Miller laughed and replied, "Goodness no. He continues to be here at 6:30 for breakfast. And we worked Sunday afternoon."[7]

Toward the end of 1986, RTMS introduced another original idea called MEGA Safe. In essence, the company packaged its safety program in the form of several training modules. Each contained a series of videotapes and other instructional material designed to assist trainers in leading company safety classes. The course stressed group participation and was developed with the assistance of two educational consultants from Northwestern University. Beyond the curriculum, MEGA Safe also included a number of decals, each intended for a specific location on a tractor and trailer. The decals included arrows pointing to certain items on the vehicle and messages regarding what needed to be checked at each particular position. Created for leasing or rental customers, MEGA Safe's first module was priced at $500, with the remaining 11 segments costing $285 each. Much like MEGA One, RTMS packed the MEGA Safe programs onto two specially painted tractor-trailer units that promoted the safety course during a 46-city national tour. Although Ruan invested $500,000 in developing the package, Miller did not view it as a moneymaker. Instead, he said, "we're approaching this from a publicity standpoint." He added that the real benefits would come because "we're known as safety conscious."[8]

Actually, RTMS already had enjoyed benefits from a renewed attention to safety. Its number of accidents per million miles declined from .096 in 1984—when it won the National Tank Truck Carriers Outstanding Performance Trophy—to .043 the following year. Continued safety improvements in 1986 led to financial rewards: company insurance rates dropped 30 percent in 1987, in part because RTMS implemented many of the guidelines that it began selling to others with MEGA Safe.[9]

With the MEGA programs well under way, Miller and Alvord began thinking that the new company direction mandated a revision of the corporate culture. Over the course of 1985 and 1986, several vendors told Miller about W. Edwards Deming and his ideas of Total Quality Management (TQM). For Deming, quality meant meeting the needs of the customer. Its achievement, he believed, required a new approach, and he turned the standard idea of quality control on its head. Rather than inspecting products for defects and disposing of those with deficiencies, he emphasized improving the system to eliminate product flaws before they occurred. Furthermore, he stressed the importance of the team approach, with everyone in the company, from top management to production people, working toward continually improving processes that in turn improved quality.[10] After hearing a Deming telecast in Des Moines, Miller and Alvord flew to a Minneapolis meeting. By coincidence, they ate dinner at the hotel where Deming had broadcast his talk earlier that day. When Miller saw Deming in the hotel lobby, he ran over, introduced himself, and said he was impressed with TQM. Deming thanked him and suggested he attend an entire Deming seminar. Miller left the conversation "fired up" about

TQM, and he and Alvord soon enrolled in such a course in San Diego.[11]

Both Miller and Alvord were inspired by the seminar, and they agreed that TQM systemized much of what Ruan had long been doing with equipment innovation, "key-stop," and, much more recently, the MEGA programs. John, meanwhile, saw the introduction of TQM and other Deming ideas as a means of cutting costs, and he supported additional training, but he jealously guarded his company's heritage and often reminded his key managers that "this was the Ruan company, not the Deming company."[12] Soon Jeff Barber and other top people were also sent to Deming seminars, and by 1987, Barber was heading up the quality improvement program in the company. Because of John's close ties to Iowa State University, company managers soon were in touch with Robert Gelina, a continuous-quality-improvement expert who taught in the school's industrial education and technology department. Barber brought in Gelina to help develop Ruan's quality approach, which not surprisingly became called MEGA Quality Improvement (MQI). Once the program was developed, Gelina and Barber set about making a series of training videos and then disseminating the ideas throughout the company. According to Gelina, "If you can improve the process, it only follows that the product or service will be automatically better. MEGA Quality Improvement is a way of managing the process differently." It combined the thinking of Deming with Stephen Covey's theories of principled leadership and statistical controls. Implementing these ideas, it was hoped, would lead to a better organization that would "deliver higher quality services . . . at a lower cost."[13]

The program was put into practice by dividing company operations into 16 components and then creating teams of managers and employees to analyze various aspects of each process. Statistics helped uncover problems, causes were identified, and solutions were formulated. These solutions were then monitored, making certain the process was actually improved. For instance, in the early 1990s, Ruan's MQI maintenance team ran a statistical study of the company's vehicle condition reports and noticed that headlights were the most frequently replaced parts on their trucks. They were replaced 6,000 times a year, largely because the bulbs burned out. The team also discovered that the 12 minutes required for changing the bulb, not the bulb itself, was the costliest part of the repair. Team members talked to vendors who suggested switching to halogen bulbs, which lasted seven times longer than standard lights. This was but one example of many that suggested MQI was working. It had uncovered a problem that would otherwise have gone undetected, and the solution led to a better-quality truck, cutting company repair costs. At the same time, employees were actively involved in decision making and saw that their ideas could lead to real improvements.[14]

Company vice president Gary Alvord thought that the MEGA Quality Improvement process had taken RTMS down the right path. He explained, "It's made our company a better place to work and it's made it more profitable. As far as we're concerned, MQI is a great success, but we know it is only the beginning. We've got to continually get better every day." In 1994, MEGA Quality Improvement followed in the tradition of the other MEGA products and was taken on a national tour. At each stop, Gelina offered a two-hour training seminar in TQM, and following the course, attendees could tour the MEGA Stealth Truck, which was crammed with the latest technology, such as a thermal night-vision system that allowed the driver to see 1,000 feet beyond the range of normal headlights.[15]

As the company benefited from the introduction of these new ideas, it also reaped the rewards of old-fashioned politics. Ever since 1939, when John successfully lobbied Iowa legislators to vote down a bill that would have hurt his new petroleum-hauling operation, he realized the importance of maintaining close ties with politicians. Such connections, coupled with a close watch on Washington, D.C., eventually led to a highly favorable tax break for RTMS. In 1986, Congress was considering a vast tax-reform package. Included among the many changes was the elimination of the investment tax credit as of January 1, 1986. Up to this point, the credit had "allowed businesses purchasing certain types of equipment to deduct 10 percent of its costs from their tax liability." A year before the tax bill was even considered— when the investment tax credit was in place—Ruan had ordered several thousand trucks, including many custom-built MEGAS, for which the company did not expect delivery until 1986 and 1987. Estimates were that under the proposed tax revision, RTMS would lose $15 to 20 million in tax exemptions it expected on new trucks when it placed the purchase order.[16]

Fortunately for John, he and RTMS president Miller were watching the progress of the tax-reform bill. When they realized the negative impact it would have on the company, they contacted Republican Chuck Grassley, one of Iowa's two U.S. senators, and asked for help. Specifically, they wanted a special provision, often called a transition rule, granting the company an exemption from the new legislation. If successful, they could preserve the tax credit for the large truck purchase. They argued that when they ordered the equipment, the tax credit was in place. Furthermore, they claimed that without the credit, they would cut back on the truck order, which in turn would force the company to cut jobs. Grassley agreed with Ruan's position and obtained a transition rule for the company. It was one of 175 special exemptions included in the bill.[17]

Although the *Des Moines Register* contended that "neither John Ruan nor Chuck Grassley did anything wrong" but only "played by the rules," many others felt differently. John Roehrick, Grassley's Democratic opponent for the Senate seat, insinuated that Grassley treated Ruan differently than other Iowa companies because of John's large contributions to the Republican senator's campaign chest. This charge was not well supported, however. While it was true that John and his political action committee had made regular donations to Grassley going back to 1980, the contributions were, according to the *Register*, "not in particularly large amounts."[18] Roehrick also complained that the tax break gave Ruan an unfair advantage against other trucking companies and could mean a loss of jobs in some of those other firms. Dan O'Connell, executive vice president for Ryder System, Inc., the largest truck leasing firm in the nation, picked up on this theme. "We're understandably upset," he said. "This transition rule creates a burden for all of Ruan's competitors. (Ruan will) be able to go out and outprice the rest of us in the marketplace."[19]

Ryder led a fierce lobbying effort against the Ruan tax break, and by September it succeeded in eliminating the exemption from the pending legislation. When another Grassley attempt at putting the Ruan exemption back in the bill failed, John decided on more direct action. He flew to Washington for some personal lobbying. He visited with old political friends, such as Republican Senate majority leader Bob Dole, whom he had known since the 1970s, and won the support of Iowa Democratic congressman Neal Smith. With the work of Smith and Grassley, a smaller, $8.5 million Ruan tax break became part of a technical corrections bill designed to fix problems with the recently passed tax-reform legislation, but members of the House Rules Committee later removed it. Then, when it looked like the exemption was dead, luck and political connections saved the tax break.[20]

At the time, Dole was considering a run for the presidency in 1988. He knew that John's support in Iowa would be important and probably thought that helping RTMS gain the exemption would be remembered in the future. An opportunity arose when a group from Massachusetts—including Speaker of the House Tip O'Neill—went to see Dole about rescuing a low-income housing provision for their state that had also been cut by the House Rules Committee. Dole suggested adding their bill along with the Ruan tax exemption to an unrelated budget bill. O'Neill agreed, and Ruan got the tax break.[21]

The $8.5 million exemption, combined with a general transition rule that applied to Ruan purchase contracts, meant a total of $12 million in after-tax benefits. John was pleased with the financial victory, but as Larry Miller explained, the widespread press coverage was also important because it "raised the stature of our company in the eyes of our customers, our vendors, and our financial partners."[22] Already perceived as aggressive and innovative, RTMS was now widely viewed as a politically savvy company with important connections and influential allies. John Smith, president of CRST Inc., a Cedar Rapids trucking firm, thought the tax exemption gave Ruan "an advantage over us he didn't have before. But, on the other hand, you have to say he worked the system better than the rest of us."[23] Most other rivals were not so magnanimous, but all took notice. Ryder's fight against the tax break suggested the leasing giant had its eye on Ruan. A year earlier, Gordon Bingham, a Ryder executive, said of Ruan, "We, of course, pay close attention to what they're doing." He added that Ruan had "a very good reputation in the industry."[24]

As RTMS's standing was increasing, so too were its revenues. In 1985, the revenues for the truck group—which combined operations of transport, leasing, and the taxi and rental car business—stood at $164 million, with net profits of $5.4 million; by 1989, these figures had risen to $231 million and $7.9 million, respectively. This growth and the firm's successful transition to the deregulated market made it a good candidate for takeover. Meanwhile, John's advancing age and the lack of a clearly identifiable successor led to a growing number of rumors that the trucking company was going to be sold. Since much of its business involved long-term equipment leases, such stories created problems. Miller reported, "There were numerous instances where our competitors had told our prospects and customers that we were selling out." This kind of information led some to opt for another transportation company.[25]

In response, RTMS came out with a clever advertisement, which first ran in the *Wall Street Journal* in May 1989. The half-page ad featured a photograph of John Ruan next to a brash quotation, which began in headline-size letters: "I'm planning on being here another 50 years, so I'll make a prediction." In smaller letters, the text continued:

We may not become the biggest—that's no great lure for me—but we'll continue to be the best. And being the best in these turbulent times takes a strong commitment. Because I am 75 years old, and we are a family owned company, I would suspect that our customers and suppliers would expect and appreciate an indication that the Ruan Companies will continue to be owned and directed by the Ruan family on into the future. That is my plan.[26]

The advertisement captured John's unabashed attitude and drew wide praise from across the country. It successfully ended the hearsay that RTMS was about to be sold, and by stating that he planned on keeping the company under family control, John also had sent a subtle message about John III. Although a formal announcement of succession remained years away, this was the first clear indication that John III, who had dutifully served in a number of posts throughout the Ruan enterprises since 1969, would eventually head the family firm.

John had been gradually moving John III up through the ranks, giving him greater and greater responsibility, largely in the Ruan Center Corporation. In 1982, he decided his son was ready for the presidency of one of the larger businesses, and he put him in charge of Carriers Insurance. The move also kept John III and Larry Miller from butting heads. Unfortunately, unbeknownst to either John or John III, the insurance company was not the stable business it appeared to be, and both father and son were in for a rocky ride.

After several months on the job learning the insurance business, John III became aware of serious problems. First of all, like many other truck insurers, Carriers was facing declining premium income, partly because a growing number of trucking companies failed after deregulation. Amid this decreasing income, the company's "loss ratio—the percentage of the premium dollar paid out in claim settlements—continued to be well over 100 percent in 1982 and 1983." Compounding the problem was Carriers' use of what was referred to as "retrospective premiums." Instead of collecting the premiums up front, it only required trucking firms to deposit two months worth of their annual premium payments. Additional funds were collected from the trucking companies if losses or the insurer's expenses surpassed the estimated premium.[27]

According to D. Michael Kelley, a former vice president of claims at Carriers, the company was beset with many problems that had hit the entire industry. "What we've had is rising underwriting losses, reduced interest rates that cut investment income, and an over-capacity in the marketplace so large that you couldn't raise premiums—it's still a buyer's market."[28]

Worse still, Carriers had been underestimating loss reserves for accidents. When an insured customer had an accident, the company created a loss reserve on its books. Even though the claim might not be paid out for years, the company reduced its net income by the loss reserve amount the year it was recorded. Underestimating loss reserves meant the company's net income and surplus appeared much higher than they were in reality. An official from its reinsurance company alerted John III to the irregularity. After finding the tip correct, John III moved quickly to remedy the situation by firing all managers in the underwriting department and calling for the development of new procedures. Meanwhile, Iowa insurance commissioner Bruce Foudree began an investigation of Carriers in 1982 and concurred that the company had indeed underestimated its claim losses, putting the figure at $16.8 million higher than Carriers had reported. The examination concluded with a stunning revelation: rather than having a $10.5 million surplus at the end of 1982, the company's liabilities exceeded its assets by $1.9 million, making Carriers theoretically insolvent. In March 1984, the company agreed with a consent order in which the State Insurance Department made its insolvency public.[29]

Although the Carriers situation concerned John, he thought it could be resolved, and with John III now serving as president, he expected to be kept well informed of the insurance company's affairs. At the same time, he had two exciting projects in mind, and he was aching to move forward with both. Always interested in sales and marketing, John often wondered why Iowa was not better at promoting its products overseas. His interest in this area had first been piqued when, with his approval, bank president Herman Kilpper established an international banking division within Bankers Trust. He became more serious about international trade when Iowa governor Terry Branstad started touting the creation of export trading companies in Iowa after recent federal legislation in the fall of 1982 had removed antitrust penalties for firms joining together in such operations. The governor also called on the private sector to help create more jobs in the state. Seeing an opportunity here, John worked with financial adviser Roger Cloutier and Kilpper on founding a company that could expand the sales of Iowa-made products abroad. As the plan developed, John decided on bringing in other investors with expertise in overseas trade, but he wanted control, noting that he expected "Ruan to own no less than 55% of the stock."[30]

After convincing several friends and top Iowa business figures of the concept's soundness, John brought six other firms into the venture. He announced the founding of Iowa Export-Import Trading Company at the governor's weekly press conference on March 28, 1983, explaining, "This . . . is an undertaking by a group of leading Iowa businesses to expand international markets for products grown, processed, or manufactured in Iowa." Based in the Ruan Center, the new company would use the trading expertise of its founding members to help small Iowa producers and manufacturers market their products internationally. Along with Ruan, the others involved were AGRI Industries, Iowa Beef Processors, Inc., Maytag Company, Pioneer Hi-Bred International, Townsend Engineering Company, and Winnebago Industries. Each investing company held seats on Export-Import's board, while John served as the company's initial president and chairman.[31]

The *Des Moines Register* welcomed the trading company because "in a world in which international trade is becoming the lifeblood of every nation, efforts like the Iowa venture hold enormous promise." Although the paper was "uncertain" about the trading company's prospects, it wrote optimistically, "John Ruan rarely gets involved in ventures in which things don't start happening soon." Prince Manufacturing Company of Sioux City, a producer of hydraulic parts for farm machinery, became the first company employing the services of Iowa Export-Import, and by the end of the year, the small trading company had over a dozen clients. Yet in the late fall, the big news was that farm-equipment manufacturer Deere and Company had joined Export-Import. According to the *Register*, "The Deere addition was seen as a boost for the trade company, both from a financial standpoint and from the view of providing additional contacts through Deere's extensive overseas marketing operation."[32]

Originally managed by international banker David Tremmel, the young company and its small staff struggled for the first couple of years, running up a debt and not yet turning a profit. When Tremmel left for another job in 1985, John realized that Export-Import needed a leader with sales and marketing experience. He found such a person in Craig Winters. Winters initially signed a two-year deal, with hopes of getting the company on its feet. If there were not signs of a turnaround by the end of the period, he knew that John would likely close down the venture. As had been hoped, Winters reported a modest profit by the end of his second year and noted that future prospects looked good. From then on, Export-Import grew steadily, and as had become typical of John, he began buying out his partners until he owned all shares of the company.[33]

On the export side, expansion up through the late 1990s was mostly based on the sale of farm machinery, such as the Iowa-made

Kinze agricultural planters. Potential buyers from Europe sometimes traveled to Iowa to talk to Winters and see the equipment firsthand. Winters soon realized that many wanted a demonstration of the machinery, and some were interested in a test-drive in a realistic farm setting. He decided that a display at Jonbar would facilitate sales. John always liked seeing his property making money, and he readily agreed to build a shelter house at Jonbar for entertaining Iowa Export-Import customers. After the structure was erected in 1996, Winters used it to promote farm equipment sales until the end of the decade, when a slowdown in the European farm economy curtailed such purchases. As the export market slowed, Winters was developing the import business, fueled by an agreement making the firm the exclusive United States distributor for the Italian company SPAL, a manufacturer of high-performance fans for automobiles and other vehicles. Ultimately, Export-Import became a valuable property, with revenues of nearly $16 million in 2000.[34]

For John, Iowa Export-Import was but the first step into the arena of international trade. His next move was much grander: he wanted a world trade center in Des Moines. Interest in such facilities had been mounting since construction of New York City's World Trade Center complex and its twin towers in the early 1970s. While John was considering a trade center for Des Moines, leaders in nearby Kansas City and Minneapolis, for instance, were thinking along the same lines for their cities. The original inspiration for the agriculturally based trade center in Des Moines grew out of the idea of turning the city into "the agri-business capital of the world" and was first discussed in 1979 by several city businessmen who regularly met for breakfast. The group included attorneys Arthur Davis and Harlan Hockenberg, Des Moines Register and Tribune Company executives Michael Gartner and Gary Gerlach, and general contractor Fred Weitz. By 1980, the group was arguing for the construction of an "architecturally unique" office building that would attract—and then house—agribusiness and farm-related firms.[35]

After establishing the import and export company, John became a proponent of a trade center for Des Moines. He first mentioned the idea at the Iowa Bankers Association meeting in September 1983, where John was one of three panelists addressing Iowa's position in global agriculture. He told the crowd that Iowa could be identified as the "Agricultural Center of the world," but "we have to earn that title—you're not going to get it by writing about it, by organizing committees or by entertaining foreign visitors." He continued, "We have to be doers and show what we can do with our Iowa agri-business economy, and then maybe we'll become a world trade center. Personally, I think we should have a world trade center which could provide the facilities needed to support foreign trade activities."[36]

Several months earlier, John had formed two organizations as preliminary steps to attaining a world trade center in Des Moines. First was the Iowa World Ag-Trade Institute, established to promote international trade from Iowa. He also formed the Iowa World Ag-Trade Center Association to lobby for the construction of such a center. These moves were followed in early September when he applied on behalf of the Ag-Trade Center Association for membership in the exclusive World Trade Centers Association. On the application, John spelled out his group's goal: "The Association will bring together, in a centralized location, activities and businesses relating to world trade. Because agriculture is Iowa's predominant product, the center will specialize in the transfer of agricultural products and knowledge, which can be utilized by other countries. The center will provide a focal point for international cultural and business exchanges with Iowa firms, universities, state and city agencies and private organizations."[37] When the Iowa association was admitted to the group a month later, there were only five world trade centers operating across the United States: they stood in New York City, Baltimore, Houston, Los Angeles, and New Orleans. With his planned multimillion-dollar Iowa world trade center, John hoped to add Des Moines to this select list.[38]

That fall, John worked behind the scenes securing support for the center from business and agricultural leaders as well as politicians and educators throughout the state. In October, he released a written statement saying a trade center was "worthy of consideration" and he would take up the project "if statewide interest continues to develop." More closed-door meetings assured him of widespread support, and early the following year, John went forward.[39]

At a crowded press conference held at his Marriott Hotel in January 1984, John unveiled his plans for a $75-million Iowa world trade center to be built adjacent to the Des Moines Convention Center currently under construction. The proposed 30-story glass-enclosed structure featured a dramatic 10-story skylighted atrium surrounded by a foreign-visitors center, a library, a television studio, and product showrooms. Atop this structure would sit a 20-story tower housing offices, restaurants, a private club, and 10 floors of hotel space. The "supermarket of services" offered at the center, John told the crowd, was all aimed at encouraging international trade and could eventually make Des Moines a "shrine or mecca" for agriculture.[40]

Designed by Ken Kendall, the architect who had done John's earlier downtown buildings, the Iowa world trade center would be unique among all such facilities because it would be the only one focusing on agribusiness. Planned as a public-private venture, John envisioned the state owning and running the exhibit portion of the center, making significant state money a project requirement. Initially very supportive, Governor Branstad said he would recommend that the legislature contribute $30 million to the trade center over a three-year period. Beyond that stake, John expected the state to pay part of the facility's annual operating costs, with its share estimated to run from $1 to $4 million yearly. He intended to obtain the remaining funds from a combination of private investment, federal money, industrial revenue bonds, and mortgage financing.[41]

After the project was announced, support appeared strong. Branstad, who had said earlier that the center held "great promise," continued stumping for it. The *Register* praised the Iowa world trade center as "the right idea, at the right time" and said that Ruan deserved "a prize for bringing forth the idea and pushing it to where it now rests—in the Legislature." Also positive were the results of its Iowa Poll, indicating that as of early January 1984, 67 percent of Iowans supported the concept of an Iowa world trade center. At the same time, *Wallaces Farmer* weighed in, challenging Iowans: "We talk of selling our way to farm prosperity. If we believe it, here's our chance. Ruan says, with state support, construction could begin yet this year, with completion in two and a half years. Full steam ahead!" And the Iowa Farm Bureau endorsed the venture, calling it "a positive step for expansion of world trade and an investment that will benefit the economy of Iowa and every citizen of this state."[42]

Yet John knew he still had an uphill battle because, as *Register* editor James Flansburg later put it, "almost everyone wanted the trade center and the economic development package as long as someone else had to pay for it."[43] John therefore traveled around the state drumming up support from a variety of groups. He told a gathering in Ames, for instance, "If you like the idea, if you think it's something that we ought to do, then do everything you can to help." He was then more specific. "Our people down (in the Legislature) are going to need a push."[44] Given the large amount of state aid he was seeking, John's concerns were warranted.

Problems cropped up from the very beginning. Early on, Branstad proposed financing the state's portion for the center through an increase in the gasoline tax. The Iowa Legislature blocked that plan and instead called for the creation of a state lottery, using the revenues it generated for the trade center package and other economic development efforts. Although the governor backed the trade center, he opposed a state lottery and vetoed the bill. Meanwhile, it was becoming clear that public support was waning. In March, the *Register* ran the results of another Iowa Poll it conducted about the trade center. The survey now indicated that only 33 percent of adult Iowans backed a trade center in Des Moines, down from 67 percent a month earlier. Even worse from John's perspective, 70 percent of Iowans opposed state aid for building the facility.[45]

The mounting opposition made John work that much harder. He stepped up his lobbying efforts, especially outside of central Iowa, where there was growing antagonism toward locating the trade center in Des Moines. John and groups such as the Iowa Development Commission labored at breaking down this resistance, while at the Statehouse, several additional efforts at funding the facility, including a corporate income surtax, failed. But John kept pressing until, near the end of the session, he broke through in the Senate. On Thursday, April 19, the Iowa Senate voted to allow Polk County residents to hold a referendum about taxing themselves to fund the center. "Voters could choose a sales tax, a wheel tax, both, or neither, to raise the money needed for the exhibition hall of the center." Estimates were that a one-cent increase in the sales tax would raise $17.9 million annually, with half earmarked for the trade center. This seemed to be it. The paper had run the story under the headline, "House Seen Likely To Go Along Today," and it thought John had all but won the long battle.[46]

Register political cartoonist Brian Duffy thought so, too. He and editor James Gannon agreed that the Sunday cartoon should deal with the end of the legislative session, and it should concern the lengthy world trade center debate. Duffy drew the cartoon Friday morning when most expected the center's funding bill to pass the House. It featured John driving a trucking rig hauling the Iowa world trade center on its trailer. Branstad was in the passenger seat, and a legislator was smashed against the front of the cab. John is exclaiming to the governor, "Now pay attention, boy! This is how you drive one of these things!!"[47]

That afternoon, the House defeated the local-option tax for Polk County, 60 to 34. Given the shift in public opinion against the trade center and the alliance of the Iowa Farm Bureau—which supported the center but opposed the local-option tax—and the Iowa Federation of Labor against the plan, a majority of representatives could not support it. This result caused a problem for Duffy, who had to prepare another cartoon depicting the world trade center defeat and then wait to see if the bill was revived in the final hours of the session. It wasn't, and the cartoon Duffy substituted for the original depicted John driving the same truck down a winding road. He has missed a "statehouse curve" and is flying off a cliff. This time, passenger Branstad speaks: "Gee, Mr. Ruan, I thought you said you knew how to drive this thing!"[48]

Duffy had to change his cartoon, but John was not ready to change his plans for a world trade center. He had failed, he thought, largely because the governor had backed away from the idea after his funding program was rejected and public opinion began shifting away from the proposal. Some thought John's "'take this and eat it' style of persuasion" and his failure to explain the need for the facility hurt his promotion efforts. Still others believed the strong anti–Des Moines feeling was the most important factor in killing the center.[49]

Over the next few months, John quietly prepared for another try at winning the Iowa world trade center, while a special legislative com-

mittee, established at the end of the session, considered the feasibility
of such a center in the state. By the summer, John was again discussing
the trade center publicly, and in September, he made a move that indicated his commitment to the cause: he shifted Herman Kilpper, who
had headed Bankers Trust since 1977, from that position to the presidency of the Iowa World Trade Center Corporation. One of John's
closest associates, Kilpper had been working on the trade center for the
past 18 months, but that was on top of his duties at the bank. Now he
would devote full attention to the trade center. John Chrystal, a banker
and agribusinessman who had previously served as the Iowa superintendent of banking, succeeded Kilpper at Bankers Trust.[50]

There was more to this move than merely beefing up his trade center team. Bankers Trust was in trouble. While in charge, Kilpper had
done just what John had wanted—he aggressively expanded the bank,
rapidly increasing its assets and loan portfolio—but such a strategy ultimately put the bank in a precarious situation. Chrystal explained,
"Bankers Trust had been in the practice of buying money [at relatively
high interest rates] and then re-loaning it [at even higher interest
rates]." With the farm crisis and the decline of the Iowa economy in the
early 1980s, many people and businesses defaulted on their Bankers
Trust loans, and the bank's strategy brought it to the brink of collapse.
With hindsight, John acknowledged that the focus on rapid growth
had caused problems. "In fast growth, you're bound to make some mistakes," he said. "Maybe we'd have been more cautious on loans had we
been able to see two or three years ago what we see now."[51]

When huge loan losses began piling up—these amounted to $15
million from the beginning of 1984 through mid-1985—state bank
regulators stepped in and placed a series of sanctions on the bank.
Beyond keeping a close eye on all of Bankers Trust's operations, the
enforcement agreement limited the types of loans the bank could
make, restricted its distribution of dividends, and placed restrictions on
hiring. Several years earlier, in fact, federal regulators had also been
concerned with the bank's practices and hit Bankers Trust with their
own enforcement agreement. Chrystal was therefore brought in to
restore confidence and return the institution to profitability. It was also
hoped that his experience as state banking superintendent could ease

the adversarial relationship that had evolved between the institution and bank regulators.[52]

If John had anticipated a quick turnaround, he was badly disappointed. In 1984, Bankers Trust lost $4.55 million; the next year it lost another $4.45 million. By 1986, Chrystal had shrunk the bank by roughly $70 million in assets and was paying out far less interest. This move, combined with stricter loan policies, led to a gradual improvement. The bank finished that year $1.18 million in the red, but that represented a huge improvement over its 1985 performance. It ended 1987 $807,000 in the black.[53]

In 1988, Chrystal managed to push net profits up to $2.58 million. While it represented a major step forward, Bankers Trust had a long way to go. For example, the bank's return on equity that year stood at 9 percent, substantially better than recent years but well below its peer group of Iowa banks, which had an average return on equity of 14.27 percent. In fact, during this bleak period, John was required to inject large amounts of his own money, more than $5.2 million, to stabilize the bank. Unhappy with the bank's condition, John could still laugh about this infusion of personal capital. "I refer to it as my charitable contribution," he joked. Nonetheless, under Chrystal's leadership as president and then chairman, the bank seemed to be making progress, and in 1989, he left the job for an unsuccessful bid at the Democratic nomination for governor. Dennis Wood, then Bankers Trust president, was named CEO, and John hoped his new appointee would keep the bank moving forward.[54]

But Wood did not do the job. After losing $427,000 in 1990, the bank lost over $1 million the following year. John could no longer laugh at the dreary picture. From 1983 through 1991, Bankers Trust suffered a net loss of $1.5 million. The dismal performance wore on the patience of state and federal regulators, and it was becoming clear that a new CEO was needed. Working behind the scenes, John III assured state banking officials that the family would hire a proven leader to right the floundering institution. Suku Radia, a partner in the accounting firm of Peat Marwick (now KMPG), which did accounting work for the Ruan companies, recommended J. Michael "Mike" Earley for the job. On that advice, John III talked with Earley several times. Impressed with the banker, he spoke with his father. After meeting the candidate, John agreed with his son's assessment, and in June 1992, he removed Wood, replacing him with the 47-year-old Earley. After heading Hawkeye Bank in Des Moines, Earley spent five years in Waterloo, Iowa, turning the poorly performing MidAmerica Savings Bank into one of the state's most profitable savings and loans. David Miller, president of West Des Moines State Bank, praised John's new CEO as "very aggressive and very articulate." He thought that if Earley was given "free rein to cut costs and run the bank he will be very effective." Des Moines developer Bill Knapp was also high on Earley, calling him "one of the top bankers in the state." John hoped these assessments were correct, and he eagerly awaited signs that his highly regarded hire could turn around Bankers Trust.[55]

Yet even during its darkest days, John focused most of his attention not on Bankers Trust but on the world trade center. With Kilpper now his full-time assistant on the matter, he was more determined than ever to build the facility. In the fall of 1984, John assured a crowd that "the time is now" for the Iowa world trade center, and it soon appeared he was right. Early in the 1985 legislative session, state lawmakers again passed a lottery bill, but this time it contained a special provision indicating that a portion of the proceeds would be used for funding the state's share of a world trade center. Also different this time was the governor's response—he signed it.[56]

Ready with $30 million in funding, state legislators set up a competitive process for the trade center. Together with the governor, they established a special committee—composed of Chairman Ned Chiodo, who at the time was the Polk County auditor, and other representatives from around the state: Richard Canella of Fort Madison, Dennis Houlihan of Dubuque, Arthur Vogel of Hamburg, and Frances Zrostlik of Garner—to study trade center proposals from developers and then make a recommendation to an executive council. This latter group was made up of governor Terry Branstad, secretary of state Mary Jane Odell, state auditor Richard Johnson, state treasurer Michael Fitzgerald, and secretary of agriculture Robert Lounsberry. Meanwhile, the Des Moines City Council decided in June that if its city's site were selected for the trade center, it would assist the developer by buying the land for the structure, building skywalks to the facility, remodeling the convention center and connecting it to the new building, and adding 1,000 parking spaces. The pieces were all falling into place, and John remembered, "The idea had real merit. I thought we had it."[57]

Seven development groups submitted trade center proposals, and in June the site committee narrowed those down to three. John's Iowa World Trade Center Corporation had been working on the project the longest and had the inside track. It still called for a downtown center next to the convention center, but costs had now risen to $85 million. The other two plans recommended building on the outskirts of greater Des Moines. A group headed by Ray Raymond, president of Danali Brokerage Services in West Des Moines, suggested an $81 million facility showcased by a 240-foot tower on 171 acres in Dallas County, approximately 15 miles west of downtown. FEH Associates, Inc., an architectural firm located in Des Moines and Sioux City, envisioned a 10-story glass pyramid on 600 acres just north of Living History Farms in Urbandale, a suburb northwest of Des Moines.[58]

John's good fortune continued. On July 30, the state selection committee chose John's plan for the world trade center but attached several conditions. Most important, the committee wanted the state's contribution limited to the $30 million from lottery proceeds. In addition, they called for downsizing the facility and giving the state an equal voice in the center's operation. The Ruan team was given a month to respond to the proposal. Overall, Kilpper was happy with the decision and talked about negotiating. "We're certainly flexible, and we are willing to look at alternatives," he said. "We're willing to stick with it and look at all kinds of compromises."[59]

As Kilpper had suggested, the Ruan group worked at complying with the state committee's conditions. It decreased the size of the building and lowered the overall cost of the structure to $65 million. Further, it agreed to put public figures on the center's decision-making board. As the deadline neared, only one sticking point remained: how the facility's operating and promotional costs were to be paid. John's original proposal had asked the state to provide up to $24 million over the center's first 10 years to cover these expenses. The state advisory committee, which had the very vocal backing of the governor, refused, and said that the $30 million for the center's construction was all the state would contribute to the project. When the revised Ruan proposal was submitted, it called for the state to pay $25 million for construction costs and then commit to paying the annual operating costs. John recommended that these costs also be paid with lottery money. With Dennis Houlihan absent from the August 30 advisory committee meeting, the panel deadlocked over the revised trade center plan— Chiodo and Canella opposed it while Vogel and Zrostlik voted in favor—but offered the Ruan group one more week to comply with its demand on the state's investment. Further, it noted that the law authorizing the use of lottery money for the project specified that it be used only for construction of the center. At this point, Richard Canella, vice chairman of the committee, thought the trade center was dead: "I feel sorry it is dead, because I think it is needed."[60]

It soon became clear that Canella was right. John held to his belief that the state should pay the operating costs, while state representatives did not budge from their notion of limiting public exposure to construction. Although the proposal had not yet been sent to the executive council for the final decision, the five-member group met and, at Governor Branstad's behest, voted unanimously in support of the advisory committee's position. As the *Des Moines Register* explained, "The Executive Council resolution was aimed at Des Moines businessman John Ruan and his associates . . . It is intended to show Ruan that Iowa officials are unified in the belief that his proposal must be modified before they will turn over $30 million in lottery profits for construction costs."[61]

Looking back, Kilpper remembered that the trade center's individual and corporate investors were worried about being asked for more money, and at least one had warned John "not to tin cup us every year." Thus, with John holding firm to the notion of not "sticking the private investors" with the center's annual operating costs, the state advisory committee convened on September 6 and voted unanimously against the plan. In a terse statement, a frustrated Kilpper summed up the significance of the committee's decision: "Today's resolution killed our proposal." After two years of trying, John could not close the deal on the Iowa world trade center, and he was both angry and upset. Architect Ken Kendall recalled, "John was irate. In his mind, the project had to happen. It was good for Iowa, and he just couldn't understand anyone turning it down." Meanwhile, much to his chagrin, other midwestern cities such as Chicago and St. Paul soon filled the void by opening their own trade centers. While he remained committed to erecting an agricultural trade center in Des Moines and resolutely pursued the project, it was a major defeat for John. In the words of Des Moines journalist Mary Tone, "For the first time in his business career there was a dent in the armor."[62]

Circumstances did not allow John to dwell on this defeat, because continuing problems at Carriers Insurance required his attention. After 1982, when the company was found to be technically insolvent, John began to inject large amounts of money into it in an attempt to shore up the floundering company. Over the next couple of years, he poured more than $10 million into Carriers, but it was not enough, and the situation went from bad to worse. Further embarrassment occurred in November 1985, when company management was taken away from Ruan control. Iowa Insurance Commissioner Foudree and John Ruan III signed an order placing Carriers under strict state supervision, with the firm being overseen by Foudree and Indianapolis insurance consultant Emil Molin. As the *Des Moines Register* reported, the order said: "'Carriers is in a condition as to render the continuance of its business hazardous to the public and the holders of its policies,' and it banned Carriers from continuing to write new or renewal insurance policies." Change was swift. The day after the agreement was signed, for instance, John Ruan III found himself locked out of his office at the Carriers Building. John, meanwhile, was busy working the phones, telling close friends and business associates that he had agreed to state control of the insurance company, but he assured them that the rest of his businesses were not affected.[63]

One of John's friends took note of the insurance company's demise, and according to Mary Tone, thought there was now a "crack in the Ruan armor." Meanwhile, finger-pointing and accusations flew back and forth. One Carriers executive blamed "misjudgment rather than mismanagement" for the company's problems, saying that when the situation grew desperate, the firm increased its premiums from 50 to 400 percent, "but it was just not enough and too late." Others were not so generous and assigned blame to leading company officials such as vice president and general manager Tom Strode. Then there were those who pointed to the Ruan family—either to John's absentee management or to John III's inexperience in the insurance business— as the root of the problem. These charges stung John, but as he had generally done in the past, he did not address them publicly.[64]

Originally the state insurance department considered selling Carriers, but with no buyer on the horizon, it decided the only option was shutting down the company. In January 1986, Carriers was turned over to Polk County District Court for liquidation. John was already humiliated, but the Carriers debacle was far from over. In June 1987, William Hager, the new Iowa insurance commissioner, filed a $63-million lawsuit against John, John III, Larry Miller, and Herman Kilpper (the latter two as Carriers board members). The four were accused of "self dealing," arising from the following specific incidents: (1) Carriers was slow to bill Ruan trucking companies, which owed the insurer more than $1.1 million in unpaid premiums; (2) Carriers bought $1 million of Bankers Trust stock in 1983 and later refused to sell it after it was notified that the purchase violated Iowa law; and (3) Carriers sold its downtown Des Moines office building to another Ruan entity with part of the payment, $6.9 million, to be spread out over time at below-market interest rates. Damages sought for these three incidents were in the $3-million range. Furthermore, the four men were charged with "gross mismanagement" when Carriers came up "$60 million short of being able to pay off claims after the state shut down the insurer."[65]

That John would respond to the charges must have surprised many observers. Usually quiet when attacked, he lashed out at what he termed an "outrageous" lawsuit. Saying he had "pumped millions" into Carriers trying to save it, John replied specifically to the charges of self-dealing. On the issue of insurance premiums owed by Ruan trucking operations, he said that his trucking firms were working with attorneys for the insurance commission, trying to establish the amount owed. As to illegally holding Bankers Trust stock, John made clear that he told the insurance commission he would buy back the stock from Carriers for the amount it paid. Finally, John explained that Carriers made a $3.4-million profit on the sale of its building. The case dragged out over a year before a partial settlement was concluded in October 1988. Although they continued to deny any wrongdoing, John, John III, Kilpper, and Miller agreed to pay $3.1 million, and John gave a personal guarantee of promissory notes from four Ruan corporations for the $6.9-million purchase of the Carriers Building in 1983. In exchange, Insurance Commissioner Hager dropped the charges of "self-dealing to the detriment of the insurance company."[66]

The remainder of the $60-million lawsuit was concluded in 1989. John and the three other defendants agreed to pay an additional $12.5 million and drop $12 million in claims—capital that Ruan firms had put into Carriers trying to save the insurance company; in return, Hager dropped the remaining charge of negligent management. John did not comment at the time on the settlement, but his attorney Roger Stetson said, "Mr. Ruan is very pleased to have this matter finally resolved." Indeed he was. John later recalled, "It was a bad deal. Things were going on at the insurance company that we were not aware of, and John III was unfairly blamed for its failure. We were just happy to get that behind us."[67]

Seemingly always in motion, John moved on to other endeavors before the lawsuit was settled. Long active in Republican politics, he began working on behalf of Bob Dole in the senator's effort to secure the 1988 GOP nomination for president. The two men had first become acquainted during President Nixon's years in the White House. Both tough and determined, they grew friendlier during the late 1970s and early 1980s, and the relationship proved beneficial for John when Dole's last-minute intervention was critical in securing the multimillion-dollar tax break for his trucking group. In May 1987, John hosted a fund-raising dinner for Dole—who for several months had been testing the waters for a presidential bid—at the Des Moines Club. Later in November, John was in Dole's hometown of Russell, Kansas, when the senator officially threw his hat into the presidential ring.[68]

Much as Dole had hoped, John appreciated the senator's "ability to exercise power," and although he would be more active in Dole's later run for the White House in 1996, he gave several speeches for the candidate and hosted a number of additional events during this campaign. John's work throughout the state, coupled with Dole's background in neighboring Kansas and his many visits to Iowa, paid off. In February 1988, Dole won the Iowa caucuses, but his campaign stumbled later that month when George Bush soundly defeated him in the New Hampshire primary. Even though he later won a primary in South Dakota and a caucus in Minnesota, Dole was in trouble. After losing all 17 states on Super Tuesday and then the primaries in Illinois and Wisconsin, Dole had had enough. On March 29, he dropped out of the race, and several days later he wrote to thank John for his support and noted how he "deeply appreciated" the Iowan's friendship. Over the next few years, John stayed in close touch with Dole and his wife, Elizabeth, and he generously complied when the senator asked on several occasions to borrow his plane.[69]

Just as Republican politics took John away from his own enterprises, so too did his continuing interest in the revitalization of Des Moines. This interest led to his sponsorship of a road race in the capital city. In 1987, the Greater Des Moines Convention and Visitors Bureau (CVB) was considering new ways of bringing people downtown. On the suggestion of its executive director, Ellen Brown, the group began thinking that a road race through the streets of downtown might be a good way of promoting the area. The CVB agreed on the idea of a race, and Brown contacted some of auto racing's top sanctioning bodies about holding such an event in Des Moines. After being turned down by the Formula One and Champion Auto Racing Teams (CART) organizations, Brown persuaded the Sports Car Club of America (SCCA) to investigate the possibility. Touring the city in the spring of 1988, the SCCA representatives were impressed with the venue and believed the city held great race potential. Equally important, George Cousins, SCCA design engineer, thought a fine racing course could be laid out on the downtown streets.[70]

Before the SCCA team left town, Brown took them over to the Ruan Center and introduced them to John. He listened intently to their evaluation of a possible race in Des Moines and the need for a title sponsor, a major financial backer whose name would be affixed to the race. John later recalled that he "knew nothing about racing but thought the idea held great possibilities." He made no commitments but remembered thinking, "It could be good for the community and therefore good for Ruan," because it would bring people and dollars downtown. Equally important, he thought, television coverage of the race was being discussed, and this could showcase the refurbished city to a large national audience. "It wouldn't hurt Ruan, either," John joked.[71]

Six months later, on a cold December evening, John saw Ellen Brown at the Des Moines Club in the Ruan Center. They were both attending the Greater Des Moines Committee's annual dinner. As the event was breaking up, John walked over to Brown and asked her about the status of the Des Moines race. She replied that plans were progressing, but they were still looking for a title sponsor. With a twinkle in his eye, John told her that Ruan would take up the major sponsorship. This chief hurdle overcome, the CVB established a separate board—the Greater Des Moines Grand Prix, Incorporated—to oversee the planning and running of the race. Robert Houser, president of Des Moines Development Corporation, headed the new organization and eventually worked out an agreement with John that Ruan Transportation Management Systems would spend $1 million to sponsor the first three years of the race. As part of the agreement, the race was to be called the Ruan Greater Des Moines Grand Prix. "John's support was critical," remembered Houser, "Without him, we couldn't have pulled it off." With Ruan on board, other Des Moines businessmen and companies soon followed with additional financial support for the upcoming event. Meanwhile, Houser and race organizers landed a commitment from cable television network ESPN to broadcast the race. Everything was in place.[72]

The three-day racing event was held in July 1989 and received rave reviews from the SCCA, which was happy with the course and the attendance. The CVB was also elated; it estimated that the Grand Prix's economic impact on Des Moines was between $10 and 12 million. Of course, the race was not without problems. Some downtown residents complained of the noise, while street closures and the rerouting of traffic aggravated others. Furthermore, this first race amassed $540,000 in operating losses, but such red ink was expected for the race's first few years. Most civic leaders, including John, were happy with the results. It brought wonderful coverage for Des Moines and boosted area businesses. More specifically for John, with the race's logo—a silhouette of the downtown Des Moines skyline prominently depicting the Ruan Center was set above the bold-lettered race title, Ruan Grand Prix—his company name was often flashed across the television screens as ESPN played and replayed the tape of the race throughout the coming year.[73]

With his name beamed into homes nationally, John looked ahead to the Ruan Grand Prix getting bigger and better, and breaking even in the coming years. As hoped, popularity grew and losses fell. John agreed in 1991 to extend his title sponsorship of the race three more years, but then disaster struck. A major flood swept through Des Moines in July 1993, and officials were forced to call off the event's main race on Sunday, July 11. Although another Grand Prix was held in 1994, losses resulting from the previously canceled race could not be overcome, and the Greater Des Moines Grand Prix Board decided it had no option but to withdraw from future racing contracts and permanently shelve the event.[74]

Even though John had little to do with the race itself and opposed its final abandonment, the ending of the Ruan Grand Prix seemed but another in a growing string of failures. Its cancellation came after his inability to win the trade center and then the liquidation of Carriers. In the meantime, *Des Moines Register* business writer Dirck Steimel suggested other evidence of the businessman's decline. He noted that John, who had been rated the most powerful person in Des Moines by a 1976 *Register* poll, dropped to second place, behind developer Bill Knapp, in the paper's 1990 "The Powers that Be" poll. And if buildings at all reflect the personality, power, and position of those who build them, then the Ruan Center as the state's tallest structure clearly represented John's clout. Yet in the fall of 1990, the rusty, 36-story monolith's title as Iowa's preeminent skyscraper gave way to the Principal Financial Group's 44-story headquarters, the 801 Grand building. To some, it was a metaphor of John's slipping influence.[75]

But images were deceptive. Even with the many problems and difficulties he faced in the 1980s and early 1990s, John had a knack of bouncing back. Not one to stop and reflect, he kept moving, often on to new projects. *Register* editor James Flansburg referred to these qualities when he once wrote of John, asking rhetorically, "What do you do with someone who won't quit?" Richard Wilkey, former Des Moines city manager, discounted the 1990 poll and thought John as influential as ever. "You can take all your surveys," Wilkey said, "but he's [still] the man." Larry Miller agreed, believing that John was more focused than ever.[76]

In fact, top management at the *Register* did not believe John had slipped at all. In January 1991, a panel consisting of publisher Charlie Edwards, editor Geneva Overholser, managing editor David Westphal, deputy managing editor Diane Graham, and business editor Rick Jost named him the *Des Moines Register's* Iowa Business Leader of the Year. The award was important to John because he believed the paper that had long opposed him was finally coming around. He reminisced, "The *Register* first changed its tune when it supported our convention center plans and then our world trade center efforts. Then it gave me this award." Sister Patricia Clare Sullivan, president of Mercy Hospital Medical Center, had similar thoughts. She wrote John: "Congratulations on the outstanding article that appeared in *The Des Moines Sunday Register.* I am enclosing the article so you can pull this out whenever you get outraged with the *Register*."[77]

Yet for all his resilience, John soon faced a situation that he could not readily shake off. It involved his daughter Jayne. By the mid-1980s, Jayne's MS had grown progressively worse, confining her to a wheelchair. Late in the decade, she became bedridden. As his daughter's condition deteriorated, John stepped up his crusade against MS. He worked harder at raising money through his golf exhibition and increased his charity's assistance to Chicago's Rush-Presbyterian–St. Luke's Medical Center, where Jayne received much of her MS therapy. Then, because of her frequent trips to Chicago, John began musing about expanding the neurological treatment opportunities in Des Moines. During a conversation with Mel Straub, chairman of the Iowa chapter of the national MS organization, John learned that Mercy Hospital Medical Center was considering increasing its orthopedic and neurological rehabilitation services. This news led him into talks with

Sister Patricia Clare Sullivan about possibly teaming up on such a project.[78]

John had several discussions with Sister Patricia Clare and others at Mercy through 1987 and into the following year. Ultimately he and hospital executives agreed to work together and establish a new MS program for central Iowa. On July 12, 1988, they called a news conference announcing their intention of building a new Mercy neurological center. John told the crowd that Iowa would now "have a first-class center for the treatment and rehabilitation of patients with MS and other neurological diseases." Toward that end, he donated $1 million—and promised to raise more if needed—for the facility, which would be located in additions to the fifth and sixth floors of Mercy Hospital Medical Center. Sister Patricia Clare then talked of John's long commitment to fighting MS and revealed that the new program would be called the Ruan Neurological Center.[79]

Opened a year later, the center included a gymnasium for patient exercise and evaluation, examination rooms, and a cool-water therapy pool, which enhanced muscle function of MS patients. In addition, because of his MS Charity work with Rush-Presbyterian–St Luke's Hospital, John promised that doctors at the Ruan Neurological Center would have "direct access" to the findings and research at the Chicago institution. At the ribbon-cutting ceremony, a proud John declared, "There is nothing like it in Des Moines." Mel Straub concurred: "This is one of the truly exciting things to happen in the medical field in the city of Des Moines."[80]

Jayne and many others throughout central Iowa and the Midwest came to take advantage of the new facility. Sister Patricia Clare remembered some of Jayne's therapy sessions at the center and recalled that "she was a real fighter" when it came to dealing with the disease. "Even though she hated the cool-water pool," Sister Patricia Clare said, "she put up with it." More than that, Rusty Hubbell Edwards observed that Jayne never complained about MS: "She was strong like her father and had a great giggle like her mother. She had a good sense of humor and was able to laugh about her situation." Yet despite her battling and the innovative treatments at the new Ruan Neurological Center, Jayne steadily declined.[81]

John felt helpless. All his efforts may have resulted in easing some of his daughter's symptoms but did nothing to reverse the degenerative effects of MS. Sadly, here again, hard work was not enough. In early June 1992, Jayne had grown so weak that she required hospitalization. She was taken to Mercy Hospital Medical Center. Although no one thought her condition was life-threatening, she did not improve, and while there, she contracted pneumonia. When that happened, John knew it might be the end. He remembered, "I thought I was prepared [for Jayne's death], but I wasn't."[82]

Jayne died at Mercy Medical Center on Sunday, June 28, 1992. The death hit John and Betty particularly hard. They had outlived their daughter. Worse still, Betty had pangs of guilt that she had passed the terrible disease on to her daughter. John stood by stoically, but inside, he was torn up by Jayne's death. Thomas Ruan, John's youngest son, noted how pale his father was at the visitation held at Dunn's Funeral Home in Des Moines: "Standing at the casket, he was visibly shaken, and I went over to give him a shoulder to lean on. He looked as if someone had stomped on his heart." Indeed, John recalled that evening as well: "Jayne looked so peaceful lying there in the coffin. She looked like she was asleep. I just couldn't believe she was gone. I couldn't understand why she had to die."[83]

The funeral was held on Wednesday, July 1, at St. Augustin's Catholic Church, where Jayne was a member. During her lengthy illness, she had grown close to several nuns at Mercy Hospital, and these encounters led to her conversion to Catholicism. Following the service, Jayne was interred at Resthaven Cemetery. The poignant event proved especially difficult for John because there, 49 years earlier, he had buried his first wife, Rose. Janis Ruan, John's daughter-in-law, remembered how dignified and composed John and Betty were at the funeral. She also knew that their appearance masked a profound sadness in them both.[84]

The period from the mid-1980s to the early 1990s was undoubtedly troubling for John. Hard work, it had become clear, did not always bring success. But through every adversity and every failure, he came back. Richard Wilkey explained this capacity simply. "John," he said, "had a tenacity that was unparalleled." Although his armor had been dented and cracked, it was still intact. Even after the loss of his daughter, John appeared undaunted to most, continuing to guide his many businesses. Those close to him knew better. "Jayne's death broke John's heart," Janis Ruan asserted, but she quickly added, "while you can break his heart, you can't break John's spirit."[85] Over the next few years, John tried working through the grief, and his fortitude carried him forward. In the twilight of his career, he would refocus his considerable energy in what was likely his most important undertaking.

8   A New Direction

John was deeply wounded by the death of his daughter in 1992; yet he seemed vigorous, and to the general public, he appeared unaffected. But family and friends saw through the facade. Jayne's passing devastated John, and the loss was compounded when close friend and associate Larry Miller died two years later. These traumas and his advancing age lessened John's characteristic resiliency. He was finally slowing down. Nonetheless, the 78-year-old quietly marked the 60th anniversary of his trucking firm in 1992, and he continued working.

By the early 1990s, John had begun shifting gears, becoming more absorbed in pursuits outside his business interests. Although he stayed active in his companies, he soon advanced John III, giving him much greater authority in the Ruan enterprises. With more of the family's empire being overseen by his son, John devoted greater attention to philanthropic endeavors, giving away some of the money he had spent a lifetime accumulating. Most significant was John's move to save and then expand the World Food Prize.

As his trucking company began its seventh decade of business that summer of 1992, John felt confident in its leadership. Larry Miller had guided Ruan Transportation Management Systems from a traditional hauling and leasing business to a company providing a wide array of transportation services. At roughly the same time, management introduced the ideas of W. E. Deming and quality improvement, soon hiring Robert Gelina to further the training throughout the company. But as Jeff Barber, former Ruan vice president of quality management, explained, the dispersed nature of the firm—with nearly 3,000 employees spread across the country in 180 terminals—made conversion to the new thinking difficult. "The victories didn't come for three or four years," noted company president Miller.[1]

When they did, the company had been completely revamped and was heading in a new direction. By 1993, RTMS was generating $300 million in annual revenues, with its "added value" services—which included driver hiring and training, fleet dispatching, fuel purchasing, and vehicle routing, as well as tasks such as handling customers' labor relations—accounting for half that figure. Some clients, in fact, rarely leased trucks and only took advantage of one or more of the afore-mentioned services. Others, like Marsh Supermarkets of Indianapolis, turned over their entire transportation unit to Ruan. Since so doing in the late 1980s, its transportation costs fell dramatically. "Basically, we give them [Ruan] a delivery schedule and they take over," said Marsh vice president David Redden. This outsourcing allowed Marsh to focus on its core business. Redden explained the relationship between his company and RTMS simply: "We know how to sell groceries. They know how to run a fleet."[2]

Clearly, John had found the right formula. His trucking operations were clicking along when the unexpected happened. In July 1994, 61-year-old Larry Miller, the athletic, health-conscious RTMS president, collapsed and died of a heart attack after his usual routine of swimming laps in the pool at the Wakonda Club in Des Moines. While he had been treated for high blood pressure, Miller was physically fit and believed to be in excellent health. Miller's death shocked his colleagues, but the company remained solid. He had put together a capable man-agement team, and Gary Alvord ably succeeded him in the presidency. Under Alvord's leadership, the company continued to grow, reaching revenues of $630 million in 2000.[3]

The trucking executive's death had a profound effect on John, however. Still not over the loss of his daughter, the 80-year-old business leader was ill prepared for another death. Over the years, it became clear that John and Larry Miller enjoyed a special relationship. "Although they could fight like tigers," remembered John's longtime friend Howard Gregory, "they shared a mutual admiration and respect for each other." Miller viewed John as a mentor, and many friends and associates felt that he saw the elder trucker as something of a surrogate father. John had similar feelings. He considered Miller "almost a son" and was impressed by his protégé's mental toughness and devotion. Like most, John was caught off guard by Miller's death, and according to secretary Jan Gillum, the news was "very upsetting to him." Alvord believed that John tried to deal with the grief as he always had, by mov-ing on and refusing "to stop and feel all that stuff."[4]

Luckily for John, his anguish was not compounded by worries about his companies, and he was especially buoyed by the resurgence

of Bankers Trust. Over the past decade, state and federal bank regulators had been bearing down on the institution, and it had been showing no significant signs of recovery. In desperation, John had made two
uncharacteristic concessions to lure the talented Mike Earley to the
bank. When John first approached him, Earley was in Waterloo, Iowa,
running MidAmerican Savings Bank, of which he was the third-largest
shareholder. While he liked the idea of returning to Des Moines and
restoring the lackluster bank, Earley had grown used to running his
own show. Earley was well aware of John's reputation for micro-
managing, and before taking the Bankers Trust job, he negotiated an
autonomy agreement that gave him complete control over the bank's
day-to-day management. Furthermore, Earley pushed John to promise
that the bank would not be sold, except to him.[5]

With these pledges in hand, Earley started at the bank in July
1992. His first month and a half was devoted to identifying the bank's
problems and drafting a 23-page report that he read to John, the board
of directors, and the regulators in September. After hearing the
account, John exploded, mainly because he had not realized the extent
of the troubles. Soon, however, he, the board, and even the regulators
threw their full support behind the new president.[6]

According to Earley, the problems dated back to the early 1980s
and occurred largely because the bank had "an impaired credit culture." He argued that Bankers Trust had not taken customers' credit-
worthiness into account when making loans, and Earley had difficulty
finding "justification" for the loan rates the bank had been charging.
Set against the backdrop of the state's farm crisis, in which many banks
experienced difficulties, this lack of policy led to millions of dollars in
bad loans and incurred the wrath of regulators. When Earley arrived
on the job, the bank was carrying $40 million in bad loans, while its
equity stood at only $30 million.[7]

If the commercial side of the bank had its problems, so too did its
trust department. Months before Earley took the job, news of a scandal involving the Iowa Trust Fund became public. The Iowa Trust was
a consortium of approximately 100 Iowa towns, counties, and municipal pension plans that pooled their excess cash for investment purposes. California financial adviser Steven Wymer managed the Iowa

Trust's nearly $100 million, while Bankers Trust acted as the fund's custodial agent. In December 1991, Wymer was charged with securities fraud when he sold $65 million in U.S. Treasury notes owned by the Iowa Fund and used the money to reimburse other clients whose money had been lost. All told, Wymer admitted to diverting $75 million from the Iowa Trust Fund. The state of Iowa brought suit, trying to recover the money, and Bankers Trust was one of the parties sued. This potentially devastating lawsuit and the millions in bad loans pushed regulators from the Federal Reserve Bank in Chicago to consider closing the bank.[8]

Earley's first goals, therefore, were to settle the lawsuit and begin following through on his plan that would get the regulatory enforcement agreements lifted. He initially focused on the lawsuit, ultimately getting an agreement to a $4-million out-of-court settlement. In Earley's mind, the constant news stories about the Iowa Trust debacle and Bankers Trust's ties to it were "undermining the confidence of depositors." He viewed the settlement as "an insurance policy" that he could move forward and deal with the regulators' concerns. To do so, he began to act upon his scheme for restoring the bank. He started with cost-cutting measures, decreasing the bank's staff by a third in three years. At the same time, he reduced the space the company leased in the Ruan Center from 85,000 square feet to 45,000 square feet. He and his new management team then carefully culled out and dropped questionable loans from the bank's portfolio and instituted a training program on good lending practices. In addition, Earley believed that the regulators could help the bank out of its troubles, and he thought the long-standing adversarial relationship that had developed between bank supervisors and employees only worsened matters. He therefore demanded that the regulators be treated with deference and respect.[9]

His efforts soon showed signs of success. In August 1993, Earley received welcome news from Iowa banking superintendent Richard Buenneke, who was pleased with the bank's turnaround. He responded by lifting the enforcement action his agency had placed on Bankers Trust in 1984. Several months later, Earley achieved another coup—in December, the Chicago Federal Reserve Bank lifted the enforcement agreement it had issued against the bank 15 years earlier. This sanction was the longest-running enforcement agreement ever issued by the Chicago branch of the Federal Reserve. Bankers Trust was now free to return to normal business practices. If these achievements were not enough, Earley topped it off by showing a $4-million profit in 1993, his first full year at the helm.[10]

John certainly felt good about the bank's new direction, but he chafed at the autonomy he had given Earley. He had always controlled his enterprises, and he had never given such independence to any of his executives. Not surprisingly, John soon tested the limits of this arrangement, which led to some fierce arguments between the two men, but Earley held firm, and John could not take issue with the bank's recovery. The arguments ceased after a couple of years, and the two developed a good working relationship.[11]

Keenly interested in the bank, John kept up-to-date on the latest developments through Earley's weekly 30-minute briefings, and it was John, as company chairman, who ran the board meetings. But he also played a more active role in the bank's continued growth. A consummate salesman, John touted Bankers Trust's many benefits whenever he had the opportunity, often mentioning his bank when speaking publicly on other matters. Earley quickly appreciated John's promotional talent and from time to time took his boss with him on sales calls.[12]

By 1995, net income was up to $6.3 million and return on equity stood at 16 percent, nearly a full percentage point higher than its peer group of banks across the state. Former bank president John Chrystal praised Earley, saying he deserved "a substantial amount of credit. He's a very competent borrower and lender." Others were impressed as well, and that year, Earley received the Ernst and Young Turnaround Entrepreneur of the Year Award. The praise was well deserved, but Earley's impressive performance was just beginning. Once having righted the ship, the banker now focused on growth. Assets, which had fallen to $491 million in 1993, topped $1 billion in 1999 and were $1.42 billion in 2001. Net income continued to climb as well, reaching $11.2 million by 2001. With this solid foundation in place, Earley plotted a course for expansion. Since John was always growth oriented, the strategy was right in line with his desires. After obtaining a national charter, Earley intended to open banks in several towns and cities throughout the state. The first one was established in Cedar Rapids in late 2002, with others planned for Ames, Newton, Iowa City, and the Quad Cities.[13]

Although pleased with the performance of both Bankers Trust and RTMS, John's primary interest was now his charitable undertakings. Part of this new focus included stepping up his battle against MS. He and Mel Straub continued to raise money with the charity golf exhibition, and they remained especially interested in the care and treatment of MS patients locally, which had been the impetus for funding the Ruan Neurological Center at Mercy Hospital. By the mid-1990s, however, it had become largely a rehabilitation center, and John was interested in a diagnostic and research program as well. He and Straub began to look for physicians to establish a neurology clinic. With the promise that the John Ruan MS Charity would fund and furnish a neurology clinic at Mercy Hospital, Straub recruited Dr. Michael Jacoby to head the clinic in the summer of 1995. Jacoby brought MS specialist Dr. Bruce Hughes into the clinic as well. Under these two doctors, the Ruan Neurology Clinic became the only Iowa participant in the multicenter trial of the drug that became known as Copaxone. The trial resulted in FDA approval for the drug now used in the treatment of MS.[14]

Over the next few years, the clinic expanded and added more neurologists, including another specialist in MS as well as specialists in the fields of epilepsy, movement, and headaches. Such growth meant that by the end of the 1990s, the clinic was seeing more MS and stroke patients than any other facility in Iowa. It was also beginning to have an impact regionally. Jacoby and his team were doing exactly what John had hoped, and he and his wife Betty showed their appreciation in 2001 by presenting a $2-million check to Mercy's Ruan Neurology Clinic. The donation was earmarked for improving its treatment of MS. Mercy CEO David Vellinga noted that many MS patients "wouldn't be alive without the improvements the Ruans have bankrolled." Even before the large gift, Bruce Hughes put John's significance in perspective: "I can't think of a single person in the State of Iowa who has had a more dramatic impact and powerful influence on MS patients than John Ruan and the Ruan MS Foundation. The continued dedication to this worthy cause is remarkable."[15]

Devoted though John was to the fight against MS, this was not the cause that really captured his imagination. It was rather the issue of food, which had been on his mind for nearly a decade, ever since he began pushing for an agriculturally oriented world trade center in Des Moines. After his first trade center proposal went down in defeat in spring of 1984, John immediately started working for legislative approval of the facility the following year. As always, he searched for any enticement or inducement that would make his plan more appealing. One such idea came to him while at Disney's Epcot Center in Florida. Passing through one of park's pavilions, John saw an exhibit about innovative ways of growing vegetables, which started him thinking about the impact of science on agriculture and the necessity of expanding the world's food supply. Then it dawned on him: "Why don't we create a global food prize that would draw international attention to the Iowa world trade center?"[16]

By that fall, he had fully fleshed out the concept and proposed the award in an address to the Des Moines Chamber of Commerce. After telling the audience of the benefits that would accrue if the trade center were built, he added, "To give credence, support, and substance to [Iowa's] designation as the agricultural capital of the world and to cause world attention to be focused on Iowa, I would propose to establish the Ruan World Food Prize. I would give $1 million to a foundation and challenge the state to match it with another $1 million." He went on, explaining that the interest on the $2 million endowment could support a biennial award of $150,000, which would be "given to the person who in the opinion of a board of trustees of world wide prominence had contributed the most to the development of food production with greatest nutritional value."[17]

With the proposed prize to be awarded at the proposed Iowa world trade center in Des Moines, John envisioned worldwide attention focused on the state. He imagined a grand ceremony covered by the national media and attended by leading "scientists, agricultural experts and political figures from around the world." John believed the concept of the prize had merit on its own, but always the promoter, he saw the award primarily as a means of winning support for his world trade center. When the center proposal was again defeated in 1985, John shelved the notion of a food prize but would continue to work for an agricultural trade facility.[18]

Oddly, at the same time John was considering the creation of a food prize, another figure was actively pursuing a similar project. His name was Norman Borlaug, and he was an agronomist who had won the 1970 Nobel Peace Prize for his lifetime of work in agriculture. Dubbed by many observers the Father of the Green Revolution, Borlaug had spent many years in Mexico and later in India and Pakistan with the Rockefeller Foundation developing a high-yield, disease-resistant strain of dwarf wheat, which could be grown across a wide range of latitudes. Aase Lionaes, president of the Nobel Peace Prize Committee, explained the significance of Borlaug's work during the 1970 award ceremony: "This year the Nobel Committee . . . has awarded Nobel's Peace Prize to a scientist, Dr. Norman Ernest Borlaug, because, more than any other single person of this age, he has helped to provide bread for a hungry world. We have made this choice in the hope that this will also give the world peace."[19]

Born just a few weeks after John in 1914, the Nobel laureate was also a native Iowan, raised on a farm near Cresco, a small community in the northeastern part of the state. Unbeknownst to John, Borlaug had been trying to create a high-visibility award for people involved in agricultural research since the late 1970s.[20]

Borlaug's first appeal was to the Nobel Board of Trustees, suggesting they create a prize for agriculture. Unfortunately for Borlaug, when the Swedish philanthropist Alfred Nobel had spelled out the parameters for the Nobel Prize in his will, he made no provision for such an award. The board had created an additional prize in economics, which was sponsored by Swedish bankers, but it was later decided that this move had been unwise because it could "open up the floodgates to an unmanageable number of prize possibilities." Holding firmly to this position, the trustees turned down Borlaug's request.[21]

Borlaug continued to advocate his idea of an agricultural prize, but he could not find a sponsor. Then, in the early 1980s, he received a telephone call from a well-connected stranger. The man introduced himself as Carleton Smith, a former director of the National Arts Foundation and founder of the International Awards Foundation. He was also interested in creating an agricultural prize and had recently come across Borlaug's name. Smith suggested they work together, thinking he could connect Borlaug with potential sponsors. Borlaug agreed and was especially pleased when he heard of Smith's recent successes in establishing new prizes. Through his International Awards Foundation, Smith concentrated on setting up awards in areas outside the purview of the Nobel Prize. He had played an important role in creating the Getty Wildlife Conservation Prize, and in the late 1970s, he convinced the Pritzker family, who owned the Hyatt Hotel Corporation, to establish a $100,000 annual award honoring outstanding architectural achievement. First given in 1979, the Pritzker Prize in architecture was soon acknowledged as the field's most important award.[22]

Indeed, Smith proved valuable in hooking up Borlaug with the company that would originally sponsor the agricultural prize. In the spring of 1984, he arranged for Borlaug to meet with James Ferguson, CEO of General Foods Corporation. The company was considering increasing its charitable giving and was looking for a worthy cause. Smith and Borlaug were to meet for dinner at a hotel in Westchester County, New York, in late May. They would talk over their ideas and then see Ferguson for lunch the following day. When Smith never arrived for the planned dinner, Borlaug became worried and called Smith's home. The housekeeper gave him shocking news: Smith had died in his sleep early that morning. Borlaug met Ferguson for lunch the next day. When he gave the General Foods executive the terrible news, the two agreed not to discuss the matter of the agricultural prize and instead decided to meet again in a month.[23]

At that second meeting, Borlaug was accompanied by old friend Robert Havener, a supporter of an agricultural prize and the head of the Winrock International Institute for Agricultural Development, an organization established by former Arkansas governor Winthrop Rockefeller to combat poverty and hunger. Ferguson and another General Foods executive listened to their proposition and said they would give it serious consideration. Several days later, Ferguson sent the prize proposal to A. S. Clausi, the company's senior vice president for research and development, for his thoughts on the matter. Clausi reported back favorably; he supported the sponsorship, but in place of an agricultural prize, he suggested a food prize "that would recognize all elements of the food chain from growing to putting it on the table of consumers." Borlaug liked the idea of a food prize, and with the approval of the company board of directors, the General Foods World Food Prize was established. The Winrock organization was brought in as the secretariat to administer the prize, while a board was established to set policy and govern the award. The board, called the Council of Advisors for the World Food Prize, was chaired by Clausi and included Borlaug, Havener, and other internationally recognized leaders on food and agricultural issues.[24]

While these structures of the organization were being laid out, the Philip Morris Companies acquired General Foods in the fall of 1985, but the new parent company was receptive to the prize, and it moved forward. The World Food Prize was formally announced in the spring of 1986, and the first award was bestowed in the fall of 1987. Borlaug's dream had come true.

In early 1989, however, Philip Morris decided to merge Kraft Foods, which it had purchased the previous year, with General Foods. The combined entity was called Kraft General Foods, and its new management team soon decided that maintaining the award was too costly. That December, the company announced it was dropping its sponsorship of the World Food Prize. Food prize officials were stunned, especially because some nominations for the 1990 award had already been received. As they began the search for a new sponsor, the *New York Times* ran an article about the prize's loss of corporate backing. Wire services picked up the piece, and the story soon ran in the *Des Moines Register,* where it caught the eye of Rox Laird, a *Register* editorial writer. Laird thought that with Iowa's close ties to agriculture, the state and its private sector should offer to fund the prize. The editorial staff agreed with him, and Laird penned an editorial challenging Iowans to take up the prize. "It seems natural," he wrote, "that this state should play a major role in keeping the prize alive and become identified with it, as Sweden and Norway are with the Nobels."[25]

State senator Elaine Szymoniak from Des Moines had followed the story and thought bringing the food prize to Iowa was a terrific idea.

Early in 1990, she called Laird for more information, and then she contacted Clausi and the Winrock Institute for details about subsidizing the award. Clausi told her that he and other prize officials were going to be on the road speaking to several potential sponsors and would be willing to add Des Moines to their list. With that, Szymoniak went to work. Soon she convinced Mike Reagen, president of the Greater Des Moines Chamber of Commerce Federation, that the public service organization should host a breakfast for the World Food Prize representatives at the Des Moines Club.[26]

Clausi, Borlaug, and Edward Williams, the Winrock administrator for the prize, traveled to Des Moines for the March breakfast with business and civic leaders—one of whom was John. After Clausi gave a brief presentation about the prize, its background, and its need for a sponsor, representatives from several Iowa businesses, including Pioneer Hi-Bred International and the Iowa Farm Bureau Federation, told him they would consider supporting the prize. John, meanwhile, was struck by how similar the food prize was to the idea he had floated for such an award several years earlier. As the event wound down, John approached Clausi and asked that he and his associates meet with him the next day. The following morning, Clausi, Borlaug, and Williams joined John in his 32nd-floor office in the Ruan Center, where the four men talked about the prize and food issues as well as John's dream of building the agricultural world trade center in Des Moines. John ended the meeting by telling his visitors he was "very interested" in sponsoring the prize. He promised to confer with some associates, and a follow-up meeting was planned. Clausi left feeling good about John's plans and Iowa in general. He sensed in the state "a grass-roots understanding of the value of food in the world" and believed that would "make Iowa a good home for the World Food Prize."[27]

John was undeniably interested in the prize, but much like before, he saw it as a potential building block toward attaining his longtime goals of making Iowa the world food capital and erecting an agricultural world trade center. After two unsuccessful efforts to get the trade center built in the mid-1980s, John put his plans on hold, but he never gave up the vision. Late in the decade, he revived the idea with a much larger proposal. This time, John called for a grandiose, $300-million,

85-story structure, topped with a huge revolving globe. The giant tower would house convention and hotel facilities as well as residential and commercial space. He hoped for major financial assistance from the federal government through the Department of Agriculture. At one point, in fact, plans called for relocating this department to Des Moines. He pitched the idea to President George Bush during a fund-raising event in 1989.[28]

Progress was slower during this third attempt at getting the trade center, and John thought the World Food Prize could prove a needed shot in the arm. Following Clausi's presentation, John and trade center point man Herman Kilpper spent a couple of weeks thoroughly investigating the possibility of sponsoring the prize.

Szymoniak was pleased with the initial reaction from business leaders at the chamber breakfast and thought there was a real chance of bringing the prize to Iowa. John, she believed, was the most likely to take up the challenge. To assist in this effort, she worked with Leonard Boswell, then chairman of the Iowa Senate Appropriations Committee, and sponsored a piece of legislation that would set aside $250,000 of state money for subsidizing the prize if a sponsor providing matching funds could be found. Before the bill came up for a vote that spring, Borlaug was invited to speak before a joint session of both houses of the Iowa State Legislature. His impassioned speech persuaded legislators to pass Szymoniak's food prize–appropriation bill.[29]

John soon decided he wanted to sponsor the prize and went after it in his usual unrelenting manner. Realizing he was competing with several other foundations across the country, he kept in close contact with World Food Prize officials, repeatedly reminding them of the advantages of moving the award to Iowa. By May 1990, John had prepared a formal proposal for taking over the prize. Late that month, he sent Robert Mickle—former Des Moines city planning director who was then serving as a consultant for the Ruan Companies—and Kilpper with two representatives from Iowa State University (ISU), which was vying to serve as the prize's secretariat, to the Winrock Institute's headquarters in Morrilton, Arkansas. There they met with Clausi, Havener, and Williams to discuss John's bid. Details were hashed out, and several days later, World Food Prize officials decided that the Ruan

Foundation would be the award's new sponsor. Under the terms of the arrangement, John established the World Food Prize Foundation and endowed it with $1.5 million. He then signed an agreement pledging that he would be responsible for the entire annual cost of the prize. At that time, the award was $200,000, and its administration added another $375,000 per year. When the state appropriation (which was also made in each succeeding year) was considered, John's yearly subsidy for the prize ran about $325,000.[30]

The change in sponsorship was announced at a Des Moines news conference on June 18, 1990. More than 300 local business figures and politicians filled a ballroom at the Des Moines Marriott Hotel to hear the news. Adolph Clausi told the crowd that beginning in 1991, the John Ruan Foundation would assume the World Food Prize sponsorship, while ISU would replace the Winrock Institute as the award's administrator. Ruan and ISU were among several strong worldwide groups seeking the prize, Clausi said, "but Mr. Ruan is a very persistent man. He aggressively pursued it and really preempted anyone else." Many in attendance had experienced John's single-minded determination firsthand, and few would have been surprised by Clausi's characterization of the prize's new benefactor.[31]

In addition to news of the Ruan sponsorship, Norman Borlaug announced that John S. Niederhauser, a plant breeder who led the development of blight-resistant potatoes, was the 1990 World Food Prize recipient. As in the past, the award would be handed out in a fall ceremony held at the Smithsonian Institution in Washington, D.C. John had agreed to contribute $50,000 toward this 1990 award, and then starting the following year, the organization would be moved to Iowa. John would take over as the new chairman of the Council of Advisors, while Kilpper would serve as executive director of the World Food Prize Foundation. The award ceremony was moved to Iowa as well.[32]

Borlaug was pleased with the prize's new midwestern headquarters. "Iowa is a lot better place for a food prize than New York [where General Foods was located]. They don't even know where food comes from in New York," he quipped. "The right setting for the World Food Prize is right here." John agreed: "Iowa has always been the heart and soul of

America. Having the World Food Prize in Iowa allows us to focus the world's attention on improving the global food system and the important role that education plays in achieving that end."[33]

Bringing the prize to Iowa garnered John plenty of praise. Chamber Federation president Mike Reagen observed: "For those of us who know John Ruan, this announcement does not come as a surprise. Throughout the years, he has proven to be a man of vision and compassion. We're honored that he chose Des Moines as the location for the World Food Prize." The *Des Moines Register* was equally generous: "It is fitting that the World Food Prize be associated with Iowa, the heart of the world's greatest agricultural region. In rescuing the prize and bringing it here, Ruan made a very significant gift to his home state, and to the world."[34]

When asked about the World Food Prize in relationship to his trade center plans, John simply said that the prize "certainly isn't going to hurt" the project. Clearly an understatement, he hoped the award would jump-start his latest try at the trade tower. John gave increasing attention to the skyscraper, but instead of moving forward, it suffered setback after setback. Although President Bush had expressed support for the idea, he was distracted by Saddam Hussein and the Persian Gulf War and then by a downturn in the economy. When Bush lost the 1992 presidential election to Bill Clinton, John lost a major supporter of federal funding for his proposed building. Two years later, his effort was further impeded when political novice Greg Ganske defeated Neal Smith for the central Iowa seat in the U. S. House of Representatives. Smith had been actively pursing congressional funding for John's trade center.[35]

None of these problems was fatal for the project, but the plan for the new version of the agricultural center did not capture the public's imagination the way it had several years earlier. John remained convinced it was a good idea, but as the 1990s wore on, he realized his dream might go unfulfilled. Still, John's enthusiasm for the World Food Prize continued.

Always the builder, John had grand visions for the prize and the events surrounding it, and he wanted to turn the festivities into something big, "like the Fourth of July for Iowa."[36] When the prize first moved to Iowa, John presided over the award ceremony at the Des Moines Marriott in October 1991. The winner that year was a nutritionist and public health doctor, Nevin Scrimshaw, and it was the first time the prize did not go to a scientist whose work had focused on increasing food production. In honoring Scrimshaw, the prize now recognized achievements beyond purely agricultural issues, much as Clausi had originally hoped.[37]

In addition to the award ceremony, John and his foundation continued the symposia that were held as part of the prize's annual program. These yearly conferences consisted of seminars and panels focused on issues surrounding food and featured experts in agriculture, nutrition, and population growth, as well as economics and public health. Previous recipients of the World Food Prize generally participated in these events as well.

John thought the first Iowa-held event was a good beginning, and over the next couple of years, he stepped up his promotional efforts, seeking to make the prize more visible and the problems of food scarcity better known. To do so, he used the same hardheaded tactics he had successfully applied in the business world. According to Michael Gartner, then part owner and editor of the *Ames Daily Tribune*, John "talks about the global food crisis with the same passion, the same badgering, [and] the same listen to me intensity that he once used in dealing with truck regulators or city councilmen."[38] Early on, John decided that he could increase the prize's prestige by adding prominent figures to the organization's council of advisers. He used his many connections and recruited former president Jimmy Carter and former secretary of defense and later head of the World Bank Robert McNamara. Later, John also persuaded former president George Bush as well as onetime secretary of transportation Elizabeth Dole to join the council.

At the same time, John and the foundation's executive director, Herman Kilpper, pondered ways of expanding the organization's agenda, and together with Norman Borlaug, they decided on publicizing the prize statewide by reaching out to Iowa's young people. In 1994, they established the World Food Prize Youth Institute. The program invited several student-teacher teams from high schools around the state to Des Moines for the symposium and award ceremony. While there, students interacted with leading scholars and World Food Prize laureates and heard panel discussions on the issues of food production and security. They also presented papers on a food-related topic of their choice—either written by themselves or a group of students from their home high school under the auspices of their faculty adviser—at the symposium. The papers were published in the *Youth Institute's Proceedings.*[39]

The Youth Institute proved immediately popular and shortly thereafter increased in size. In October 2002, more than 150 Iowa students and teachers as well as students from Ukraine, Brazil, and the International School in Washington, D.C., participated in the three-day, all-expenses-paid program focusing on issues of global water quality. Besides promoting the World Food Prize and increasing awareness of international food concerns, the institute soon established an annual internship program offering a select group of Iowa teenagers a hands-on experience with scientists in the field. Travis Franck, a student who had earlier participated in the institute, suggested the idea. Kilpper was instantly taken by the proposal. John was also enthusiastic, and the program began in 1998. Participants in the Youth Institute were eligible to apply, and those selected were sent overseas for summer internships, where they worked with world-renowned food scientists at research centers in developing countries. The first year, two Iowa high school students participated in the eight-week program: Amanda James of Creston traveled to Nairobi, Kenya, where she interned at the International Centre for Insect Physiology and Ecology, while Matthew Feldmann of Cedar Rapids spent his summer in Mexico City at the International Maize and Wheat Improvement Center.[40]

Many observers thought the prize's embracing of Iowa's young people was a smart move. James W. Hubbell Jr., for example, wrote John, saying he was "impressed with all of the students that are involved in this new outreach which you are sponsoring." He believed the internship would be "well received throughout the state" and was certain "it should be attractive to many students who have an interest in agriculture and its future." Hubbell was right. From its small beginning, the program grew, sending 13 high school students to research centers in developing countries in 2002. Soon widely regarded as the "most pres-tigious internship in the state," the program proved eye-opening for participants. Two former interns, for instance, explained its value. Meredith Nelson, a Bettendorf High School student who spent her internship in Mexico, said she gained a "greater perspective on life and a greater appreciation of the human experience," while Zachary Vos-burg of Hampton-Dumont High School found that in Kenya, "I have learned as much about myself as I have about food security." Beyond broadening the experience of select young Iowans, this program and the Youth Institute also encouraged some top Iowa students to con-sider careers in agriculture, food science, or other related disciplines.[41]

While John was delighted with the growing involvement of Iowa youth in World Food Prize activities, he was also interested in drawing more attention to the prize festivities themselves. He knew from expe-rience with his MS Golf Exhibition that celebrities had great appeal, and he sought out star power. At the prize's 10th anniversary in 1996, for instance, the award ceremony featured singer John Denver, who played to a packed Des Moines Civic Center.[42] The following year, Iowa-born opera singer Simon Estes performed, and Elizabeth Dole, then president of the American Red Cross, addressed the crowd. But it was John who had attracted the headlines that year. While in Wash-ington, D.C., in June 1997 for an American Trucking Associations (ATA) ceremony honoring him for his years of service by naming their new Capitol Hill complex the Ruan Center for Transportation, John announced that he was increasing the World Food Prize award from $200,000 to $250,000. Furthermore, he explained, he was working on an idea to assure that the prize continued well into the future and stayed in Iowa.[43]

A couple of months later, John unveiled his plan: he was giving $10 million to permanently endow the World Food Prize Foundation. He said, "This ensures that the World Food Prize will remain a Des Moines-based organization." Of the prize's future, he noted, "It's hard to fathom where it's going to be in 10 years, but I'm sure it's going to grow. Food is so basic; it's the lifeblood of everything else. You don't need a television, or electricity, or roads, but you've got to eat." The *Register* reported that the donation was "one of the largest single charitable gifts by an individual in state history" and cheered the act as one of "uncommon generosity . . . for a noble cause." The paper continued, "It's not unusual for big-time benefactors to begin looking for building projects when they're reached the top of successful careers, as John Ruan has. But rather than wanting to see his name carved in granite, Ruan has had a passion for assuring that the world's exploding population will somehow be fed in the future. He has invested generously of his time, talent, and his personal bank account to see that the job is done."[44]

This act seemed in line with what Larry Miller had suggested several years earlier when he noticed a change in John's demeanor. He believed his boss had started thinking about posterity. "Maybe it's the sense that he's running out of time that is causing him to pick up the pace," Miller surmised. John's advancing age and the additional time he was devoting to the World Food Prize led him to a major decision. In the summer of 1998, he turned over greater power to John III, advancing his son from vice chairman to chairman of RTMS. Although John maintained ultimate control of his business empire through his chairmanship of two holding companies—Ruan Financial Corporation and Ruan, Incorporated—the move was an unmistakable sign of change. The process of passing the torch from one Ruan generation to another was beginning. Furthermore, John gave his son full public backing, telling the *Des Moines Register* that John III had all "the tools, and I have no concern that he can't take what we've put together and do a lot better with it than I've done." With more than 30 years at the companies, John III felt he was "groomed, maybe even overgroomed," but the weight of the mantle was heavy, and he considered his father's comments "pretty tall marching orders."[45]

With the process of succession at the Ruan Companies under way, John continued to focus on the World Food Prize. With a solid foundation and new programs, it was becoming more widely known. John believed he had the organization moving in the right direction, but he remained interested in making it more visible, and he publicized it at every opportunity. Toward the end of the 1990s, John was receiving growing praise from friends and associates for his efforts on behalf of the prize. Tom Donohue, president of the United States Chamber of

Commerce and former head of the ATA, told John he should be "very proud" of the progress he had made with the prize, while David Vellinga, chief executive officer of Mercy Medical Center in Des Moines, wrote: "The citizens of Des Moines, and in fact, the State of Iowa, are fortunate, indeed, for your leadership. The [World Food Prize] award has given international acclaim to Des Moines, Iowa, as it will for generations to come."[46] In early January 2000, the American Farm Bureau Federation recognized John's accomplishments with the World Food Prize by giving him its Distinguished Service to Agriculture Award. John gratefully acknowledged the honor, but in characteristic fashion, he was still not satisfied with the stature of the World Food Prize.[47]

Meanwhile, when Herman Kilpper started to think about retirement in the late 1990s, John realized the importance of the upcoming hire: the new director would most likely lead the World Food Prize after he was gone. It was crucial, therefore, that he find the right person, someone who could "take the prize to the next level." At the same time, thousands of miles away in Southeast Asia, Ken Quinn was contemplating retirement from the State Department.[48]

Quinn had grown up in Dubuque and had attended Loras College there. After graduate work at Marquette University and the University of Maryland, he joined the American Foreign Service, beginning his career as a rural development officer in Vietnam. This job was followed by a stint on Henry Kissinger's National Security Council staff. From 1978 through 1982, Quinn took advantage of a special program giving federal employees an opportunity to work for state or local governments, and he returned to Iowa to join Governor Robert Ray's administration. Quinn played a major role in the governor's Indochinese refugee resettlement program and served as the executive director of Iowa Shares, a humanitarian program that sent food as well as doctors, nurses, and medical supplies to Cambodia. Then it was back to State Department duty, with assignments in Austria, the Philippines, and Cambodia, where he served as the U.S. ambassador from 1996 to 1999.[49]

While working in Des Moines, Quinn had impressed a number of people who had followed his subsequent career. When word got out that Kilpper was preparing to step down, Michael Gartner, Mike

Reagen, and former governor Ray all suggested Quinn as a possible successor. Encouraged by these recommendations, Kilpper contacted Quinn, and after several telephone conversations, he arranged to meet the ambassador during one of his trips back to the United States. The two enjoyed a good discussion, but Quinn was hesitant about heading the World Food Prize.[50]

John met the candidate as well and was impressed with his international experience, political connections, and links to Iowa. "He was," thought John, "a perfect fit for the prize." After conferring with John III, who agreed with his father, the two Ruans worked to hire the experienced diplomat. John III took the lead, finally persuading Quinn to take the position over dinner in Washington, D.C. For his part, Quinn had never sold the home he had purchased in Des Moines when he was with the Ray administration, and he saw great potential for the prize. Furthermore, he had found his first state department assignment, working with farmers in Vietnam, rewarding. While there, he had introduced new technology that increased their crop yields and lifted many Vietnamese out of poverty. Quinn remembered these efforts as fulfilling and "wanted to have the opportunity to make that kind of difference again and be involved with something that brings about change." John III convinced Quinn that he could effect such change with the World Food Prize, and the former ambassador accepted the position as executive director of the foundation in August 1999.[51]

Quinn took up his new position in January 2000. Charged with raising the standing of the prize, the new director kept a book about the Nobel Prize in his office as a reminder that the goal was to make the World Food Prize "the equivalent of the Nobel Prize for food and agriculture."[52] Shortly after retuning to Des Moines, Quinn used his diplomatic connections for the benefit of the prize. In April, he arranged for the World Food Prize to cosponsor one of 60 U.S. Department of State town meetings held around the country that year. Convened in Des Moines at the Marriott Hotel, the conference was titled "Refugees and Immigration: Humanitarian Response and Work-force Implications" and gave participants an opportunity to examine the state's successes and failures in dealing with recent immigrants.

Later, he moved the laureate award ceremony, which had been held the previous year at Hoyt Sherman Auditorium, to the golden-domed State Capitol. "By holding the award presentation at the Iowa State Capitol, one of the most beautiful buildings in North America," Quinn explained, "we took an important step in the direction of emulating the Nobel Prize, which is presented in the grandeur of one of Europe's most elegant buildings."[53]

This was only the beginning of Quinn's aggressive promotional efforts. Following the ceremony at the capitol, he looked to heightening international awareness of the prize. On October 16, World Food Day, the two recipients who shared the 2000 World Food Prize, Dr. Surinder Vasal of India and Dr. Evangelina Villegas of Mexico, were honored at a luncheon for the United Nations diplomatic corps at the Rockefeller Center in New York City. Richard Holbrooke, U.S. ambassador to the United Nations, addressed the gathering about problems of world hunger, while Dan Glickman, U.S. secretary of agriculture, also spoke about such issues and paid homage to the World Food Prize: "[It] is an important recognition of those who have dedicated their professional lives to narrowing the gap between the world's nutritional haves and have nots."[54]

In the spring of 2002, Quinn and the World Food Prize Foundation persuaded the Iowa State Legislature to pass a law designating October 16 as Norman Borlaug/World Food Prize Day in Iowa.[55] This move heightened visibility of the World Food Prize and was part of a strategy to expand its offerings beyond the laureate ceremony and symposium into a monthlong series of activities and events held in various locations throughout the state. Later that October, the World Food Prize offered the more expansive program, which included lectures by a number of past laureates, panel discussions, art shows, museum exhibits, plays, and documentaries carried on Iowa Public Television.

During his first three years at the foundation, Quinn made great strides in raising the visibility of the World Food Prize, and many observers thought he was well on the way to his goal of making the food prize "the signature event for the state of Iowa." Michael Gartner, for one, believed he could do it. "He's just a very smart guy," Gartner noted, "and he's got a little bit of P. T. Barnum in him. He's a showman and a promoter as well as a true intellectual." Norman Borlaug was also delighted with Quinn's leadership, explaining that the former ambassador had "lifted it to the level that I never thought was possible." John was impressed as well, although he worried about the lavish spending Quinn's efforts required. Nonetheless, he and his family promised more monetary support when an opportunity arose that could increase the profile of the prize.[56]

After the downtown Des Moines Public Library decided to erect a new facility, John Ruan III and Ken Quinn turned their attention toward acquiring the 1903 building on the Des Moines River. Kilpper had considered the library building as a possible home for the prize organization, but plans for a new library did not really come together until Quinn was on board. Quinn believed that if it were fully restored to its original grandeur, the structure would serve as a magnificent headquarters for the World Food Prize. Quinn explained, "Having a headquarters in a distinguished building parallels the way the Nobel Prize operates in Stockholm. If the building lends great dignity and prestige to the prize, it becomes a solid foundation for the prize, making it even more essential to the community." Besides housing foundation offices, the facility would include a hall honoring World Food Prize laureates and other Iowa agricultural leaders as well as changing exhibits on loan from the Smithsonian Institution. Working closely with John III, and with John's approval, the World Food Prize Foundation secured a promise of $5 million from Polk County for the project. Then, during the 2001 laureate ceremony, John III announced that the family was pledging $5 million for the undertaking. Beyond this $10 million, prize officials were seeking an additional $13 million in federal grants needed to complete the renovations and establish an endowment for the building. Yet federal money was not immediately forthcoming, and even as ground was broken for the new Des Moines Public Library in late 2002, the future of housing the World Food Prize Foundation in the old library building remained in doubt.[57]

As the World Food Prize grew in prestige, John's health declined. Several months after Jayne's death in 1992, John experienced a slight tremor in his right hand. Shortly thereafter, his facial expressions began growing more rigid. These conditions worsened after Miller's death and were followed by John's increasing tendency to lose his balance and fall. While physicians debated over the diagnosis, the symptoms continued. Finally Dr. Fred Ball, a neurologist, decided John was suffering from Parkinson's disease and began to treat him for the neurological disorder.[58]

Medication soon masked the most noticeable symptoms, but John was clearly slowing down. Age, emotional trauma, and now Parkinson's disease took their toll, and John gradually started cutting back on his unforgiving work schedule. He still went down to the office early each morning, but he started leaving earlier in the afternoon. At the same time, friends and family perceived a softening in John's personality. Bob Mickle remarked that John's once hot temper was cooling: "He used to be a lot more short-tempered. It didn't take long and he was pounding his fist on the table. Now he doesn't do that as much." Others noticed that John's playful sense of humor, although always present, was becoming more pronounced. Friends were regularly treated to funny stories, limericks, and jokes. And John's interest in music started showing through as well. Once rarely displayed, his piano playing became a common occurrence, and he also developed a reputation for singing in public. He was most often heard crooning "You're a Heavenly Thing," usually to wife Betty but also to friends on various social occasions. Sometimes, while out at restaurants, John even serenaded the wait staff. One day in the spring of 2001, for instance, he and Betty were out for a drive with Ely Brewer, an executive with the Boy Scouts, and good friends Ralph and Charlotte Schlenker when they stopped for lunch at the Town and Country Café in Madrid, a small town 25 miles north of Des Moines. While there, John surprised his waitress by singing to her, and the spectacle was reported by columnist Marc Hansen in the *Des Moines Register*.[59]

In general, John was spending greater amounts of time with friends and apparently appreciating it all the more. He now held dinner parties regularly, but it was the birthday celebrations he hosted that were noteworthy. During months when several of his friends or colleagues had birthdays, John gathered them together for dinner, most often at his Marriott Hotel. The event soon took on a familiar format. John went around the table and asked each person celebrating a birthday to say a few words. He responded with a funny quip or two and then gave each a birthday present. The gifts were all the same, presented in the same manner, and yet each was customized to the particular individual. Standing next to each honoree, John threw a wad of crisp, new, dollar bills—the amount always corresponded with the person's age—into the air where they fluttered down around the recipient. He always enjoyed this trademark stunt, and newcomers to the event were captivated by the cascading dollars.[60]

More socializing did not mean that John gave up working, however, and even in the twilight of his career, he remained keenly interested in the disposition of his companies. Yet as the 1990s progressed, John turned his considerable wherewithal to philanthropic activities. Like his earlier involvement in the development of downtown Des Moines, the MS charity work and the World Food Prize originally appealed to him because of personal interests. Later, they both became priorities as John developed a genuine concern for each of the causes.

For decades, he had focused chiefly on building and then expanding his companies. It wasn't until he bought a majority share of Bankers Trust that he really began to think outside the narrow confines of his own business interests. The bank's main branch and offices were located in Des Moines's declining downtown, and John realized that the bank's prospects were closely tied to that of the central business district. First to protect his own interests and then for the good of the community, John became involved in downtown redevelopment, leading the way with the Ruan Center. As his concern for the business district mounted, John's participation in downtown civic groups increased, and he was championing projects such as the skywalks and the convention center that clearly benefited the entire community.

In a similar fashion, his battle against MS began for personal reasons. He embraced the cause because the disease had struck both his wife and his daughter. But his commitment to the fight deepened even after his family could no longer derive direct benefits from his work. From the funding of research to the founding of the Ruan Neurology Clinic, John's battle against MS helped victims of the disorder in Iowa and throughout the Midwest.

John's ties to the World Food Prize had comparable origins. Initially his support for the award was related to his long-held dream of building a world trade center. While that idea gradually faded away, John's affinity for the prize and the significant work it honored deepened. Clearly, he agreed with former president Jimmy Carter's position. "The World Food Prize," Carter said, "does three things. It recognizes achievement, inspires others to do greater work, and acquaints the public with the importance of providing high-quality food to the world's growing population."[61] By the late 1990s, the international prize was taking up a majority of John's time, and through this commitment, his influence was felt worldwide.

Epilogue

A sunny and mild afternoon in January 2002 found John Ruan relaxing by the pool at his North Palm Beach home. In his signature bow tie, the aging Iowa business legend was sipping a glass of merlot and reminiscing with Betty and friends about his eventful past. The conversation flowed freely, and John offered many colorful anecdotes, but time and again, he returned to a simple explanation for his success: "Things just happened one after another, and I just took opportunities when they came."[1] Never a reflective person, John had always looked forward, pondering the expansion of a current business or considering an entirely new idea. Now a few weeks shy of his 88th birthday, he was in the process of thinking back and taking stock, something he had gradually begun to do over the course of the 1990s. Such review had been further prompted by the deaths of several close friends and his diminishing health. At the same time, John continued to relinquish more and more control of the empire he had built over the past 70 years.

Ever since the untimely death of his daughter in 1992, John became increasingly sensitive to the loss of those close to him. Inevitably, as he grew older, more of his longtime colleagues passed away, but 2000 was especially difficult. That year, three important figures in his life died.

In January, 74-year-old John Chrystal, former president and then chairman of John's Bankers Trust, died of cancer. A farmer turned banker with an interest in agricultural economics, Chrystal was widely known for his frequent trips to the Soviet Union and later Russia where he advised state officials on agricultural policy. When asked by the *Des Moines Register* for his reaction to Chrystal's death, John said simply, "Iowans will not only miss him; the world will miss him."[2] Several months later, John honored his friend's international efforts by establishing an annual John Chrystal Internship Award at the World Food Prize for the student whose summer internship work best exemplified "Mr. Chrystal's lifelong commitment to improving international understanding and cooperation."[3]

In April, John was struck by an even sharper blow when 95-year-old Bob Root, one of his oldest and dearest friends, died. Their rela-

tionship dated back to the late 1930s, when the two met as neighbors
in Des Moines's south-of-Grand neighborhood. An investment banker
by profession, Root eventually joined John at Ruan Transport in 1943,
remaining there until retiring in 1978. Shortly afterward, he began
working at Bankers Trust, and his longevity at the Ruan companies
once led John to joke that he kept Root on the payroll "because he
knows too much about me."[4] Unlike Chrystal, whom John honored in
death, Root had been repaid for his many years of loyal service by
John's keeping him employed in the bank's personal banking department. Root loved the job and worked at his Bankers Trust desk five
days a week until shortly before his death.[5]

Later that spring, 96-year-old Joe Rosenfield died of congestive
heart failure. John had first become acquainted with Rosenfield in
1937 when the then young attorney handled a labor case for his trucking company. After practicing law for a number of years, Rosenfield
joined Younkers Department Stores, which had earlier been merged
with his family's retail business. Over the years, Rosenfield became an
adviser and mentor to many leading figures in Des Moines. John was
among that group, and he grew particularly close to the lawyer turned
merchant and benefactor. Rosenfield led John into a number of major
investments outside of trucking, and it was his tip that eventually put
him onto buying the lucrative Intel stock. As with Chrystal, John was
interested in honoring his close friend, and plans for a memorial were
developed even before Rosenfield died.[6]

Several months earlier, during the 2000 Iowa caucus, John and Des
Moines attorney Steve Roberts began talking about Rosenfield.
Roberts, a past president of the local Boy Scouts Council, told John
that when Rosenfield was 12, he and his mother had made arrangements for his scout troop to meet and be photographed with Theodore
Roosevelt, who was in Des Moines in 1918. Eighty years later, actor
John Davidson, who was touring as Theodore Roosevelt in the one-
man play "Bully, An Adventure with Teddy Roosevelt," contacted Ely
Brewer, the executive director of the Boy Scouts Mid-Iowa Council,
and asked if Roosevelt had any connections with central Iowa. Brewer
mentioned many ties and faxed him the 1918 photograph of the president with the Boy Scouts. When Davidson arrived in Des Moines for
the play, he agreed to sit in as Roosevelt with current Boy Scouts and

reenact the photograph. Everything was done to re-create the original, except that Rosenfield, who had been in the first photograph, joined Davidson's Roosevelt and the young scouts for the 1998 version. The Mid-Iowa Council had a plaque containing the two photographs made for Rosenfield, and Roberts invited John to go along when he and Brewer presented the gift.[7]

Rosenfield loved the present. He identified all but one of the boys in the 1918 photo and talked about each one. During the conversation, Rosenfield discussed his scouting experience, going to summer camp at central Iowa's Camp Mitigwa, and claimed he was probably the "oldest Boy Scout." When it was time to leave, Rosenfield asked Brewer to hang the picture for him. The three visitors then walked out of the apartment, and John, clearly interested, asked about Rosenfield being the oldest scout. Brewer said it would be difficult to verify but thought he could easily be called the council's "longest tenured scout." John liked the sound of that, and it gave him an idea. He said, "I want to do something for Joe. He likes the scouting program and I like him." In the car on the way back to the Ruan Center, John continued, "Can you get a plaque or something for him saying that he is the old-est scout?" Brewer nodded; he was glad to help and promised a list of several ideas from which John could choose. "Great," John replied. "I want this to be something nice, something between 50 and 100." From the backseat, Roberts raised an eyebrow: "You mean $50,000 to $100,000, John?" "Yes," was the reply.[8]

A month later, John picked what he wanted. The memorial hon-oring Joe Rosenfield would stand at the main entrance to Camp Mi-tigwa, a Boy Scout camp about 30 miles northwest of Des Moines. It would consist of a new sign for the camp set behind a recasting of the life-size statue called "The Boy Scout" originally sculpted in 1914 by artist R. Tait McKenzie. After plans were finalized, John visited with Rosenfield. He was now bedridden and could no longer talk, but after John described the project for the camp entrance, Rosenfield responded by squeezing his hand. That was the last time John saw Rosenfield alive.[9]

Although the memorial was not quite completed, John asked for a preview of the statute, and one morning in the spring of 2001, Brewer took him, along with Betty and friends Ralph and Charlotte

Schlenker, to Mitigwa. As they approached the site, John grew excited. "Betty," he exclaimed, "that's it right there, and it looks just like those boys told me it was going to look." He got out of the car, went up to the statue, and put his arm around it. Then, as if actually talking to his departed friend, John said, "Joe, you're looking pretty good."[10]

Honoring these friends made John feel better, but their loss gave him pause, and he began to consider his own mortality. This reflection led to frequent musings over his personal history and amplified John's interest in his ancestors. His efforts at connecting to this past had increased in recent decades and included several treks to the Caribbean island of St. Croix, where he visited the remains of the family's sugar plantation, Hannah's Rest. He could trace his family's line back to the late 1730s, when William Ruan (his fourth-great-grandfather) arrived on the island. Although believed to have come from England, possibly from French Huguenot stock, William Ruan's origins were murky. In the early 1990s, therefore, while on a business trip to Europe, John stopped in England and France, where he made inquiries into his family's background. In England, he went to the medieval parish of Ruan Major in Cornwall, hoping for information about his ancestors. He found nothing definitive, but while visiting the local church, he struck up a conversation with the caretaker's wife. Fascinated that her visitor's last name was Ruan, the woman gave John an old door knocker, which she claimed was taken from the nearby Ruan Castle before it had been torn down. Whether or not he had any familial connection to the former castle, John enjoyed the story and put the artifact on display in the family room of his Des Moines home.[11]

So intrigued was he by his roots, in fact, that John had his two oldest grandchildren, Jonathan Ruan Fletcher and John Ruan IV, research and write a family history. The result was a 200-plus-page manuscript following the Ruan line and its branches as far back as possible. Unfortunately, gaps in the record meant that no authoritative answers about the Ruan origins were forthcoming.[12]

Although his attempts at tracing the family's European lineage had failed, John's mounting interest in his heritage took him in other directions as well. He visited his hometown of Beacon more often, even though his boyhood home had been razed long ago. Similarly, he frequently drove by the family's old home on Ninth Street in Des Moines, sometimes taking his children and grandchildren with him. Ultimately, working with John III and consultant Bob Mickle, John purchased the home in 2002. Once the structure was acquired, plans for its future, including restoring the house for use by the company or the community or demolishing it and building a park on the site, were considered.[13]

Likewise, John decided to organize the many boxes and binders of documents, photographs, and newspaper clippings covering the development of his companies. Haphazardly collected and categorized since the 1960s, the material was handed over to Bill Giles—recently retired Ruan vice president of research and engineering—in 2000 for the task of arranging the collection into a series of leather-bound scrapbooks.[14]

Such review of one's life was not unusual for a person John's age. Nor was his desire of keeping management of the companies in the family after he was gone. Yet his moves in transferring power had been slow. The vast majority of his life had been devoted to these enterprises, and giving up control, even to his son, was hard for him. Des Moines developer Bill Knapp noted, "It's difficult for John to turn over the reins. He's a very take charge guy." Although he ultimately planned to pass control to John III, he had no intention of stepping aside until declining health forced him to do so. By 2000, however, the effects of advancing age and Parkinson's were finally catching up with him. Even though habit and the old drive kept John going to the office early every morning, his eldest son gradually took on greater responsibility.[15]

Symbolic of the changing of the guard was John III's attempted rescue of the Des Moines-based airline AccessAir. Founded by former Eastern Airlines executive Roger Ferguson, AccessAir was a widely hailed local effort to lower the high fares major carriers charged in the noncompetitive Des Moines market by offering an attractively priced alternative. The upstart airline opened for business in 1999. It initially provided nonstop flights from Des Moines to New York and Los Angeles and planned to extend its service to other major metropolitan areas. Unfortunately, after "management missteps and low ridership, [the airline] suspended regular passenger flights and filed for bankruptcy from creditors in November after only 10 months of operation."[16]

The Ruan companies had originally invested $3 million in Access-Air, and John III still thought that the airline was a good idea for the community. For the first time, he, rather than his father, was out in the public eye, making the family's big decisions. With John's assent, John III worked out a plan for the revival of AccessAir. Under the proposal, the Ruan family and its companies would put up $12 million needed to get AccessAir back in operation, and John III would take over as the airline's chairman. The *Des Moines Register* believed AccessAir's "original goal of offering competitive airfares" was important and thought John III "deserved a ton of credit" for taking on "the challenge of resuscitating the bankrupt airline when most everyone else was prepared to write it off as a failure." Similarly, former Des Moines insurance executive David Hurd said that if AccessAir succeeded, John III would "be a hero." So important was the endeavor, in fact, that Hurd assumed John III would be held in high regard even if the company failed.[17]

AccessAir reopened for business in November 2000 with flights to Chicago. Much as it tried, the reorganized airline could not "overcome image problems, high debt and continued low ridership," and in February 2001, it shut down for good. Although disturbed by the airline's closure and the loss of millions in Ruan money, John was proud of his son's efforts on behalf of the community.[18]

This move by John III into a greater leadership role at the Ruan companies did not go unnoticed and prompted many comparisons with his father. Whereas John had been described as aggressive, tough, smart, and shrewd, people saw John III as bright but quiet and thoughtful. Michael Gartner agreed the two had "totally different personalities" but thought they had "the same smarts" and "the same love of Des Moines." As John III settled into running the Ruan enterprises, additional comparisons were inevitable, but for the time being, observers agreed that the two possessed different skills and that John was leaving some very large shoes to fill.[19]

As the torch was being passed, John's lifetime of achievement was being recognized. In September 2001, he was given the Iowa Award, the state's highest citizen award. The prize had been created in 1948 to recognize "Iowans for outstanding service in the fields of science, medicine, law, religion, social welfare, education, agriculture, industry, government and other public service," and John was only the 17th person ever to receive the honor.[20]

The presentation took place at the governor's ceremonial offices in the Iowa State Capitol. There Governor Vilsack addressed the crowd: "John Ruan is a testimony to how dreams can come true in this state. Whether it's being a tremendous business leader, someone who has invested time and energy building this capital community and this state, someone who understands the importance of medical research, someone who has a world vision. Very rarely do you find those combinations in a single man." When John spoke, the promoter in him could not help but comment on the issues surrounding the World Food Prize. Briefly talking about global population outstripping food production, he told the audience, "If we don't change, there will be nothing left of the planet. So we've got to get on it now." Later his somber tone changed. After the governor hung the medal around his neck, John's sense of humor emerged. With a twinkle in his eye, he quipped, "I thought this was going to be cash."[21]

Several months later, John received yet another tribute, this time by Iowa State University. The institution he attended for one year before being forced to drop out now acknowledged his long service to the school and the state of Iowa generally. At ISU's December 2001 graduation ceremony, John was awarded an honorary doctorate of humane letters, finally donning the cap and gown that circumstances had kept him from wearing 65 years earlier.

The timing of the awards could not have been better, for over the next few months, it became clear that John's health was failing. Late one morning in July 2002, John had already been at his office for several hours when he complained of being dizzy and disoriented. Those around him noticed that he was slurring his speech and had great difficulty walking. Friends and family feared he had had a stroke, and after consulting with his local physician, John was rushed to the Mayo Clinic in Rochester, Minnesota, for tests and treatment. Doctors found no evidence of a stroke and decided that the symptoms were caused by transient ischemic attacks—these episodes are caused by disruption of blood to the brain, but unlike strokes, the symptoms usually last less than 24 hours and do not cause brain damage—and advancing Parkinson's disease. After several weeks of additional tests and adjustments in his medication, John returned to Des Moines, where he spent another few weeks in rehabilitation at Mercy Hospital. This health episode proved to be a life-altering event, and when he finally went home in August 2002, John's world was forever changed.

The man who had spent all his adult life working and was always on the job at his Ruan Center before dawn was now assisted by full-time attendants around the clock, and he was largely confined to his home. Rare were appearances at the office, and for the first time since beginning the John Ruan MS Charity in 1975, John missed its annual benefit dinner. Similarly, he did not attend the World Food Prize laureate ceremony that October. Frustrated by his situation, he often repeated the adage, "Getting old is hell."[22]

Still, his active mind did not rest, and John set up shop at the head of his dining room table, where he spent several hours each day. Here he spread out piles of yellow notepads, and as he had done for years, he jotted down ideas about the Ruan foundations, charities, and the companies. His hopes for these entities now mingled with digressions about their origins and the long way he had come from hauling gravel in 1932. As the autumn days grew shorter, John could look back on a lifetime of achievement. The *Des Moines Register* certainly thought such reflection was well deserved. He was, the paper observed, "a great Iowan" who with his various businesses and philanthropic work had made "his community, his state, his nation, and the world a better place."[23] Even though looking back had become more common and from time to time brought a fleeting smile to his face, John remained focused on the future. Where, he wondered, would his companies be down the road? How should RTMS navigate through the continuing poor economy? What would expansion mean for the bank? Where would the breakthroughs occur in the fight against MS? What was in store for downtown Des Moines? And how, he mused, would the growing global population be fed?

Much of his life had recently changed, but John found solace in his old habit of working, pondering future possibilities and considering new opportunities. That had always been his way.

Notes

Introduction

1. Rosenfield quoted by John Ruan, interview by author, Des Moines, Iowa, 17 April 2002; Jan Gillum, interview by author, Des Moines, Iowa, 17 April 2002.

2. From Joseph Schumpeter, *Theory of Economic Development* (Cambridge: Harvard University Press, 1934), as quoted in Jameson Doig, *Empire on the Hudson: Entrepreneurial Vision and Political Power at the Port of New York Authority* (New York: Columbia University Press, 2001), 19.

3. Quoted in Matt Kelley, "Turning Gravel into Gold: The Amazing Enterprises and Spirit of John Ruan," *Brighter Ideas,* April 2001, 8.

4. Quotation from *Des Moines Register,* 8 October 1976.

5. Cownie's story is recounted in *Des Moines Register,* 4 March 1984. Ruan quotation from *Des Moines Business Record,* 13-19 March 1989.

6. Quoted in Kelley, "Gravel into Gold," 9.

7. Ralph Schlenker, interview by author, Indianola, Iowa, 30 November 2001.

8. John Ruan, interview by author, Des Moines, Iowa, 12 September 2001. Ruan's statement about opportunities is taken from *Des Moines Register,* 14 January 1990.

9. Sam Kalainov, interview by author, Des Moines, Iowa, 30 May 2002. Gillum quotation from *Des Moines Register,* 4 March 1984.

10. Richard Wilkey, interview by author, West Des Moines, Iowa, 21 February 2002; Bill Knapp quotation from *Des Moines Business Record,* 13-19 March 1989; Michael Gartner quotation from *USA Today,* 20 October 1993.

11. Mickle quotation from *Des Moines Register,* 18 October 1981.

12. Walter Neumann, interview by author, Des Moines, Iowa, 30 November 2001.

13. Mooney quotation from *Des Moines Register,* 27 January 1991; Houser quotation from *Des Moines Register,* 1 September 1985; Robert Ray's comment from "Ruan International Companies," Ruan Companies pamphlet, circa 2000.

14. Norman Borlaug, interview by author, Des Moines, Iowa, 6 February 2002; Elaine Szymoniak, interview by author, Des Moines, Iowa, 16 August 2002.

15. Ibid. Ruan quotations from Ruan, interview, 17 April 2002; and *Des Moines Business Record,* 4-10 June 1990.

16. Ruan quotation from *Des Moines Business Record,* 28 May 2001.

17. Quotation from *Des Moines Register,* 23 August 1998.

18. "The Richest Man in Town," *Worth,* March 2002, 76-77; quotation about Ruan getting what he wanted is from Szymoniak, interview. The *Worth* story was soon followed up by a piece in the *Register* by David Elbert, challenging Ruan's position as the city's wealthiest person. Elbert noted that John Pappajohn, a Des Moines venture capitalist, was estimated to have a fortune worth $1 billion; see *Des Moines Register,* 11 March 2002, sec. D, p. 1.

19. Bill Guy, telephone conversation with author, 7 December 2001.

20. John Ruan, telephone conversation with author, 22 January 2003; B. J. Lester, telephone conversation with author, 22 January 2003; Jan Gillum, telephone conversation with author, 22 January 2003.

Chapter 1

1. See Mark Twain, *The Adventures of Tom Sawyer* (New York: Viking, 2000); Mark Twain, *The Adventures of Huckleberry Finn* (New York: Penguin, 1986); Sherwood Anderson, *Winesburg, Ohio* (New York: Penguin, 1978); Sinclair Lewis, *Main Street* (New York: Bantam Books, 1996); Hamlin Garland, *A Son of the Middle Border* (New York: Macmillan, 1962). For more on writers of the period and their portrayals of small-town life, see Lewis Atherton, *Main Street on the Middle Border* (Bloomington: Indiana University Press, 1954).

2. See Dorothy Schwieder, *Black Diamonds: Life and Work in Iowa's Coal Mining Communities, 1895-1925* (Ames: Iowa State University Press, 1983), 118-19, 168; and Dorothy Schwieder, Joseph Hraba, and Elmer Schwieder, *Buxton: Work and Racial Equality in a Coal Mining Community* (Ames: Iowa State University Press, 1987), 198-99.

3. Tom Morain, *Prairie Grass Roots: An Iowa Small Town in the Early Twentieth Century* (Ames: Iowa State University Press, 1988), 56. On Ruan's position as Beacon's only physician, see *Colman's Oskaloosa City Directory, 1914-15* (Oskaloosa, IA: Oskaloosa Herald Co.), 337. The 1895 census listed three doctors practicing in Beacon; see D. Schwieder, *Black Diamonds,* 171.

4. John Ruan IV and Jonathan Ruan Fletcher, "The Family of John Ruan," typescript, 1996, 123, 153-57, in John Ruan Papers, private collection held by John Ruan, Des Moines, Iowa [hereafter cited as Ruan Papers].

5. John A. Ruan, "My Little Country School," handwritten, undated poem, Ruan Papers.

6. Central Medical College was founded in St. Joseph, Missouri, in 1881 as Northwestern Medical College. In 1895, several members of its faculty left to create Central Medical College, and Northwestern Medical College soon closed. Central Medical merged with Ensworth Medical College in 1906 but then closed in 1914. For the history of Central Medical College, see *St. Joseph News-Press,* 29 April 1916 and 5 June 1983; and Howard Conrad, ed., *Encyclopedia of the History of Missouri,* vol. 4 (New York: Southern History Company, 1901), 593. For Ruan and the medical school, see *Oskaloosa Weekly Herald,* 23 February 1888 and 23 September 1899; and Ruan and Fletcher, "Family of John Ruan," 157.

7. *Oskaloosa Herald*, 13 July 1904.

8. Ruan and Fletcher, "Family of John Ruan," 109-10; and John Ruan, interview by author, Des Moines, Iowa, 5 April 2001.

9. Ruan, interview, 5 April 2001; "John Ruan Biography," undated typescript, Ruan Papers; Marybeth Hoffman, interview by author, Oskaloosa, Iowa, 31 March 2001; John Bedillon, interview by author, Oskaloosa, Iowa, 31 March 2001; J. A. Ruan, *She Always Had a Date* (Chicago: Success Music Company, 1906), in Ruan Papers.

10. Atherton quoted in Morain, *Prairie Grass Roots*, 57.

11. See *Oskaloosa Weekly Herald*, 30 March 1916; "Attention, Voters!" handbill, Ruan Papers.

12. Ruan, interview, 5 April 2001.

13. For women and their position in society, see Dorothy Schwieder, *Iowa: The Middle Land* (Ames: Iowa State University Press, 1996), 159-60. For more on Rachel Ruan, see Bedillon, interview; Marie Ogden Ahlbrecht, telephone conversation with author, 11 April 2001; Rex Jenkins, telephone conversation with author, 4 April 2001; and Hoffman, interview.

14. Quotation comes from Ahlbrecht, telephone conversation. See also Hoffman, interview; and Dorothy Nott, interview by author, Monrovia, California, 12 March 2001.

15. "John Ruan Biography"; Ruan, interview, 5 April 2001; Ahlbrecht, telephone conversation. Relatives living in or around Beacon during John's childhood included grandmother Elizabeth Llewellyn, grandfather Thomas Llewellyn, grandfather William H. K. Ruan, and aunt Golda (Ruan) and uncle Ora Carrell.

16. Ahlbrecht, telephone conversation; "John Ruan's Recollections," 11 March 1997, typescript, Ruan Papers.

17. Bedillon, interview; "John Ruan Biography."

18. "John Ruan Biography"; Ruan, interview, 5 April 2001; Ahlbrecht, telephone conversation.

19. The memories of Hoover are taken from Atherton, *Main Street*, 200. On Ruan and the family farm, see Ruan, interview, 5 April 2001; "John Ruan Biography"; and *Oskaloosa Herald*, 14 September 1929. Quotation from John Ruan, interview by author, Des Moines, Iowa, 31 July 2001.

20. Ruan, interview, 5 April 2001; Ahlbrecht, telephone conversation. See also letters from N. A. Reinert to Dr. J. A. Ruan, 11 December 1917 and 11 April 1918, and Catlett-Davis Oil Corporation to Mr. J. A. Ruan, 10 May 1919, Ruan Papers.

21. Ruan, interview, 5 April 2001.

22. Ibid.

23. See Calvin W. Coquillette, "The Struggle to Preserve Iowa's State Banking System, 1920-1933," *Annals of Iowa* 59 (winter 2001): 52-54; and Ruan, interview, 5 April 2001.

24. Ahlbrecht, telephone conversation; Ruan, interview, 5 April 2001.

25. Ruan, interview, 5 April 2001; Marie Ahlbrecht, telephone conversation with author, 22 January 2003; and "Draft copy of information on Model T," Ruan Papers.

26. "John Ruan Biography"; Ruan, interviews, 5 April and 5 June 2001; Rex Jenkins, telephone conversation with author, 4 April 2001; "Maroon Memories," Oskaloosa High School Yearbooks, 1928, 28, 36; 1929, 28; 1930, 21.

27. On baseball in small towns, see Atherton, *Main Street*, 200-202. See also Jenkins, telephone conversation; and Ruan, interview, 5 April 2001.

28. "John Ruan Biography." On the advent of radio and its impact, see Hugh G. J. Aitken, *The Continuous Wave: Technology and American Radio, 1900-1932* (Princeton, NJ: Princeton University Press, 1985); Erik Barnouw, *A Tower of Babel* (New York: Oxford University Press, 1966); and Christopher Sterling and John Kittross, *A Concise History of American Broadcasting* (Belmont, CA: Wadsworth, 1978).

29. Transcript of John Ruan Interview for Des Moines Oral History Project, 12 August 1999, Ruan Papers; "John Ruan Biography"; Ruan, interviews, 5 April and 31 July 2001.

30. Ibid. For a listing of Dr. McClean, see *Polk's Des Moines City Directory, 1931* (Des Moines, IA: R. L. Polk and Co., 1930), 647.

31. *Des Moines Register*, 10 September 1998.

Chapter 2

1. John Ruan, interviews by author, Des Moines, Iowa, 18 and 31 July 2001; *Polk's Des Moines City Directory, 1931* (Des Moines, IA: R. L. Polk and Co., 1930), 647; *Des Moines Register*, 14 January 1931; *Oskaloosa Time-Globe*, 15 January 1931; *Annals of the Grand Lodge of Iowa A. F. & A. M.* 40 (1932): 318.

2. "John Ruan Memorabilia from Birth to Present," undated typescript, John Ruan Papers, private collection held by John Ruan, Des Moines, Iowa [hereafter cited as Ruan Papers]; *Polk's Des Moines City Directory, 1933* (Des Moines, IA: R. L. Polk and Co., 1932), 384.

3. Quotation from "John Ruan's Recollections," 11 March 1997, typescript, Ruan Papers. See also "John Ruan Biography," undated typescript, Ruan Papers; *Des Moines Register*, 4 March 1984; *Supplement to the North High Oracle* 23 (June 1931): 17; and Ruan, interview, 18 July 2001.

4. Quotation from *Des Moines Register*, 10 September 1998. See also John Ruan, interview by author, 26 July 2001.

5. Larry Hanes, telephone conversation with author, 23 May 2001; Al DeCarlo, telephone conversation with author, 23 May 2001; Ruan, interview, 18 July 2001; *Supplement to the North High Oracle*, 25; *Des Moines Register*, 4 July 1996.

6. See "John Ruan Biography" and *Des Moines Register*, 19 May 2001.

7. Ibid.

8. John Ruan, interviews by author, Des Moines, Iowa, 5 April 2001 and 5 October 2002; *Polk's Directory, 1933*, 689.

9. See John Ruan's class schedule for fall 1931; *Iowa State College of Agriculture and Mechanical Arts Official Publication Catalogue, 1930-31* 28 (12 March 1930): 190-91; *Iowa State College of Agriculture and Mechanical Arts Official Publication Catalogue, 1931-32* 29 (25 February 1931); fall grades for John Ruan, Iowa State College, 1931; and various exams and papers from Ruan's year at college; all in Ruan Papers.

10. "John Ruan's Recollections"; *Des Moines Register*, 4 March 1984 and 10 September 1998; Transcript of John Ruan Interview for Des Moines Oral History Project, 12 August 1999 [hereafter cited as Oral History transcript]; Ruan, interview, 5 April 2001.

11. Ruan, interviews, 5 April 2001 and 5 October 2002. Young and Harvey Company received another contract to provide gravel for covering country roads in Richmond and Prairie townships; see *Oskaloosa Tribune*, 9 December 1932.

12. William Childs, *Trucking and the Public Interest: The Emergence of Federal Regulation, 1914-1940* (Knoxville: University of Tennessee Press, 1985), 35-36; *Des Moines Register*, 8 June 1933.

13. Quotation from Ruan, interview, 5 April 2001. See also Ruan, interview, 5 June 2001; "John Ruan Biography"; Oral History transcript.

14. Quotation from Ruan, interview, 5 June 2001. See also "Ruan: The Company and the Man," internal company publication, typescript, Ruan Papers; *Des Moines Register*, 4 March 1984. Several strip mines were being opened in this part of Iowa at the time; see discussion of one new coal mine in the *Eddyville Tribune*, 28 July 1932.

15. Childs, *Trucking and Public Interest*, 39.

16. Des Moines coal dealers charged a fairly standard rate of $4 a ton for the delivery of Iowa lump or range coal. See, for instance, advertisements for Carbon Coal Company, Economy Coal, or Bloomfield Coal Company in *Des Moines Register*, 2 January 1933.

17. "John Ruan's Recollections."

18. Ruan, interview, 5 June 2001.

19. Quotations from *Des Moines Business Record*, 31 March–6 April 1989; and *Des Moines Register*, 11 December 1977, respectively.

20. Quotation from *Des Moines Register*, 4 March 1984. See also Ruan, interviews, 5 April and 5 June 2001.

21. Childs, *Trucking and Public Interest*, 31; Ruan, interview, 5 April 2001; Duff, Anderson, and Clark, "Report Ruan Transport Corporation, 1950," 1, Ruan Papers.

22. The Euclid State Bank was located at Sixth and Euclid Avenues, but its president, George Jensen, had an office in the Utica Building in the central downtown business district. In 1936, the bank's name was changed to Des Moines Bank and Trust Company.

23. See Oral History transcript. For more on Jensen, see William J. Petersen, *The Story of Iowa: The Progress of an American State, Family and Personal History,* vol. 3 (New York: Lewis Historical Publishing Co., 1952), 618.

24. Ruan, interview, 5 June 2001. On Bernie Evans and Iowa Trailer Sales, see *Polk's Des Moines City Directory, 1934* (Des Moines, IA: R. L. Polk and Company, 1934), 403, 972.

25. Kenneth D. Durr and Philip L. Cantelon, *Never Stand Still: The History of Consolidated Freightways, Inc. and CNF Transportation Inc., 1929-2000* (Rockville, MD: Montrose Press, 1999), 75.

26. Ruan quotation from "John Ruan Recollections." For the Motor Carrier Act, see Childs, *Trucking and Public Interest,* 139-49; D. Daryl Wyckoff and David H. Maister, *The Motor Carrier Industry* (Lexington, MA, and Toronto: D. C. Heath, 1977), xxxvii-xxxix; and Durr and Cantelon, *Never Stand Still,* 74-76.

27. The two-dollar-bill story is recounted in Leon Alexander, interview by author, Omaha, Nebraska, 15 August 2001. Alexander was Bernstein's son-in-law. The first time I met John Ruan, in spring 2000, he signed a two-dollar bill and handed it to me. The framed bill now hangs in my office. It was not until later that I learned the origin of this John Ruan tradition.

28. See "The Ruan Story"; Duff, Anderson, and Clark, "Report," 1,38; and *Polk's Des Moines City Directory, 1938* (Omaha: R. L. Polk and Company, 1938), 672.

29. "The Ruan Story."

30. John Ruan, interview by author, Des Moines, Iowa, 21 August 2001.

31. Ibid. On the Mainliner, see also Ralph Bumpilori, telephone conversation with author, 2 August 2001.

32. See "Iowa Partnership Return of Income, 1946," 13 March 1947, Ruan Papers; "John Ruan Biography"; Ruan, interview, 5 June 2001; George Oldenburger, telephone conversation with author, 10 August 2001; and Duff, Anderson, and Clark, "Report," 1, 38.

33. See Oral History transcript; Ruan, interviews, 5 April and 5 June 2001; "A Story of Mr. John Ruan and His New Des Moines Terminal," *Iowa Oil Spout* 9 (April 1948): 14-15; and *Polk's Directory, 1938,* 704.

34. *Des Moines Register,* 11 December 1977.

35. Quotations from Oral History transcript and Ruan, interviews, 5 April and 5 June 2001. On the general nature of the trucking bill, see *Des Moines Register,* 23 and 27 April 1939.

36. John Ruan, telephone conversation with author, 22 January 2003.

37. Dorothy Nott, telephone conversation with author, 10 August 2001; Ina Rae Ruan, telephone conversation with author, 10 August 2001.

38. "Ruan and His Terminal," 14. See also "The Ruan Story" and "History Ruan Transport Corporation Operations," Ruan Scrapbook, 1932-1948, Ruan Papers.

39. "History Ruan Transport" and "Operating Statements, 1938-1941," Ruan Scrapbook, 1932-1948, Ruan Papers.

40. "John Ruan Biography"; Ruan, interview, 5 June 2001; *Polk's Des Moines City Directory, 1940* (Omaha: R. L. Polk and Co., 1940), 235; Marriage Certificate, John Ruan and Rose Duffy, Sioux Falls, South Dakota, 5 October 1940.

41. In September 1940, Congress passed the United States' first peacetime draft, requiring all males from 21 through 35 years of age to register for military service. Three weeks after conscription became law, John Ruan registered for the draft while on his honeymoon in Absarokee, Montana. For more on conscription, see Justus D. Doenecke and John E. Wilz, *From Isolation to War, 1931-1941* (Arlington Heights, IL: Harlan Davidson, 1991), 90-92, 107-9.

Chapter 3

1. *Des Moines Register*, 8 October 1976.

2. Originally established as the Office of the Petroleum Coordinator for National Defense in 1941, the name was changed to Office of the Petroleum Coordinator for War in the spring of 1942 and to the Petroleum Administration for War in December 1942. The Midwestern District where John worked encompassed North and South Dakota, Nebraska, Kansas, Oklahoma, Missouri, Iowa, Minnesota, Wisconsin, Illinois, Indiana, Michigan, Ohio, Kentucky, and Tennessee.

3. Duff, Anderson, and Clark, "Report, Ruan Transport Corporation, October, 1950," 18, John Ruan Papers, private collection held by John Ruan, Des Moines, Iowa [hereafter cited as Ruan Papers].

4. On transferring railroad tank cars from the Midwest to the East Coast, see *Des Moines Register*, 14, 20, and 31 May 1942; and *Time*, 18 May 1942, 73. Hickenlooper story is recounted in "John Ruan Memorabilia from Birth to Present," undated typescript, Ruan Papers.

5. On Phillips's service for the Office of Petroleum Coordinator, see *Des Moines Register*, 25 May 1942.

6. Holger Ridder, "Oil Transporter Sets Up 'Key-Stop' Plan to Deliver Products to Unattended Plants," *National Petroleum News* 42 (8 February 1950): 23-29.

7. On Denkhoff, see LeRoy Brown, interview by author, Des Moines, Iowa, 28 August 2001; James Gabriel, interview by author, Des Moines, Iowa, 30 August 2001; *Ruan Transreporter*, January 1952, 8; and *Des Moines Register*, 27 August 1950. For information on Bob Root, see *Des Moines Register*, 13 March 1995.

8. McGinn quotation from S. Francis McGinn to John Ruan, 25 March 1969, Ruan Scrapbook, 1969, Ruan Papers; "The Ruan Story," Ruan Papers; John Ruan, interview by author, Des Moines, Iowa, 21 August 2001.

9. *Ruan Transreporter*, November 1953, 4. See also Bill Giles, interview by author, Des Moines, Iowa, 27 August 2001; *Des Moines Register*, 13 March 1995; "The Ruan Story."

10. For the World War II home front in Iowa, see Dorothy Schwieder, *Iowa: The Middle Land* (Ames: Iowa State University Press, 1996), 275-85.

For a balanced account of the home front generally, see John W. Jeffries, *Wartime America: The World War II Home Front* (Chicago: Ivan R. Dee, 1996).

11. See the Corydon *Times-Republican*, 26 September, 10, 17, 24, and 31 October, and 7 and 21 November 1940. Ruan quotation from John Ruan, telephone conversation with author, 30 August 2001.

12. Corydon *Times-Republican*, 7 November and 5 December 1940; Roger and Jan Winslow, telephone conversation with author, 1 September 2001; Ruan, telephone conversation, 30 August 2001. For the going-out-of-business sale advertisement, see Corydon *Times-Republican*, 9 October 1941. Interestingly enough, another Corydon grocer, Parish Grocery, closed the following week (*Times-Republican*, 16 October 2001), suggesting how competitive the market was in this small community.

13. The Nixons' time in Ottumwa is covered in Roger Morris, *Richard Milhous Nixon: The Rise of an American Politician* (New York: Henry Holt and Company, 1990), 245-46; and Stephen Ambrose, *Nixon: The Education of a Politician, 1913-1962* (New York: Simon and Schuster, 1987), 106. Nixon's quotation on the air station is from Morris, *Richard Milhous Nixon*, 245. See also "John Ruan Memorabilia": Ruan, telephone conversation, 30 August 2001; and *Polk's Ottumwa (Wapello County, Iowa) City Directory, 1943* (Omaha: R. L. Polk and Co., 1943), 384, 390.

14. See James and Genevieve Wren, *Motor Trucks of America* (Ann Arbor, MI: University of Michigan Press, 1979), 171; Kenneth Durr and Philip Cantelon, *Never Stand Still: The History of Consolidated Freightways, Inc. and CNF Transportation Inc., 1929-2000* (Rockville, MD: Montrose Press, 1999), 109, 120-21; and Gladys Mitchell, telephone conversation with author, 22 October 2001.

15. See "History Ruan Transport Corporation Operations," in Ruan Scrapbook, 1932-48, Ruan Papers.

16. "Report, Ruan Transport," 6-7.

17. See *Polk's Des Moines City Directory, 1943* (Omaha: R. L. Polk and Company, 1943), 64, 124; Virgil Debettignies, telephone conversation with author, 6 September 2001; John Ruan, interview by author, 31 July 2001; and Minutes of the First Meeting of the Board of Directors of Ruan Transport Corporation, 10 April 1943, corporate records of Ruan Transport, private collection held by Belin Lamson McCormick Zumbach Flynn, a Des Moines, Iowa, law firm. Ream continued doing work for Ruan Transport, and he eventually handed over the account to Roger Cloutier, a young associate at the accounting firm.

18. Quotation from Ruan, interview, Des Moines, Iowa, 31 July 2001. See also *Des Moines Register*, 12 May 1943; and *Des Moines Tribune*, 11 May 1943.

19. Story recounted in Jan Gillum, interview by author, Des Moines, Iowa, 12 September 2001.

20. John and Betty Ruan, interview by author, Des Moines, Iowa, 26 July 2001.

21. See ibid.; "John Ruan Memorabilia"; John Ruan, interview, 12 September 2001; agreement between John Corsaut and Lotta Leister and John Ruan, 14 April 1945, Ruan Corporation; and e-mail from Susan Schuler, Cerro Gordo Auditor's Office, to author, 13 September 2001. For Grenville Dodge, see Leland Sage, *A History of Iowa* (Ames: Iowa State University Press, 1974), 111, 112, 145, 154, and 176; and Stanley P. Hirshson, *Grenville M. Dodge: Soldier, Politician, Railroad Pioneer* (Bloomington: Indiana University Press, 1967). Several years after the original purchase, John also bought the adjacent Dodge family cottage, tripling the size of his Clear Lake property.

22. "The Ruan Story"; Agreement between C. & W. Transport Company, a partnership composed of Lanceford H. Wood and Sigfred Carlson, and Ruan Transportation Company, owned by John Ruan, 19 February 1945; and Bill of Sale, C. & W. Transport to Ruan Transportation Company, 28 February 1945, Ruan Papers. The purchase price was $102,869.66.

23. See "History Ruan Transport Corporation Operations;" *Annual Report of the Iowa State Commerce Commission,* vol. 66 (Des Moines: State of Iowa, 1943), 508-9, 524-25; and *68th Annual Report of the Iowa State Commerce Commission* (Des Moines: State of Iowa, 1945), 469, 480.

24. Ruan quoted by Orville Long, telephone conversation with author, 17 September 2001.

25. John Ruan, interview by author, Des Moines, Iowa, 6 June 2001.

26. "John Ruan Recollections," 11 March 1997, typescript, Ruan Papers. On Roosevelt's death and Truman's being sworn into office, see David McCullough, *Truman* (New York: Simon and Schuster, 1992), 340-47.

27. See "Report, Ruan Transport," 2.

28. John and Betty Ruan, interview, 26 July 2001.

29. See ibid.; and *Des Moines Register,* 6 August 1986.

30. See Betty Ruan, interview by author, North Palm Beach, Florida, 19 January 2002.

31. See John and Betty Ruan, interview, 26 July 2001.

32. "John Ruan Memorabilia."

33. Ibid., and wedding announcement in *Des Moines Register,* undated clipping in Ruan Papers.

34. John and Betty Ruan, interview, 26 July 2001; Dorothy Nott, interview by author, Monrovia, California, 12 March 2001; Ina Rae Ruan, interview by author, Monrovia, California, 12 March 2001. On the Commodore Hotel, see *Des Moines Register,* 2 January 2002.

35. Ridder, "Oil Transporter," 23-24; "Operation Safely Around the Clock," *International Trail,* March 1951, 1-4. The 15 major oil companies being serviced in the region by Ruan Transport's "key-stop" were Anderson Prichard, Cities Service, Continental Oil, Johnson Oil and Refining, Kan-

otex, Mid-Continent, Paraland, Phillips, Pure Oil, Shell Oil, Sinclair, Skelly, Socony-Vacuum, Standard Oil of Indiana, and the Texas Company.

36. *National Petroleum News,* September 1957, 6.

37. "Report, Ruan Transport," 10-15.

38. On sale of Ruan Motor Freight, see *Des Moines Register,* 7 December 1947; and *Carroll Times-Herald,* 9 December 1947. For John selling his interest in McCoy Trucking, see "McCoy Cartage Company Dissolution Agreement," 22 July 1947, Ruan Papers; George Oldenburger, telephone conversation with author, 10 August 2001; and *Polk's Waterloo City Directory, 1948* (Omaha: R. L. Polk and Co., 1948), 418. Joe Hall paid $37,500 for John's share of McCoy. For more on Western Grocer being purchased by a larger wholesaler and dropping Ruan, see *Polk's Des Moines City Directory, 1947* (Omaha: R. L. Polk and Co., 1947), 766; and *Ruan Transreporter,* June 1949, 7, and October 1949, 3.

39. On changing locations of Ruan's Des Moines operations, see *Polk's Directory, 1943,* 562; and *Polk's Des Moines City Directory, 1944* (Omaha: R. L. Polk and Company), 566. See also "Report, Ruan Transport," 27; "The Ruan Story"; and "A Story of Mr. Ruan and His New Des Moines Terminal," *Iowa Oil Spout,* April 1948, 14-15.

40. *Ruan Transreporter,* December 1950, 7; Minutes of a Special Meeting of the Board of Directors of Ruan Transport Corporation, 17 October and 1 December 1949; John Stiger to S. T. Carlson, 24 April 1945, Ruan Papers.

41. *Des Moines Register,* 20 March 1952.

42. Quotation from *Des Moines Register,* 10 July 1949. See also *Transport Topics,* 18 July 1949, 35; and *Ruan Transreporter,* June 1949, 4-5.

43. For terminals, see *Ruan Transreporter,* October 1949, 3. Revenue figures are for the combined operations of Ruan Transport, Terminal and Supply, and Eastside Service. For revenues, see "History Ruan Transport Corporation Operations"; and "Report, Ruan Transport," 43-44.

44. Orville Long, telephone conversation with author, 17 September 2001.

45. "Business Takes to the Air in Iowa," *Iowa Business and Industry,* July 1949, 21; Jerry Ware, telephone conversation with author, 18 September 2001.

46. See Ruan Cab Company photographs, Ruan Scrapbook, 1949-50, Ruan Papers.

47. Quotation from *Ruan Transreporter,* April 1950, 2. See also *Des Moines Tribune,* 21 September 1949.

48. Ruan quotation from *Des Moines Register,* 12 June 1949. On Hutchison, see "Report, Ruan Transport," 40.

49. "Ruan Safety Plan Proves Profitable to All Concerned," *Iowa Oil Spout,* June 1949, 16; and Holger Ridder, "Oil Tank Trucker Finds Driver Safety Program Pays Off in Good Will," *National Petroleum News,* 12 October 1949, 27-28, 30-33, 35.

50. Ridder, "Oil Tank Trucker," 27; and "Ruan Safety Plan," 16.

51. *Transport Topics,* 18 July 1949, 35.

52. *Transport Topics,* 8 August 1949, 3.

53. See *Des Moines Register,* 21 July 1949. For the *Register's* influence, see William Friedricks, *Covering Iowa: The History of the Des Moines Register and Tribune Company, 1849-1985* (Ames: Iowa State University Press, 2000).

54. *Transport Topics,* 17 October 1949.

55. *Transport Topics,* 31 October 1949, 6; *Iowa Motor Truck Association: Delivering 50 Years of Progress* (Des Moines, IA: Iowa Motor Truck Association, 1992), 3, 6; Scott Weiser, interview by author, Des Moines, Iowa, 25 April 2002.

56. *Motor Truck News,* November 1948, n.p., Ruan Papers; Bill Giles, telephone conversation with author, 21 September 2001.

57. John's status as a millionaire is difficult to judge. Since he was the sole stockholder of Ruan Transport Corporation, my statement here is based on the firm's earned surplus, which at the end of 1949 stood at $606,000.

Chapter 4

1. Dick Herman, telephone conversation with author, 3 October 2001.

2. Margaret Ann Bastian, interview by author, West Des Moines, Iowa, 1 November 2001.

3. See John and Betty Ruan, interview by author, Des Moines, Iowa, 26 July 2001; and *Des Moines Register,* 27 January 1991. Rosenfield quotation from *Des Moines Register,* 4 March 1984.

4. The accounting firm of Ream, Martin, Cloutier, and Sanderson had split off from Bemis, Ream, and Knobbe (the firm John had originally engaged in 1943) when it was taken over by Ernst and Ernst, and it continued to serve the Ruan companies. For figures, see "Appraisals of Ruan Transport Corporation and Terminal and Supply Corporation, December 31, 1950," John Ruan Papers, private collection held by John Ruan, Des Moines, Iowa [hereafter cited as Ruan Papers].

5. Ruan's becoming the nation's largest hauler of petroleum products by 1957 is cited in the *Des Moines Business Record,* 13-19 March 1989.

6. LeRoy Brown, interview by author, Des Moines, Iowa, 28 August 2001.

7. John and Betty Ruan, interview, 26 July 2001. John's hospitalization and time away from the office were reported in the *Ruan Transreporter,* April-May 1951, 3.

8. Brown, interview.

9. Duff, Anderson, and Clark, "Report, Ruan Transport Corporation, 1950," 33-37, 53, Ruan Papers.

10. On the purchase of Union Service, see Minutes of Special Meeting of the Board of Directors of Ruan Transport Corporation, 25 July and 7 August 1950, Ruan Papers; and Rex Fowler to C. W. Emken, 31 August 1951, Ruan

Papers. For Petroleum Carriers Corporation, see Minutes of the Special Meeting of the Board of Directors of Ruan Transport Corporation, 25 January and 17 April 1951, Ruan Papers.

11. "Report, Ruan Transport," 31.

12. Lenore Bible, telephone conversation with author, 22 October 2001; Gladys Mitchell, telephone conversation with author, 22 October 2001; Peggy (Kempster) Broer, telephone conversation with author, 22 October 2001; James Gabriel, interview by author, Des Moines, Iowa, 30 August 2001.

13. "Report, Ruan Transport," 31; *Ruan Transreporter,* July 1949, 8, and September 1949, 7.

14. See *Cedar Rapids Tribune,* 18 January 1951; *Dubuque Leader,* 19 January 1951; and *Des Moines Tribune,* 13 February 1951.

15. On the Clear Lake retreats, see Ruan Scrapbook, 1932-48, Ruan Papers; Managers' Meeting, *Ruan Transreporter,* 6, 7, and 8 September 1957; and Brown, interview.

16. Quotation from *Ruan Transreporter,* January 1952, 2, June-July 1952, 2-3; Ruan Scrapbook, 1951-53, Ruan Papers; *Des Moines Register,* 4 June 1951.

17. "Ruan Receives Trailmobile Award," clipping from unidentified source, April 1951, Ruan Scrapbook, 1951-53, Ruan Papers; *Des Moines Register,* 21 October 1951; *Ruan Transreporter,* October-November 1951, 2, October 1952, 7, May 1954, 5.

18. Quotation from "Drive Right Campaign Scheduled in Iowa Soon," undated clipping, Ruan Scrapbook, 1951-53, Ruan Papers. See also *Transport Topics,* 22 October 1951.

19. For more on Harold Baker, see *Ruan Transreporter,* September 1952, 7; and *Des Moines Register,* 21 September 1952.

20. On Geraghty, see *Ruan Transreporter,* February 1954, 6. On the hiring of Fabritz, see *Ruan Transreporter,* September 1953, 9; and for Harrington and the earlier public relations function of the company attorney, see "Report, Ruan Transport," 34.

21. Story and quotations are all recounted in Brown, interview.

22. "Pulling Together: Foto Facts about Ruan," internal company publication, 1953, 17, Ruan Papers; "Map and Street Directory of Des Moines: Compliments of Ruan Rent-A-Car Service," in Ruan Scrapbook, 1951-53, Ruan Papers; *Des Moines Evening Tribune,* 20 May and 19 June 1952; Minutes of Special Meeting of the Board of Directors of Capitol Cab Co., 20 September and 29 October 1954, Ruan Papers. For information on the relationship between Ruan and Avis Rent-A-Car, see Jim Garlock, telephone conversations with author, 7 and 14 November 2001; and John Ruan, interview by author, 7 November 2001.

23. Bill Giles, telephone conversation with author, 17 October 2001.

24. "Pulling Together," 16.

25. *Des Moines Register*, 4 March 1984.

26. John Ruan U.S. Individual Income Tax Return, 1947; Joe Rosenfield to John Ruan, 29 May and 30 September 1947; John Boler to John Ruan, 15 July 1948, Ruan Papers. See also Charles Duchen, interview by author, Des Moines, Iowa, 14 December 2001; and *Des Moines Register*, 8 October 1976.

27. Gertrude Cloutier, interview by author, Des Moines, Iowa, 13 October 2001; Dan Cloutier, interview by author, Des Moines, Iowa, 13 October 2001; Roger Cloutier II, interview by author, Des Moines, Iowa, 13 October 2001; Virgil DeBettignies, telephone conversation with author, 6 September 2001.

28. "John Ruan Memorabilia from Birth to Present," undated typescript, Ruan Papers; John Ruan, interview by author, 9 October 2001.

29. John Ruan, U.S. Individual Income Tax Return, 1952; John Ruan 1952 Oil Drilling Operations—Income & Expenses, Ruan Papers; Minutes of Special Meeting of Board of Directors of Ruan Transport Corporation, 2 January 1952, Ruan Papers; Minutes of Annual Meeting of Directors, Ruan Transport Corporation, 10 March 1953, 9 March 1954, 8 March 1955, Ruan Papers; Ruan, interview, 9 October 2001; R. Cloutier, interview.

30. See John and Betty Ruan, interview, 26 July 2001.

31. Dan Golightly, interview by author, Waukee, Iowa, 3 October 2002; John Ruan interview by author, Des Moines, Iowa, 5 October 2002; John Ruan III, interview by author, Des Moines, Iowa, 5 October 2002; Howard Gregory, telephone conversation with author, 17 October 2002.

32. On company picnics, see LeRoy Brown to John Ruan/Jan Gillum, 25 May 2001, Ruan Papers.

33. For biography of Settlemyer, see *Ruan Transreporter*, December 1954, 2. On R & S Oil Company, see R & S Oil Company, Des Moines, Iowa, Financial Statements, 1952, 1953, Ruan Papers.

34. *Polk's Des Moines City Directory, 1953* (Omaha: R. L. Polk and Company, 1953), 641; and Audit Report, R & S Oil Company of Des Moines, 31 December 1960; Audit Report, R & S Oil Company of Waterloo, 31 December 1960; and Audit Report, 2301 Lafayette Corporation, 31 December 31, 1960, Ruan Papers.

35. For background on Keeshin, see John Lewis Keeshin, *No Fears, No Tears: A Memoir of Four Score Years, The Autobiography of John Lewis Keeshin* (Oshkosh, WI: Castle-Pierce Press, 1983). On Ruan takeover, see "Ruan Wins Approval of ICC for Control of Keeshin Companies," *Transport Topics*, 14 June 1954, 1, 3; *Davenport Times*, 6 February 1954; and Bill Giles, interview by author, Des Moines, Iowa, 20 August 2001.

36. This story is recounted in Transcript of John Ruan Interview for Des Moines Oral History Project, 12 August 1999 [hereafter cited as Oral History transcript]; and "John Ruan Biography," undated typescript, Ruan Papers.

37. "Application for Right to Purchase Keeshin System Filed at ICC," *Transport Topics*, 30 November1953, 1, 7; *Des Moines Evening Tribune*, 19 February 1954.

38. "Ruan Wins Approval of ICC," 1, 3; *Chicago Daily Tribune*, 9 June 1954; *Des Moines Register*, 9 June 1954.

39. John Ruan, interview by author, Des Moines, Iowa, 5 June 2001; "Keeshin System Adds 300 Vehicles as Step in Rehabilitation Plan," *Transport Topics*, 2 August1954, 1-2; *Chicago Daily News*, 19 July 1955; General Expressways Scrapbook, Ruan Papers.

40. Orville Long, telephone conversation with author, 17 September 2001; Brown, interview; "Keeshin Appoints Shields Executive Vice President," *National Hiway Shipper*, October 1954.

41. "Out of the Red, by Plane and Truck," *Fortune*, September 1955, 44. See also General Expressways in-house publication, *General Express*, October 1956, 2-5; and Orville Long, telephone conversation with author, 15 October 2001.

42. Company financial information from *Transport Topics*, 25 March 1957, 32. The story of John's yelling at the General Expressways executive is recounted in *Des Moines Register*, 8 October 1976.

43. Quotation from *Des Moines Register*, 8 October 1976. See also *Transport Topics*, 3 August 1959, 1, 16.

44. General Expressways' net loss in 1958 was $860,000 and more than $1.5 million in 1959. Over the course of Ruan ownership, Ruan Equipment advanced the freight carrier $3.4 million. On the deal, see John Ruan to Samuel Goldberg, 22 July 1960, Ruan Papers; Minutes of Special Meeting of Board of Directors of Ruan Transport Corporation, 25 April 1960, Ruan Papers; and Agreement between Navajo Freight Lines, Inc., General Expressways, Ruan Transport Corporation, Ruan Equipment Company, and John Ruan, 26 April 1960, Ruan Papers. Quotation from "Navajo Asks Control, Option to Purchase General Expressways," *Transport Topics*, 23 May 1960, 1, 5.

45. William E. Grace to John Ruan, 6 March 1970, Ruan Papers.

46. John Ruan, telephone conversation with author, 22 January 2003; Jan Gillum, telephone conversation with author, 22 January 2003. The gold-plated golf clubs currently adorn John's office suite, leaning against the side of his fireplace hearth. The framed letter from Bill Grace sits atop the golf bag.

47. John Ruan to Sam Simpson, 26 April 1955, and Sam Simpson to John Ruan, 28 April 1955, Ruan Scrapbook, 1954-55, Ruan Papers; Minutes of meeting to form a trucking industry insurance company, 5 May 1955, Ruan Papers; *Ruan Transreporter*, October 1955, 9.

48. Minutes of Annual Meeting of Transport Underwriters, Inc., 18 April 1955; Transport Underwriters, Inc., Statement of Financial Condition, 31 October 1956; and Auditor's Report, Carriers Incorporated, 31 March 1960; all in Ruan Papers.

49. Ruan Scrapbook, 1954-55, Ruan Papers; *Ruan Transreporter,* October 1954, 5, and September 1960, 5.

50. On the Brule Lake facility, see "Welcome to Ruan Isle" pamphlet, Ruan Papers.

51. Ruan, interview, 9 October 2001.

52. See *Ruan Transreporter,* July 1954, 2; *Transport Topics,* 10 March 1958, 24; and "The Ruan Story." On the sale of the Brule Lake property, see Minutes of Meeting of Ruan Transport Board of Directors, 2 April 1963; Prent Savage to John Ruan, 20 December 1962; Ray Iverson to John Ruan, 13 March 1963; and Eloise Helmerick to L. P. Neff, 3 April 1963, Ruan Papers.

53. Minutes of [Ruan Transport] Executive Committee Meeting, 3 January, 7 and 21 March, and 11 April 1955, Ruan Papers; *Ruan Transreporter,* June 1955, 8; and Bill Giles, interview by author, Des Moines, Iowa, 8 October 2001.

54. John Ruan to Bob Root and Harold Baker, 5 November 1958, Ruan Papers.

55. On acquisition of Terminal Transport, see *Transport Topics,* 20 February 1956, 20. The quotation from the ruling is taken from *Ruan Transreporter,* May 1956, 7. See also Giles, interview, 8 October 2001.

56. *Transport Topics,* 19 August 1957, 34; *Ruan Transreporter,* November 1957, 3.

57. *Transport Topics,* 10 March 1958, 4; *Ruan Transreporter,* April 1958, 3.

58. Ibid.; *Ruan Transreporter,* May 1959, 5.

59. *Ruan Transreporter,* February 1960, 6.

60. Bill Giles, interview by author, Des Moines, Iowa, 6 November 2001.

61. Ibid; John Ruan, interview by author, 2 October 2001; *Ruan Transreporter,* February/March 1962, 3, June 1961, 6-7. See also Cement Division, Weekly Reports, 1960; Cement Personnel, 30 October 1959; John Ruan to R. L. Seeley, 16 August 1960; Rex Fowler to H. L. Fabritz, 8 June 1960; and Rex Fowler to Glenn Wallace, 2 June 1960; all in Ruan Papers.

62. Orville Long, telephone conversation with author, 15 October 2001; John Ruan to All Employees, 6 January 1960, Ruan Papers. On cement tanks, see *Mason City Globe Gazette,* 13 January 1961; *Ruan Transreporter,* June 1961, 6-7; and "Ruan: The Company and the Man," internal company publication, typescript, Ruan Papers.

63. Ruan, interview, 9 October 2001.

64. Leon Alexander, interview by author, Omaha, Nebraska, 15 August 2001.

65. Ibid. Problems with the aluminum tanks are first discussed in Minutes of Executive Committee Meeting, 21 November and 12 December 1955, Ruan Papers. See also "Ruan: Company and Man" and Ruan Transport Corporation, Analysis of Aluminum Tank Failures, both in Ruan Papers.

66. See Minutes of Executive Committee Meeting, 23 May 1955; Giles, interview, 8 November 2001; and "Ruan Has Been a Pioneering Leader," typescript, Ruan Papers.

67. See Ruan Transport Corporation, Its Subsidiaries, and Associated Companies, Combined Financial Statements, 1960, Ruan Papers. Carriers Insurance, General Expressways, Ruan Equipment, and John's smaller investments such as R & S or the development of oil property are not included in this financial statement.

68. *Transport Topics,* 27 April 1953, 10; *Ruan Transreporter,* June 1953, 3.

69. *Des Moines Register,* 23 January 1958. See also Iowa Power and Light News Release, 22 January 1958; Bankers Trust Company pamphlet, 31 December 1960; and Transportation Center Report, 1959-60; all in Ruan Scrapbooks, 1958, 1960, Ruan Papers. John's nomination to Transportation Center's advisory board is covered in Frank Kremmel to J. R. Miller, 26 November 1958, Ruan Scrapbook, 1987, Ruan Papers.

70. Evelyn Benson, interview by author, Des Moines, Iowa, 11 October 2001.

71. Peggy (Kempster) Broer, telephone conversation; John Ruan III, interview by author, Des Moines, Iowa, 23 October 2001.

72. John Ruan III, interview by author, Des Moines, Iowa, 4 December 2002.

73. John Ruan III, interview, 23 October 2001; and Kingsley Macomber, telephone conversation with author, 12 November 2001.

74. Ibid.; Elise "Squeak" (Macomber) Geraghty, telephone conversation with author, 7 November 2001; and John and Betty Ruan, interview, 26 July 2001.

75. Ibid.; Rusty (Hubbell) Edwards, interview by author, Des Moines, Iowa, 6 November 2001; Maggi Moss, interview by author, Des Moines, Iowa, 5 November 2001; Marion Blount, interview by author, Cumming, Iowa, 16 November 2001; Barbara (Weeks) Phinney, telephone conversation with author, 30 November 2001; James W. Hubbell Jr., interview by author, North Palm Beach, Florida, 17 January 2002.

76. I've used the club members' names as they appeared at the time. Several names have since changed because some of the women remarried. John and Betty Ruan, interview, 26 July 2001; Bastian, interview; Virginia Pearsall, interview by author, West Des Moines, Iowa, 1 November 2001; "Squeak" Geraghty, telephone conversation; Peggy (Percival) Friedman, telephone conversation with author, 12 November 2001.

77. John and Betty Ruan, interview, 26 July 2001; John and Betty Ruan, interview by author, Des Moines, Iowa, 18 August 2002; "Life for a Lovely Lady," *International Trail,* February 1952, 20-21.

78. The Yellowstone family vacation is mentioned in *Ruan Transreporter,* August 1952, 5; John and Betty Ruan, interview, 26 July 2001; and John Ruan III, interview, 23 October 2001.

79. John Ruan to Arthur Ruan, 28 November 1953 and 15 April 1954; Arthur Ruan to John Ruan, 2 December 1953, all in Ruan Papers; Dorothy Nott, telephone conversation with author, 5 October 2001; John Ruan III, interview, 23 October 2001.

80. John Ruan to Arthur Ruan, 15 May 1955, and John Ruan to Arthur Ruan, undated letter; Dorothy Ruan to John Ruan, 1 June 1954; all in Ruan Papers.

81. John and Betty Ruan, interview, 26 July 2001.

82. Quotation from ibid. See also *Des Moines Register*, 8 August 1988.

83. John and Betty Ruan, interview, 26 July 2001.

Chapter 5

1. Conversation recounted by Bill Giles, interview by author, Des Moines, Iowa, 25 January 2001.

2. John Ruan, interview by author, North Palm Beach, Florida, 17 January 2002.

3. Mel Straub, interview by author, Des Moines, Iowa, 27 November 2001.

4. *Des Moines Register*, 4 March 1984.

5. *Des Moines Register*, 8 October 1976.

6. Ruan Transport paid Denver Chicago $1.2 million for the liquid products division and took over $590,000 of the unit's obligations due the First National Bank of Denver. See Ruan Transport Corporation, Special Meeting of Directors, 9 November 1961 and 28 April 1962, John Ruan Papers, private collection held by John Ruan, Des Moines, Iowa [hereafter cited as Ruan Papers].

7. *Des Moines Register*, 17 December 1961; *Wall Street Journal*, 13 December 1961; *Colorado Motor Carrier*, 25 May 1962, 15.

8. Quotation from Bill Giles, interview by author, 12 December 2001. See also *Ruan Transreporter*, April-May 1962, 2-3.

9. John Ruan to All Employees, 4 May 1962, Ruan Scrapbook, 1962-63, Ruan Papers; *Ruan Transreporter*, April-May 1962, 6.

10. John Ruan to All Terminal Managers, 25 June 1963, Ruan Scrapbook, 1962-63, Ruan Papers.

11. Ibid.; John Ruan, interview by author, Des Moines, Iowa, 2 October 2001; James W. Hubbell Jr., interview by author, North Palm Beach, Florida, 17 January 2002; *Ruan Transreporter*, February-March 1962, 3, June 1961, 6-7. See also Cement Division, Weekly Reports, 1960; Cement Personnel, 30 October 1959; John Ruan to R. L. Seeley, 16 August 1960; Rex Fowler to H. L. Fabritz, 8 June 1960; and Rex Fowler to Glenn Wallace, 2 June 1960, all in Ruan Papers.

12. Ruan to All Terminal Managers.

13. *Metropolis* (Illinois) *News*, 7 November 1963, Ruan Scrapbook, 1962-63, Ruan Papers.

14. Quotations are from Fruehauf press release, 6 November 1963, Ruan Papers. See also Giles, interview, 12 December 2001.

15. See *Des Moines Register*, 3 May 1964; *Motor Truck News*, May 1964, 6; Giles, interview, 12 December 2001; Robert Hicklin, interview by author, Des Moines, Iowa, 6 August 2001; and John Walker, interview by author, Kansas City, Missouri, 15 August 2001.

16. *Iowa Business and Industry*, June 1964, 10; *Truck Power*, October-November 1964, 1; John Hamm, "Marketing Accomplishments, 1967-68, Ruan Transport," 12, Ruan Papers.

17. *Power Parade*, January 1964, 18.

18. Virgil Anderson, interview by author, Clear Lake, Iowa, 3 September 2002; Tony Phyle, interview by author, West Des Moines, Iowa, 6 September 2002; *Des Moines Register*, 15 and 16 July 1994; John Ruan To All Regional Managers and All Terminal Managers, 6 December 1962, Ruan Papers.

19. *Petroleum Marketer*, September 1964, 33.

20. *Iowa Business and Industry*, June 1964, 11.

21. *Des Moines Register*, 16 July 1994.

22. See *Full-Power Living*, April 1965, 4, a publication for customers of Iowa Power and Light Company. Quotation is taken from *Dana Digest*, January 1970, 6-7.

23. See *International Trail*, March 1965, 4; Ken Kendall, interview by author, Des Moines, Iowa, 9 January 2002; and Bill Giles, telephone conversation with author, 7 January 2002.

24. Bill Fultz, telephone conversation with author, 10 January 2002; John Ruan, interview by author, Des Moines, Iowa, 9 January 2002; *Ruan*, September-October 1972, 2. *Ruan* was a new in-house publication begun in 1971. It replaced the *Ruan Transreporter*, which had ceased publication in the early 1960s. See also *International Trail*, March 1965, 4.

25. Ruan Transport Corporation Its Subsidiaries and Associated Companies, Combined Financial Statements, 1963, 1967; John Ruan to All Staff, 29 December 1962; all in Ruan Papers.

26. Ibid.; *Des Moines Register*, November 25, 1964; and Ruan Transportation Corporation 1977 Report/1978 Forecast, John Ruan Papers. Carriers Insurance's net income increased from $373,000 in 1963 to $824,000 in 1967. Carriers Insurance Exchange and its management company Carriers, Incorporated, merged in 1964, and the new entity was called Carriers Insurance. See Carriers Insurance Company, Auditors' Report, December 31, 1967, John Ruan Papers.

27. *Des Moines Register*, 9 February and 2 June 1963.

28. John Ruan Memorandum regarding Bankers Trust Company, 1 January 1965, Ruan Papers; Transcript of John Ruan Interview for Des Moines Oral History Project, 12 August 1999, John Ruan Papers [hereafter cited as

Oral History transcript]; "Bankers Trust Company, Des Moines" pamphlet, n.d.; Robert Fleming, interview by author, Carlisle, Iowa, 26 November 2001.

29. Ibid.; News Bulletin from Northwestern Banker, 9 December 1964, Ruan Scrapbook, 1964, Ruan Papers; Hubbell, interview, 17 January 2002. Bankers Trust shares were initially valued at $120 per share. See also *Des Moines Register*, 12 May 1968.

30. Ruan Memorandum regarding Bankers Trust.

31. Ralph Jester to Trans. Supply Corporation, 29 March 1965, Ruan Papers; *Des Moines Register*, 16 January 1968; "Welcome to banking a-la-car," Bankers Trust advertising pamphlet, n.d., Ruan Scrapbook, 1970, Ruan Papers.

32. John Ruan to W. E. Grace, 8 March 1965, Ruan Papers.

33. William C. Talen to Mr. Ruan, 24 September 1971, and photographs of promotion, Ruan Scrapbook, 1971, Ruan Papers. On the corn roasts, see Robert Hicklin, interview by author, Des Moines, Iowa, 7 August 2001. See also photographs of dinner for John Majors at Hicklin's building, 16 December 1970, Ruan Scrapbook, 1970, Ruan Papers.

34. Bankers Trust Company Financial History, Bankers Trust Company, Des Moines, Iowa; *Des Moines Register*, 16 January and 12 May 1968, 8 October 1976.

35. John Ruan, interview by author, Des Moines, Iowa, 24 December 2001; Giles, interview, 12 December 2001.

36. John Ruan, interview by author, North Palm Beach, Florida, 19 January 2002.

37. *Des Moines Business Record*, 13-19 March 1989.

38. "John Ruan Memorabilia from Birth to Present," undated typescript, Ruan Papers.

39. Quotation comes from *Des Moines Register*, 4 March 1984. See also Ruan, interview, 19 January 2002; and "Greetings Book, 2nd Annual Frank Fitzsimmons Invitational Golf Tournament, 15-19 September 1971," Ruan Scrapbook, 1971, Ruan Papers.

40. Ruan, interview, 19 January 2002; Fleming, interview; Ralph Schlenker, interview by author, Indianola, Iowa, 30 November 2001.

41. John Ruan III, interview by author, Des Moines, Iowa, 23 October 2001.

42. On John's letters to his children, see Cathy Macomber, telephone conversation with author, 10 December 2001.

43. John Ruan III, interview.

44. Ibid.; Maggi Moss, interview by author, Des Moines, Iowa, 5 November 2001; Barbara (Weeks) Phinney, telephone conversation with author, 30 November 2001.

45. *Horsemen's Advisor*, June 1966, 25.

46. See Moss, interview; and *Horsemen's Advisor,* December 1967, 5.

47. See Stephens College web page, www.stephens.edu/www/pr/tour/ ctstables.html.

48. Macomber, telephone.

49. Darlene Willis, interview by author, Des Moines, Iowa, 10 January 2002.

50. Howard Gregory, interview by author, Des Moines, Iowa, 28 November 2001.

51. John and Betty Ruan, interview by author, Des Moines, Iowa, 26 July 2001; Kendall, interview.

52. Ibid. On construction of Interstate 80 from Earlham eastward toward Des Moines, see the *Des Moines Tribune,* 17 August 1966.

53. Dorothy Nott, interview by author, Monrovia, California, 12 March 2001.

54. Willis, interview; obituary of Rachel Ruan, unidentified clipping, Ruan Papers.

55. John and Betty Ruan, interview; Kendall, interview; Willis, interview.

56. *Des Moines Register,* 8 October 1976; Ruan, interview, 19 January 2002; Hubbell, interview.

57. Gregory, interview.

58. *Des Moines Register,* 3 October 1968.

59. John Ruan, interview by author, Des Moines, Iowa, 15 November 2001.

60. Gregory, interview.

61. Ibid.; and W. T. Dahl, interview by author, Des Moines, Iowa, 22 January 2002.

62. *Des Moines Register,* 10 November 1973 and 15 August 1981; Donald Cordes to John Ruan, 31 July 1979, Ruan Scrapbook, 1979, Ruan Papers.

63. "The Ruan Phenomenon: It Started with a Dump Truck," *Contrails,* February 1977, 10.

64. See Press Release from the Greater Des Moines Chamber of Commerce, 16 January 1969, Ruan Scrapbook, 1969, Ruan Papers; B. B. Druker to Robert Sterling, 31 July 1969, Ruan Scrapbook, 1972, Ruan Papers; and Kendall, interview.

65. Ruan quotation recounted in Bill Guy, telephone conversation with author, 7 December 2001. See also *Des Moines Register,* 15 January 1969.

66. Guy, telephone conversation; Kendall, interview.

67. Oral History transcript.

68. Guy, telephone conversation.

69. See Kendall, interview; and Walter Neumann, interview by author, Des Moines, Iowa, 30 November 2001. On Eero Saarinen and the Deere & Company Building, see pamphlet, "Challenge to an Architect," in Ruan Scrapbook, 1965-66, Ruan Papers.

70. Neumann, interview.

71. David Neugent, interview by author, Des Moines, Iowa, 4 December 2001; *Des Moines Register*, 18 December 1972.

72. See *Ruan* January-February 1973, 2; and Kendall, interview.

73. *Des Moines Register*, 5 June 1973.

74. Quotations from *Modern Bulk Transporter*, December 1975, 25; and *Des Moines Register*, 2 August 1974 and 1 June 1975. See also *Northwestern Banker*, January 1973, 64; and "Bankers Trust. Reaching high for a greater Des Moines and a growing Iowa," undated Bankers Trust pamphlet in Ruan Scrapbook, 1975, Ruan Papers. COR-TEN steel is still widely used today. The current bridges being erected in the reconstruction of Interstate 235, which runs through Des Moines, for instance, are made of COR-TEN steel; see Ken Kendall, telephone conversation with author, 22 October 2002.

75. "Topping Ceremony, March 15, 1974," Ruan Scrapbook, 1974, Ruan Papers.

76. On Northwestern Bell, see *Omaha World-Herald*, 24 May 1974; and Jack MacAllister to John Ruan, 9 July 1974, Ruan Scrapbook, 1974, Ruan Papers. For Iowa Power and Light, see *Des Moines Tribune*, 31 July 1975.

77. *Des Moines Tribune*, 7 October 1974; *Des Moines Register*, 8 October 1976.

78. See invitation for Open House, Ruan Scrapbook, 1975, Ruan Papers.

79. Jill Southworth Rolek, "Two for the Skyline," *Iowan*, spring 1976, 41-45.

80. *Des Moines Register*, 29 November 1973.

81. Quotation from *New York Times*, 7 November 1973. See also *Washington Star-News*, 6 November 1973.

82. *Des Moines Register*, 31 October 1972.

83. On the North High Band's participation in the inaugural parade, see *Des Moines Register*, 16 January 1973; and Nolden Gentry to John Ruan, 24 January 1973, Ruan Scrapbook, 1973, Ruan Papers.

84. "John Ruan Memorabilia." See also various invitations to White House dinners and parties, Ruan Scrapbooks, 1972-1974, Ruan Papers.

85. *Des Moines Register*, 26 October 1973.

86. *Des Moines Register*, 29 November 1973.

87. *Washington Star-News*, 6 November 1973.

88. *Des Moines Register*, 2 December 1973.

89. The Boston company was originally awarded the WHDH-TV license in 1957, but the losing parties soon appealed, and the fight dragged on until it was finally settled in 1972. See *New York Times*, 18 March 1972.

90. *Wall Street Journal*, 19 March 1964.

91. The FCC's ruling was based on the principle of media diversity. Since the Boston Herald Traveler owned one of the city's four major dailies, it had what was considered one of the "primary sources" of information in the city. Therefore, it was not allowed to own one of Boston's six television channels,

also "primary sources" of information. For information on the battle over WHDH-TV, see *New York Times*, 24 January and 25 February 1969; 15 June 1971, and 18 March 1972; "Making Bad in Boston," *Life*, 29 September 1972, 18; and Sterling Quinlan, *The Hundred Million Dollar Lunch* (Chicago: J. Philip O'Hara, 1974).

92. See Eugene Mullin Jr. to John Ruan, 10 December 1969; George Lyon to John Ruan, 6 October 1971; Escrow Agreement among John Blair & Company and Manufacturers Hanover Trust Company, 2 April 1973; and Minutes of WHDH Corporation Directors' Meeting, 29 March and 11 April 1973; all in Ruan Papers; *Des Moines Register*, 1 June 1972; and Quinlan, *Hundred Million Dollar Lunch*, 230.

93. For more on Noyce and the development of microchips, see T. R. Reid, *The Chip: How Two Americans Invented the Microchip and Launched a Revolution* (New York: Random House, 2001); and Robert Burgelman, *Strategy is Destiny: How Strategy-Making Shapes a Company's Future* (New York: Free Press, 2002).

94. Ruan, interview, 19 January 2002; Stan Madson, telephone conversation with author, 10 September 2002.

95. Ruan, interview, 19 January 2002; John Ruan, interview by author, Des Moines, Iowa, 27 March 2002; and John Ruan financial records, Ruan Papers.

96. James Hoak Sr., interview by author, North Palm Beach, Florida, 19 January 2002; Ruan, interview, 27 March 2002; Barbara Beving Long, *Des Moines and Polk County: Flag on the Prairie* (Northridge, CA: Windsor Publications, 1988), 127; *Des Moines Register*, 5 January 1975.

97. Hoak Sr., interview; Ruan, interview 27 March 2002. See also James Hoak Jr., telephone conversation with author, 1 March 2002; John Ruan III, interview by author, Des Moines, Iowa, 4 December 2002; and *Des Moines Register*, 1 July 1987.

98. *Des Moines Register*, 4 March 1984.

Chapter 6

1. Louis Dennig, telephone conversation with author, 4 March 2002.

2. James Flansburg, "Without Lobbyist Favors It's 'Burger Chef' Session," *Des Moines Register*, 9 January 1978.

3. *Modern Bulk Transporter*, December 1975, 25.

4. Greater Des Moines Partnership, "Corporate Overview" (typescript, n.d.).

5. Quotation from *Des Moines Register*, 10 October 1976. See also *Des Moines Register*, 13 November 1974 and 11 November 1975.

6. *Des Moines Tribune*, 21 and 28 August 1973; James W. Hubbell Jr., interview by author, North Palm Beach, Florida, 17 January 2002; Dick Olson, interview by author, West Des Moines, Iowa, 10 May 2002; "Some Significant Dates in History of Des Moines," Robert Houser Papers, private

collection held by Robert Houser, Des Moines, Iowa [hereafter cited as Houser Papers].

7. Quotation from William Friedricks, *Covering Iowa: The History of the Des Moines Register and Tribune Company, 1849-1985* (Ames: Iowa State University Press, 2000), 193-94. See also Robert Houser, interview by author, Des Moines, Iowa, 23 January 2002; Robert Houser text of speech, 29 January 1991, Houser Papers; and Herman Kilpper, interview by author, Urbandale, Iowa, 22 March 2002.

8. Charles Duchen, interview by author, Des Moines, Iowa, 14 December 2001; Ken Kendall, interview by author, Des Moines, Iowa, 9 January 2002; Edgar Hansell, interview by author, Des Moines, Iowa, 29 March 2002; *Des Moines Tribune*, 25 October 1976.

9. Ibid.; Olson, interview; *Des Moines Tribune*, 13 January 1975.

10. *Des Moines Register*, 3 October 1976.

11. Quotation from *Des Moines Tribune*, 13 January 1975. On the Grand Avenue Garage and connecting skywalk, see "Ruan Center" informational packet, Ruan Scrapbook, 1972, in John Ruan Papers, private collection held by John Ruan, Des Moines, Iowa [hereafter cited as Ruan Papers]; *Des Moines Tribune*, 18 December 1972 and 18 November 1974; Houser notes, Houser Papers; and Robert Houser, telephone conversation with author, 26 March 2002.

12. Duchen, interview; Richard Wilkey, interview by author, West Des Moines, Iowa, 21 February 2002; Michael Hayes, interview by author, Des Moines, Iowa, 17 April 2002; Olson, interview; Kendall, interview by author, Des Moines, Iowa, 17 April 2002.

13. Hansell, interview; Kenneth Haynie, interview by author, Des Moines, Iowa, 8 April 2002; Transcript of John Ruan Interview for Des Moines Oral History Project, 12 August 1999, John Ruan Papers [hereafter cited as Oral History transcript]; "Skywalk Progress Continues," *Greater Des Moines Business Action Report* 92 (3 December 1979): 3; undated *Des Moines Register* clipping, Ruan Scrapbook, 1982, Ruan Papers.

14. Hayes, interview; Wilkey, interview.

15. *Des Moines Register*, 3, 10, and 17 October 1976.

16. Ibid.; Hansell, interview.

17. Quotation about model from Walter Neumann, interview by author, Des Moines, Iowa, 30 November 2001. On City Center Corporation, see Hansell, interview; and City Center Corporation Stockholder Lists, 8 February and 13 March 1978, Ruan Papers.

18. *Des Moines Tribune*, 23 February and 19 and 30 April 1977. Quotations from unmarked clipping, *Des Moines Register*, Ruan Scrapbook, 1977, Ruan Papers.

19. *Des Moines Tribune*, 24 February 1977.

20. Ibid. See also *Des Moines Tribune*, 21 April and 16 October 1977.

21. *Des Moines Tribune,* 21 April and 16 October 1977. Quotation from *Des Moines Tribune,* 13 February 1978.

22. *Des Moines Tribune,* April 28, 30, 1977.

23. *Des Moines Register,* 9 and 10 September 1977 and 31 January and 12 February 1978.

24. Quotation from *Des Moines Register,* 12 February 1978. For report of the vote, see *Des Moines Register,* 7 February 1978. For specifics on the hotel, see John Ruan Hotel Press Conference notes, 11 February 1978, and City Center Corporation Press Release, 11 February 1978, Ruan Scrapbook, 1978, Ruan Papers; and John Ruan, interview by author, 27 March 2001.

25. See list of hotel investors, Ruan Papers.

26. See Wilkey, interview; *Des Moines Tribune,* 23, 24, and 30 March 1978.

27. Houser quoted in *Des Moines Register,* 1 April 1978. See also Robert Houser, interview by author, Des Moines, Iowa, 25 March 2002. On ACORN, see *Des Moines Register,* 31 March 1978.

28. *Des Moines Tribune,* 15 February, 14 and 17 April, and 5 May 1978; *Des Moines Register,* 9 June 1978.

29. *Des Moines Register,* 24 July and 6 September 1978 and 28 June 1979; *Des Moines Tribune,* 9 August and 7 September 1978 and 29 June 1979. Hubbell quotation from *Des Moines Register,* 27 January 1991.

30. *Des Moines Register,* 27 October 1978.

31. Quotations from *Des Moines Tribune,* 2 March 1979. See also Kendall, interview, 9 January 2002; and Hansell, interview.

32. Quotation from *Des Moines Register,* 28 June 1979. *Des Moines Tribune,* undated clippings, Ruan Scrapbook, 1979, Ruan Papers; and *Des Moines Register,* 16 March 1979.

33. *Des Moines Register,* 21 July 1979. See also Haynie, interview.

34. *Des Moines Register,* 3 and 21 January 1979; *Des Moines Tribune,* 20 April 1979.

35. Wilkey, interview; Hansell, interview; Haynie, interview; *Des Moines Register,* 9 and 13 May and 14 and 24 June 1980.

36. Quotation from *Des Moines Register,* 4 September 1980. See also John Ruan, interview by author, Des Moines, Iowa, 27 March 2002; and undated letter, "We Fourteen to John Ruan or whoever is in charge," John Ruan Scrapbook, 1980, Ruan Papers.

37. Des Moines Marriott Fact Sheet, Ruan Scrapbook, 1981, Ruan Papers; *Des Moines Register,* 21, 27, and 29 January 1981; *Des Moines Tribune,* 22 and 28 January 1981.

38. Peter Hubschmitt, telephone conversation with author, 7 October 2002; and Marriott Hotels Press Release, 28 January 1981, Ruan Scrapbook, 1981, Ruan Papers.

39. See *Des Moines Tribune*, 28 January 1981. Michael Gartner's remarks as well as a photograph of his gift to John appeared in *Des Moines Tribune*, 31 January 1981.

40. *Des Moines Tribune*, 22 January 1981.

41. *Des Moines Tribune*, 21 and 29 January and 6 November 1979.

42. *Des Moines Tribune*, 2 November 1979. On Des Moines Development Corporation, see Robert Houser Notes, Houser Papers.

43. Wilkey quotation from *Des Moines Tribune*, 5 November 1979. See also Wilkey, interview. Editorial quotation from *Des Moines Tribune*, 16 November 1979.

44. Haynie, interview.

45. See Edgar Hansell, interview; and Ruan, interview, 27 March 2002.

46. *Des Moines Register*, 3 and 9 November 1979.

47. "Office Building Announced for Downtown," *Greater Des Moines Business Action Report* 92 (3 December 1979): 1.

48. John Ruan III, interviews by author, Des Moines, Iowa, 27 March and 4 December 2002; *Des Moines Tribune*, 4 March 1981.

49. *Des Moines Tribune*, 24 March 1981; Ruan, interview, 27 March 2002.

50. *Des Moines Register*, 25 March 1981; *Des Moines Tribune*, 8 April and 21 May 1981.

51. *Des Moines Register*, 2 June 1981.

52. Quotation from text of speech to Pioneer Club, Ruan Scrapbook, 1981, Ruan Papers. On continued newspaper support, see *Des Moines Tribune*, 27 July 1981.

53. All quotations except John's comments are from *Des Moines Register*, 1 July 1981. John's remarks are from text of his speech, Ruan Scrapbook, 1981, Ruan Papers. For more on award and event, see *Northwestern Banker*, August 1981, 70; *Des Moines Register*, 22 May 1981; and *Des Moines Tribune*, 25 June and 1 July 1981.

54. Phrase is from *Des Moines Register*, 27 January 1991.

55. John Ruan III, interviews by author, Des Moines, Iowa, 7 and 27 March 2002.

56. Ibid.; Janis Ruan, interview by author, Des Moines, Iowa, 26 April 2002.

57. Ibid.; Gary Alvord, interview by author, West Des Moines, Iowa, 25 April 2002; *Ruan*, March-April 1972, 2, and January-February 1973, 4-5; *Des Moines Register*, 15 March 1982.

58. Janis Ruan, interview; John Ruan III, interview, 27 March 2002; and Gary Fletcher, interview by author, Des Moines, Iowa, 28 February 2002.

59. Gary Fletcher, interview.

60. Ibid.; Gary Fletcher, telephone conversation with author, 22 April 2002; Betty Ruan, interview by author, Des Moines, Iowa, 26 July 2001.

Quotation from *Des Moines Register*, 6 August 1988. According to Michael Jacoby, M.D. and medical director of the Ruan Neurology Clinic, there is a genetic connection to the disease, and while the exact link remains a mystery, children of MS patients are at a much greater risk than the rest of the population of being diagnosed with MS; see Michael Jacoby, interview by author, West Des Moines, Iowa, 14 September 2002.

61. John Fitch to John Ruan, 10 May 1974, Ruan Scrapbook, 1974, Ruan Papers; Mel Straub, interview by author, Des Moines, Iowa, 27 November 2001.

62. This was one of John's most successful methods of fund-raising. Quotation from Scott Weiser, interview by author, Des Moines, Iowa, 24 April 2002.

63. *Des Moines Tribune*, 18 August 1975. See also *Ruan*, July-August 1975, 2-3; and *John Ruan MS Golf Exhibition* program, 17 August 1975, Ruan Papers.

64. Straub, interview. Information on donation to Rush-Presbyterian–St. Luke's as well as quotation are from *Des Moines Tribune*, 19 July 1982. See also text of John Ruan remarks for 1988 MS Press Conference, 12 July 1988, Ruan Scrapbook, 1988, Ruan Papers.

65. Typescript of president's remarks for *Remark* magazine, n.d., Ruan Papers; Gary Fletcher, interview.

66. Quotation from *Iowa State–Colorado Homecoming* (football game program), 1 November 1975, 17. See also *Des Moines Register*, 31 October 1975; Howard Gregory, telephone conversation with author, 24 April 2002; and Thomas Ruan, interview by author, Clive, Iowa, 19 February 2002.

67. Darlene Willis, interview by author, Des Moines, Iowa, 10 January 2002; B. J. Lester, telephone conversation with author, 4 September 2002; *Des Moines Register*, 6 August 1988.

68. Kendall, interview, 9 January 2002; Betty Ruan, interview by author, North Palm Beach, Florida, 18 January 2002; John Ruan, interview by author, North Palm Beach, Florida, 17 January 2002.

69. Ruan Transportation Corporation, 1977 Report/1978 Forecast; Ruan Transportation Group 1981 Report/1982 Forecast, Ruan Papers.

70. Michael H. Belzer, *Sweatshops on Wheels* (Oxford: Oxford University Press, 2000), 64-65, 78.

71. Ibid., 82.

72. Weiser, interview.

73. Bill Giles, telephone conversation with author, 29 April 2002; *Des Moines Register*, 17 November 1985 and 22 June 1986. See also 1981 Report/1982 Forecast. It should be noted that operating profits (which do not include profits from company investments, etc.) went from a loss of $77,000 in 1979 to a profit of $37,000 in 1980 and then fell to a large $1.5 million loss in 1981.

74. Alvord, interview; Jeffrey Barber, interview by author, West Des Moines, Iowa, 25 April 2002; Ken Penaluna, interview by author, Ankeny, Iowa, 3 May 2002; *Remark,* December 1981, 1, 7-8.

75. Penaluna, interview.

76. Ibid.; *Des Moines Register,* 14 November 1981; *Remark,* December 1982, 3.

77. Ruan Leasing's revenues rose from $55.7 million in 1979 to $68.8 million in 1981. Over the same period, operating profits moved from $1.45 to $3.0 million, while net profits climbed from $4.5 to $6.5 million. See 1981 Report/1982 Forecast.

78. Carriers Insurance Company and Subsidiaries, Consolidated Financial Statements for 1980; and Carriers Insurance Company, Pro Forma Income Statement, 1982, Ruan Papers.

79. *Des Moines Register,* 14 September 1977; Bankers Trust Company News Release, 13 September 1977, Ruan Scrapbook, 1976, Ruan Papers.

80. Kilpper, interview. Financial numbers are taken from Bankers Trust Financial History, Bankers Trust Company, Des Moines, Iowa.

81. Bankers Trust Financial History. In 1985, the investment department was spun off as Ruan Securities Corporation, which specialized in underwriting Iowa municipal securities and marketing U.S. government securities; see Tom Mehl, telephone conversation with author, 18 October 2002.

82. Jeremiah Milbank to John Ruan, 10 December 1976, John Ruan Scrapbook, 1976, Ruan Papers; *Des Moines Register,* 1, 6, and 22 January 1980; *Des Moines Tribune,* 18 and 22 January 1980.

83. *Remark,* July 1982, 1, 3-4.

84. *Des Moines Daily Business Record,* 12 December 1982.

85. For Wright quotation, see *Des Moines Register,* 3 May 1981. Offenburger's statement is from *Des Moines Register,* 4 October 1983. See also Stuart and Martha Krohn to John Ruan, 3 January 1981, Ruan Scrapbook, 1981, Ruan Papers.

Chapter 7

1. *Des Moines Register,* 18 November 1991.

2. Gary Alvord, interview by author, West Des Moines, Iowa, 25 April 2002; Jeff Barber, interview by author, West Des Moines, Iowa, 25 April 2002.

3. Ibid.; see also Ken Penaluna, interview by author, Ankeny, Iowa, May 3, 2002.

4. *Des Moines Register,* 10 September 1985.

5. *Des Moines Register,* 22 June 1986.

6. Ruan Transportation Management Systems 1990 Business Plan, John Ruan Papers, private collection held by John Ruan, Des Moines, Iowa [hereafter cited as Ruan Papers].

7. Penaluna, interview. Miller quotation from *Des Moines Register*, 11 June 1986.

8. Quotation from *Des Moines Register*, 17 December 1986. See also *Des Moines Business Record*, 22-28 December 1986.

9. Ibid.

10. See, for instance, W. Edwards Deming, *Out of the Crisis* (Cambridge: Massachusetts Institute for Technology, Center for Advanced Engineering Study, 1991).

11. Alvord, interview.

12. Ibid.

13. Ibid.; Barber, interview; "MEGA Task Force Takes TQM Tour on the Road," 1994 press release, Ruan Papers.

14. MQI Pamphlet, revised 11/1994, Ruan Papers.

15. "MEGA Task Force Takes TQM Tour."

16. *Des Moines Register*, 28 June 1986.

17. *Des Moines Register,* 30 June and 1 July 1986.

18. In 1980, Ruan Transport's Political Action Committee for Effective Government gave $4,000 to the Grassley campaign. In 1985 and then again in 1986, it gave Grassley donations of $1,000. Over the 1985-86 year, Betty Ruan gave Grassley $500, while another $333.33 came from John III. Other contributions closely tied to the Ruan companies included $1,000 from Larry Miller and $250 from his wife, Jean Miller. See *Des Moines Register*, 2 July 1986.

19. *Wall Street Journal*, 18 September 1986.

20. *Des Moines Register*, 1, 16, and 17 October 1986.

21. *Des Moines Register,* 21 October 1986.

22. Ruan Transportation Management Systems 1987 Plan, Ruan Papers.

23. *Waterloo Courier*, 7 July 1986.

24. *Des Moines Register*, 17 November 1985.

25. Revenue figures are from Ruan Transportation Management Systems, 1990 Business Plan, Ruan Papers. Miller quotation from *Des Moines Register*, 20 May 1989.

26. *Wall Street Journal*, 19 May 1989. The advertisement also ran in *Transport Topics, Forbes*, and the *Harvard Business Review*.

27. *Des Moines Register*, 18 March 1984.

28. Ibid.

29. John Ruan III, interview by author, Des Moines, Iowa, 27 March 2002; *Des Moines Register*, 17 November 1985.

30. Herman Kilpper, interview by author, Des Moines, Iowa, 22 March 2002; "Comments by Governor Branstad on Announcement of Export Trading Company," 28 March 1983, Ruan Scrapbook, 1983, Ruan Papers; *Des Moines Register*, 3 April 1983. Quotation is from John Ruan to Herman Kilpper and Roger Cloutier, 28 February 1983, Ruan Scrapbook, 1983, Ruan Papers.

31. Quotation from "Ruan Announces New Export Trading Company," 28 March 1983, press release, Ruan Scrapbook, 1983, Ruan Papers.

32. Quotations are from *Des Moines Register*, 3 April 1983 and 3 January 1984, respectively.

33. Craig Winters, interview by author, Des Moines, Iowa, 14 June 2002.

34. Ibid.; Dan Golightly, interview by author, Waukee, Iowa, 3 October 2002.

35. *Des Moines Register*, 13 July 1998.

36. Text of John Ruan's remarks, Iowa Bankers Association Panel, 19 September 1983, Ruan Scrapbook, 1983, Ruan Papers. See also *Des Moines Register*, 20 September 1983.

37. Iowa World Ag-Trade Center Association Application for Membership in the World Trade Centers Association, 8 September 1983, Ruan Scrapbook, 1983, Ruan Papers.

38. *Des Moines Register*, 26 October and 23 November 1983.

39. Ibid.

40. Quotation is from *Des Moines Register*, 7 January 1984. See also Press Release, "Plans Unveiled for Iowa World Trade Center," 6 January 1984; promotional pamphlet for trade center, "Iowa: Because Our Market Is The World . . . Our Vision Must Be World Wide," John Ruan Scrapbook, 1984, Ruan Papers.

41. John Ruan, interview by author, Des Moines, Iowa, 25 June 2002; *Des Moines Register*, 30 December 1983.

42. *Des Moines Register*, 30 December 1983 and 15 January 1984; *Wallaces Farmer*, 28 January 1984, 14; Iowa Farm Bureau Federation News Release, 31 January 1984.

43. *Des Moines Register*, 29 April 1984.

44. *Des Moines Register*, 19 January 1984.

45. *Des Moines Register*, 4 March and 25 October 1984.

46. For more on the growing opposition to a Des Moines trade center, see *Des Moines Register*, 4 March and 10 October 1984. On other funding plans and Senate passage of the Polk County tax, see *Des Moines Register*, 20 April 1984.

47. *Des Moines Register*, 27 April 1984.

48. Ibid.

49. Herman Kilpper, telephone conversation with author, 19 June 2002; John Ruan, interview by author, Des Moines, Iowa, 8 May 2002; *Des Moines Register*, 23 April and 1 May 1984.

50. *Des Moines Register*, 16 May and 6 September 1984; Kilpper, interview.

51. See Kilpper, interview; and Ruan, interview, 25 June 2002. Chrystal quotation from Lori Erickson, "Homespun Hero," *America West Airline*

Magazine, May 1988, 29; Ruan quotation from *Des Moines Register*, 8 September 1985 and 28 August 1993.

52. *Des Moines Register*, 28 August 1993; Tom Bengtson, "The Turn-Around at Bankers Trust," *Northwestern Financial Review* 178 (23 October 1993): 10; Monte Olmsted, "A Miracle Worker," *Northwestern Financial Review* 185 (22 January 2000): 11.

53. *Des Moines Business Record*, 13-19 February 1989. See also Bankers Trust Financial History, Bankers Trust Company, Des Moines, Iowa.

54. Bankers Trust Financial History; *Des Moines Register*, 4 September 1989; Sam Kalainov, interview by author, Des Moines, Iowa, 30 May 2002.

55. Miller's first quotation from *Des Moines Register*, 30 June 1992; Miller's second quotation and Knapp quotation from *Des Moines Business Record*, 27 July–2 August 1992. See also John Ruan III, interviews by author, Des Moines, Iowa, 5 October and 4 December 2002; and Bankers Trust Financial History.

56. *Des Moines Register*, 25 October 1984.

57. Ruan, interview, 25 June 2002.

58. *Des Moines Register*, 25 June and 1 July 1985.

59. Kilpper quotation from *Des Moines Register*, 31 July 1985. See also *Des Moines Register*, 4 August 1985.

60. *Des Moines Register*, 31 August 1985.

61. *Des Moines Register*, 4 September 1985.

62. First Kilpper quotation from Kilpper, interview; Ruan quotation from Ruan, interview, 25 June 2002; second Kilpper quotation from *Des Moines Register*, 7 September 1985; Kendall quotation from Ken Kendall, telephone conversation with author, 15 July 2002; Tone statement from *Des Moines Business Record*, 18-24 November 1985.

63. *Des Moines Register*, 17 November 1985. See also John Ruan III, interview, 27 March 2002.

64. Ibid. See also *Des Moines Business Record*, 18-24 November 1985.

65. *Des Moines Register*, 12 June 1987.

66. See *Des Moines Register*, 1 October 1988. The $3.1 million was paid in two installments: $2 million at the time of the settlement and $1.1 million the following March. Other important aspects of the settlement included: (1) the 10,000 shares of Bankers Trust stock held by the liquidator would be turned over to Ruan Financial Corporation after the March payment; and (2) John dropped his appeal to recoup the profits from the sale of Intel and Heritage Communications stock that had been pledged to Carriers. The judge in the case had already decided that the profits belonged to Carriers liquidators.

67. *Des Moines Register*, undated clipping [1989], Ruan Scrapbook, 1989, Ruan Papers. John's comments are from Ruan, interview, 25 June 2002.

68. Bob Dole to John and Betty Ruan, 26 June 1987; Ruan Scrapbook, 1987, Ruan Papers.

69. On Dole's campaign in 1988, see Jake H. Thompson, *Bob Dole: The Republicans' Man for All Seasons* (New York: Donald E. Fine, 1994), 157-73. See also Bob Dole to John Ruan, 6 April 1988, Ruan Scrapbook, 1988, Ruan Papers; Ruan, interview, 25 June 2002; and Jan Gillum, interview by author, Des Moines, Iowa, 23 July 2002.

70. Robert Houser, telephone conversation with author, 25 July 2002; Ellen Brown, telephone conversation with author, 25 July 2002.

71. Brown, telephone conversation; John Ruan, interview by author, Des Moines, Iowa, 15 July 2002.

72. Ibid. Houser quotation from Houser, telephone conversation. See also *Des Moines Register*, 28 February 1989; and *Progress* 5 (March 1989): 1, 4, 5.

73. *Des Moines Register*, 6-10 July 1989 and 3 July 1991.

74. *Des Moines Register*, 17 April and 3 July 1991 and 8-13 July 1993; *MEGANEWS*, August 1993, 2-3. See also Brown, telephone conversation; and Ruan, interview, 15 July 2002.

75. *Des Moines Register*, 27 January 1991. For story on 1990 "The Powers That Be," see *Des Moines Register*, 14 January 1990. On completion of 801 Grand building, see *Des Moines Register*, 21 October 1990.

76. On John's determination and tenacity, see Kalainov, interview. Comments from Wilkey and Miller are from *Des Moines Register*, 27 January 27, 1991. Flansburg's statement is from *Des Moines Register*, 22 April 1984.

77. The award was announced in the *Des Moines Register*, 27 January 1991. See also Ruan, 25 June 2002; and Sister Patricia Clare Sullivan to John Ruan, 29 January 1991, Ruan Scrapbook, 1991, Ruan Papers.

78. Gary Fletcher, telephone conversation with author, 31 July 2002; Betty Ruan, telephone conversation with author, 1 August 2002; Mel Straub, interview by author, Des Moines, Iowa, 27 November 2001.

79. Ibid.; transcript of remarks at Neurological Center Press Conference, 12 July 1988, Ruan Scrapbook, 1988, Ruan Papers. See also *Des Moines Register*, 13 July 1988; and "Patients Rebuilding Lives at New Rehabilitation Center," *Mercy Hospital Medical Center/Des Moines Journal*, October 1989, 1, 14.

80. *Des Moines Register*, 28 July 1989.

81. Patricia Clare Sullivan, telephone conversation with author, 31 July 2002; Rusty Edwards, interview by author, Des Moines, Iowa, 6 November 2001; Fletcher, telephone conversation; John and Betty Ruan, interview by author, Des Moines, Iowa, 26 July 2001; Straub, interview.

82. Ruan, interview, 15 July 2002; Fletcher, telephone conversation.

83. Thomas Ruan, interview by author, Clive, Iowa, 19 February 2002; John Ruan, interview, 15 July 2002.

84. Gary Fletcher, interview by author, Des Moines, Iowa, 28 February 2002; Sullivan, telephone conversation; and Janis Ruan, interview by author, Des Moines, Iowa, 26 April 2002. See also obituary in *Des Moines Register*, 30 June 1992.

85. Richard Wilkey, interview by author, West Des Moines, Iowa, 21 February 2002; Janis Ruan, interview.

Chapter 8

1. Miller quotation in *Des Moines Register*, 24 October 1993. See also Jeff Barber, interview by author, West Des Moines, Iowa, 25 April 2002.

2. Redden quotation in *Des Moines Register*, 24 October 1993.

3. For more on Miller's death, see *Des Moines Register*, 15 and 16 July 1994. Company revenues from *Transport Topics*, 23 July 2001, 19.

4. Howard Gregory, interview by author, Des Moines, Iowa, 28 November 2001; Gary Alvord, interview by author, West Des Moines, Iowa, 25 April 2002; John Ruan, interview by author, Des Moines, Iowa, 5 October 2002; Jan Gillum, telephone conversation with author, 30 September 2002. For more information on the relationship between John and Larry Miller and John's reaction to his death, see also Janis Ruan, interview by author, Des Moines, Iowa, 26 April 2002; Dave Neugent, interview by author, Des Moines, Iowa, 4 December 2001; and Scott Weiser, interview by author, Des Moines, Iowa, 25 April 2002.

5. Mike Earley, interview by author, Des Moines, Iowa, 13 September 2002; *Des Moines Business Record*, 20 September 1999.

6. Ibid.

7. *Des Moines Business Record*, 20 September 1999.

8. For background of the Iowa Trust Fund and the scandal, see *New York Times*, 16, 18, and 20 December 1991 and 1 January and 3 February 1992. See also Tom Bengtson, "The Turn-Around at Bankers Trust," *Northwestern Financial Review* 178 (23 October 1993): 11, 29.

9. Quotations from Earley, interview. See also Monte Olmsted, "A Miracle Worker?" *Northwestern Financial Review* 185 (22 January 2000): 11-12.

10. Ibid.; *Des Moines Register*, 28 August 1993; Bankers Trust Financial History, Bankers Trust Company, Des Moines, Iowa.

11. Earley, interview.

12. Ibid.

13. Chrystal quotation from *Des Moines Business Record*, 20 September 1999. See also Bankers Trust Financial History; and *Des Moines Register*, 25 June 2002.

14. Mel Straub, interview by author, Des Moines, Iowa, 27 November 2001; Michael Jacoby, interview by author, West Des Moines, Iowa, 14 September 2002.

15. Vellinga quotation from *Des Moines Register*, 3 April 2001; Hughes quotation from unmarked clipping, Ruan Scrapbook, 2000, John Ruan Papers, private collection held by John Ruan, Des Moines, Iowa [hereafter cited as Ruan Papers]. To avoid continued confusion and to distinguish it from the Ruan Neurology Clinic, the Ruan Neurological Center's name was changed to the Ruan Rehabilitation Center in May 2001.

16. Elaine Szymoniak recounted this story; Elaine Szymoniak, interview by author, Des Moines, Iowa, 16 August 2002.

17. Transcript of John Ruan speech, "Why a World Trade Center for Iowa," n.d., Ruan Papers. See also *Des Moines Register*, 25 October 1984.

18. Ruan, "Why World Trade Center"; John Ruan, interview by author, Des Moines, Iowa, 23 August 2002.

19. Lionaes quotation from *Des Moines Register*, 14 October 2001. See also Norman Borlaug, interview by author, Des Moines, Iowa, 6 February 2002.

20. Ibid.; *USA Today*, 15 October 1996; *Des Moines Register*, 16 October 1997.

21. Borlaug, interview. Quotation is from a transcript of A. S. Clausi, "Oral History of the World Food Prize from Its Inception to Its Assumption by the Ruan Foundation," n.d., World Food Prize Foundation, Des Moines, Iowa.

22. Borlaug, interview; A. S. Clausi, telephone conversation with author, 11 September 2002; Carleton Smith obituary, *New York Times*, 1 June 1984.

23. Borlaug, interview.

24. Ibid.; Clausi, "Oral History."

25. Ibid.; *New York Times*, 15 December 1989; *Des Moines Register*, 24 December 1989.

26. Szymoniak, interview.

27. Clausi, "Oral History." See also Ruan, interview, 23 August 2002; and *Des Moines Business Record*, 4-10 June 1990.

28. Herman Kilpper, interview by author, Des Moines, Iowa, 22 March 2002; John Ruan, interview by author, Des Moines, Iowa, 25 June 2002; *Des Moines Register*, 13 July 1998.

29. Elaine Szymoniak, telephone conversation with author, 23 September 2002.

30. Jan Gillum, telephone conversation with author, 23 September 2002; Herman Kilpper, telephone conversation with author, 11 October 2002.

31. *Des Moines Register*, 19 June 1990. See also *New York Times*, 19 June 1990.

32. Ibid.

33. Borlaug quotation from *Des Moines Register*, 19 June 1990. Ruan quotation from *Greater Des Moines Progress*, 9 July 1990.

34. Reagen quotation from *Greater Des Moines Progress*, 9 July 1990; *Des Moines Register* editorial, 19 June 1990.

35. Ken Kendall, interview by author, Des Moines, Iowa, 9 January 2002; Kilpper, interview; Ruan, interview, 25 June 2002; *Des Moines Register*, 20 February 1995.

36. *Des Moines Register*, 23 July 1991.

37. *Des Moines Register,* 15 October 1991.

38. *USA Today*, 20 October 1993.

39. Kilpper, telephone conversation.

40. Ibid.; Jan Douglas, telephone conversations with author, 14 October and 1 November 2002.

41. Douglas, telephone conversation, 14 October 2002. Quotation on internship being highly regarded is from *Des Moines Business Record*, 28 May 2001. Hubbell quotation from James W. Hubbell Jr. to John Ruan, 18 October 1999, Ruan Scrapbook, 1999, Ruan Papers. For more on Nelson and Vosburg, see *Des Moines Register*, 17 October 1999; and World Food Prize Youth Institute pamphlet, n.d.

42. John Denver had performed at two previous World Food Prize award ceremonies. He died in a plane crash in October 1997 and was honored with a tribute at the food prize ceremony a week later.

43. *Des Moines Register*, 16 October 1997; *Omaha World-Herald*, 20 June 1997.

44. When the endowment was originally established, it consisted of 500,000 shares of Intel stock, which was trading at approximately $20 per share at the time; see Ralph Schlenker, interview by author, Indianola, Iowa, 30 November 2001. For the announcement of the endowment, see *Des Moines Register*, 25 September 1997. The editorial appeared in *Des Moines Register*, 1 October 1997.

45. Miller quotation from *Des Moines Register*, 27 January 1991. John Ruan and John Ruan III quotations from *Des Moines Register*, 23 August 1998. For John III's comment about being "over-groomed," see *Des Moines Register*, 4 June 2000.

46. Thomas J. Donohue to John Ruan, 22 October 1999; and David Vellinga to John Ruan, 15 October 1999; both in Ruan Scrapbook, 1999, Ruan Papers.

47. Ruan Scrapbook, 2000, Ruan Papers.

48. Ruan quotation from John Ruan, interview by author, Des Moines, Iowa, 18 October 2002. See also Ken Quinn, interview by author, Des Moines, Iowa, 19 November 2002.

49. Quinn, interview. See also Dubuque *Telegraph Herald*, 30 November 1998, 24 August and 15 October 1999, 19 April 2000, and 8 January 2001.

50. Kilpper, telephone conversation with author, 22 October 2002; Quinn, interview.

51. John Ruan quotation from Ruan, interview, 18 October 2002; Quinn quotation from *Des Moines Business Record*, 28 May 2001. See also John Ruan III, interview by author, Des Moines, Iowa, 4 December 2002; and *Des Moines Register*, 25 August 1999.

By the time Quinn took the position, Iowa State University was in the process of ending its relationship with the World Food Prize. In 1990, it had signed a 10-year agreement to serve as the prize's secretariat. Toward the end of that period, its relationship with the World Food Prize Foundation had become strained after ISU had begun to use some of the $250,000 state appropriation earmarked for the foundation to cover costs associated with its role as secretariat. When the university and the foundation failed to come to an agreement on how the state money should be allocated, ISU discontinued its role as secretariat after the awarding of the 2000 prize. Once the secretariat was taken over by the World Food Prize Foundation, Judith Pim, former administrator of the Center for Agriculture and Rural Development at Iowa State University, was hired as its director and began in August 2000.

52. *Des Moines Register*, 23 April 2001.

53. Quinn quotation from *Des Moines Business Record*, 28 May 2001. See also *World Food Prize Report*, July 2000; and *Des Moines Register*, 10 September 2000.

54. *World Food Prize Report*, December 2000.

55. On Norman Borlaug/World Food Prize Day, see *Des Moines Register*, 14 May 2002.

56. Gartner and Borlaug quotations from *Des Moines Register*, 27 October 2002. For John's views, see Ruan, interview, 25 June 2002.

57. Quinn quotation from *Des Moines Business Record*, 28 May 2001. See also Quinn, interview; Ken Kendall, telephone conversation with author, 22 October 2002; Kilpper, telephone conversation, 22 October 2002.

58. Gillum, telephone conversation, 30 September 2002.

59. Mickle quotation from *Des Moines Register*, 27 January 1991. See also Margaret Ann Bastian, interview by author, West Des Moines, Iowa, 1 November 2001; Virginia Pearsall, interview by author, West Des Moines, Iowa, 1 November 2001; Ralph Schlenker, telephone conversations with author, 15 January and 6 November 2002; and Ely Brewer, interview by author, Des Moines, Iowa, 11 November 2002. Marc Hansen's column appeared in *Des Moines Register*, 19 May 2001.

60. I attended one of these birthday celebrations at the Marriott Hotel on March 4, 2002.

61. Carter quotation from "Ruan International Companies," company promotional brochure, n.d. [ca. 2000].

Epilogue

1. John Ruan, conversation with author, North Palm Beach, Florida, 19 January 2002.

2. On Chrystal's death, see *Des Moines Register*, 21 January 2000.

3. For the John Chrystal Internship Award, see *Des Moines Register*, 14 April 2000. Quotation describing award is from "The World Food Prize 2002 Laureate Ceremony" program.

4. *Des Moines Register*, 13 March 1995.

5. Quotation about keeping Root on the payroll from *Des Moines Register*, 13 March 1995. On Root's death, see *Des Moines Register*, 4 April 2000.

6. *Des Moines Register*, 8 June 2000.

7. Ely Brewer, interview by author, Des Moines, Iowa, 11 November 2002.

8. Ruan quoted in Brewer, ibid.

9. Ibid. See also Ely Brewer, telephone conversation with author, 20 November 2002.

10. Ibid. See also Ralph Schlenker, telephone conversation with author, 6 November 2002. The monument, which ultimately cost $73,000, was dedicated on July 17, 2001.

11. John Ruan, interview with author, Des Moines, Iowa, 4 November 2002.

12. See John Ruan IV and Jonathan Ruan Fletcher, "The Family of John Ruan," 1996, John Ruan Papers, private collection held by John Ruan, Des Moines, Iowa [hereafter cited as Ruan Papers]. See also Pattie Tidwell, interview by author, Carlsbad, New Mexico, 15 November 2001.

13. John Ruan III, interview by author, 26 October 2002; and Ruan, interview, 4 November 2002. For more on John's Ninth Street home in Des Moines, see *Des Moines Register*, 10 September 1998.

14. Bill Giles, telephone conversation with author, 1 November 2002.

15. *Des Moines Register*, 23 August 1998.

16. *Des Moines Register*, 4 June 2000.

17. *Register* quotation from editorial, *Des Moines Register*, 21 August 2000. Hurd quotation from *Des Moines Register*, 4 June 2000. See also *Des Moines Register*, 11 April, 20 and 22 May, and 4, 12, and 18 August 2000.

18. *Des Moines Register*, 4 June and 15 November 2000.

19. For descriptions of John III, see *Des Moines Register*, 4 June 2000. Michael Gartner quotation from *Des Moines Register*, 23 August 1998.

20. The award is described in *Des Moines Register*, 3 September 2001.

21. Author's notes. See also *Des Moines Register*, 6 September 2001.

22. Author's notes.

23. *Des Moines Register* editorial, 6 September 2001.

Index